Trinity After Pentecost

Trinity After Pentecost

WILLIAM P. ATKINSON

PICKWICK *Publications* · Eugene, Oregon

TRINITY AFTER PENTECOST

A proportion of the material in chapter 2 has previously been published as "Angels and the Spirit in Luke-Acts." This appeared in the *Journal of the European Pentecostal Theological Association* XXVI.1 (2006) 76–90. It is reproduced here with permission.

Pickwick Publications
An Imprint of Wipf and Stock Publishers
199 W. 8th Ave., Suite 3
Eugene, OR 97401

www.wipfandstock.com

ISBN 13: 978-1-62032-779-1

Cataloging-in-Publication data:

Atkinson, William, 1961–.

Trinity after Pentecost / William P. Atkinson.

viii + 186 pp. ; 23 cm—Includes bibliographical references and indexes.

ISBN 13: 978-1-62032-779-1

1. Trinity. 2. Holy Spirit. 3. God (Christianity). 4. Pentecostalism. I. Title.

BT111.3 A85 2013

Manufactured in the USA

Contents

Preface

I WOULD LIKE TO preface this book with a word about its title: *Trinity After Pentecost*. Those who are familiar with the traditional church year will recognize a slight word play here, for Trinity Sunday falls one week after Whitsun, or Pentecost Sunday. Beyond that, however, the title indicates my own experience and thinking, for I am Pentecostal, and I want to explore trinitarianism in the light of my Pentecostalism. When I say that I am Pentecostal, I mean this denominationally. I was ordained within the Elim Pentecostal Church in 1990. I also mean it experientially, in that I believe I have been baptized with God's Spirit—an act of God's grace distinct from and logically subsequent to my entering the sphere of Christian salvation. I mean it ecclesially, as well: I believe that God's church on earth can only fulfill its mission when enabled by the Spirit in ways that echo God's act at Pentecost.

There is, however, yet a third sense in which I find this book title appropriate. In terms of developing trinitarian scholarship, I want to take up Max Turner's implied challenge, echoed by Gordon Fee, that rich pickings exist for our understanding of the Trinity in the events of Pentecost. Turner has a chapter in his excellent book *The Holy Spirit and Spiritual Gifts: Then and Now* entitled "Towards Trinitarian Theology—Perspectives from Pentecost." I intend in this work to step further towards that trinitarian theology, precisely by traveling along the lines Turner implies: by pursuing the thoughts that the events of Pentecost inspire.

This book was mainly written during the summers of 2011 and 2012. Only when the book had been virtually completed did I learn about the forthcoming publication by Eerdmans of *From Pentecost to the Triune God: A Pentecostal Trinitarian Theology* by Steven M. Studebaker. Therefore, my work does not interact with the latter book. I hope that readers may find it interesting to compare the two independent works.

Finally, I draw to readers' attention the fact that nearly all New Testament translations in this book are, for better or for worse, my own. In a sense, this entire book is simply an extended theological exposition of Acts 2:33. With that in mind, I offer here my rendering of that text in English:

Having been exalted, then, to God's right hand,
and having received the promise
of the Holy Spirit from the Father,
he has poured out what you both see and hear.

William P. Atkinson,
London School of Theology,
November 2012

1

Introductory Matters

AIMS

THIS BOOK AIMS TO offer an account of the Trinity from a Pentecostal viewpoint. My theological perspective as a classical Pentecostal, in line with other expressions of charismatic and wider renewal Christianity, pays particular attention to the Holy Spirit. That is, it is pneumatologically orientated. Thus I seek to offer an account of the Trinity that is pneumatologically driven, and more specifically, that takes full account, in church history and in believers' personal histories, of "Pentecost," which term I will consider later in this chapter. I agree with Amos Yong that "theology is only fully trinitarian when due attention is given to pneumatology."[1] Such attention I will seek to provide.

In doing this, I do not claim to be proposing an understanding of the Trinity that differs markedly from those that have preceded it. There are certain fresh emphases and insights but overall the picture of the Trinity that emerges is fairly traditional. What is new is its method.[2] It is not new to start trinitarian explorations "from below," in other words from the history of Jesus of Nazareth and the thinking of his first followers, as opposed to "from above," in the sense of beginning with mysterious abstractions about

1. Yong, *Spirit Poured Out*, 225; cf. 146 n. 4.

2. If in fact a different method of research leads to the same results as previous methods, this is a cause not for disappointment but for reassurance. Modern science is committed to testing the replicability of results. If new experiments, using different methods, confirm existing results, the conclusions can be regarded, naturally enough, as confirmed: "triangulation" has been achieved.

being, person, and process that bear no observable relation to human experience of God. What is less explored, however, is detailed thinking about the Trinity that starts with Pentecost. This I attempt here.

As with my previous book, I also have a more general aim. I will simply repeat here what I stated then:

> I trust that this book will help to bridge the divide that exists between academic theological study and current Pentecostal church practice and mission. In my own context, this divide is still wide and deep: it needs all the long, strong bridges that can be mustered! I hope to show that academic theological study does have its uses, and that those uses are relevant to Pentecostals who for whatever reason do not intend to or do not have the opportunity to engage in such study themselves. With this in mind, I try to write in a way that is reasonably accessible for people who may not be used to scholarly language.[3]

Aims do not arise in a vacuum. My own aim arises from three particular challenges that I perceive facing Pentecostal trinitarianism and from the potential I see for Pentecostal insights to contribute significantly to trinitarian thinking in general. In other words, I think Pentecostal trinitarianism needs to be robust so that it can provide an answer to those who regard trinitarianism as misguided or unnecessary, and beyond that I think that general trinitarian thinking can perhaps be enhanced through the application of Pentecostal thinking.

CHALLENGES

Trinitarian Pentecostalism faces three challenges that make it especially important for a rigorous Pentecostal trinitarianism to be advanced. The first and second of these arise from within Pentecostalism itself; the third lies further afield.

From within Pentecostalism, I see two problems. First, Pentecostals who are trinitarian ignore the Trinity *in practice* if not in theory. Secondly, the "unitarian" voices of Oneness Pentecostalism raise a challenge. If one can be Pentecostal without being trinitarian, what if any is the significance of our trinitarianism? From the wider theological realm comes another

---

3. Atkinson, *Baptism in the Spirit*, 2. Not all technical terminology can be avoided; also, in trinitarian discussion some common terms such as "person" take on technical use.

more diffuse and less definable challenge: a form of trinitarianism that in reality is not far removed from "binitarianism." I will introduce these challenges a little more fully before proceeding to consider how this book will go about mounting its advance of a Pentecostal trinitarianism.

The "Trinitarian" Challenge

The first challenge we face is that the Trinity has largely been ignored by Pentecostals. Academic Pentecostal theology has come on in leaps and bounds in the generation since Clark Pinnock wrote, "Watch out you evangelicals—the young Pentecostal scholars are coming!"[4] While a wealth of subjects has been tackled by the new generation of Pentecostal scholars, it is unsurprising that much of this focus has been on pneumatology. Thus the chapter in Keith Warrington's *Pentecostal Theology* titled "God," which is 113 pages in length, devotes no fewer than eighty-seven of these pages to a section titled "The Holy Spirit."[5] What is perhaps more surprising is that this interest in the Holy Spirit has not been translated into more interest in the Trinity. Indeed, Warrington's chapter on "God," just mentioned, has a section titled "Trinity" that is a mere four pages long. Warrington is no exception here. While whole books—and many of them, at that—have been written by Pentecostals on the Spirit and the Spirit's activities, little serious scholarly work has been offered from a Pentecostal perspective on the nature of the Trinity.[6]

This gap is to be found not only in academic writing but also in Pentecostal church practice. Mark Cartledge's observations of a typical British Pentecostal church in its worship identify that there is focus on the person of Jesus but that this focus is only placed in "a general theistic context" rather than being placed in "an explicitly Trinitarian framework."[7] Anybody with a reasonable acquaintance of what Cartledge calls "ordinary Pentecostal theology"[8] will, I imagine, readily recognize that his findings could be multiply replicated. Pentecostals "in the pew" are not encouraged to think

---

4. Pinnock, "Foreword," vii.

5. Warrington, *Pentecostal Theology*, 44–130.

6. Examples that do exist include Yong, *Spirit Poured Out* and *Spirit-Word-Community*; and Macchia, *Baptized in the Spirit*.

7. Cartledge, *Testimony in the Spirit*, 47.

8. Cartledge's *Testimony in the Spirit* is subtitled *Rescripting Ordinary Pentecostal Theology*.

about the Trinity, either by the church year with its Trinity Sunday, or by the wording of prayers led extempore in public worship, or by the wording of many contemporary worship songs.[9] I do not mean to suggest that this weakness is unique to Pentecostalism. I was recently in a Methodist church in which the preaching on the Trinity was by no means profound. But at least the fact that it was Trinity Sunday that day led to a choice of hymns and a sermon topic that acknowledged and celebrated trinitarian doctrine.

One is justified in wondering whether ignoring the Trinity matters. After all, even Pentecostalism's pneumatological distinctives are pragmatic rather than ontological—we concern ourselves more with what the Spirit *does* than with who or what exactly the Spirit *is*. And when it comes to the Father and the Son, trinitarian Pentecostalism does not generally offer distinctive viewpoints. Thus, one might argue, it is sufficient for Pentecostals to rely on the theologizing of previous generations on the one hand and contemporaries from other ecclesial and theological streams on the other.

I am not convinced, however, that such a policy is the best way forward. Jürgen Moltmann has criticized the church for being, in recent times, too pragmatic.[10] This criticism is especially true of us Pentecostals. To those of my tribe who argue that theological study of the Trinity can play no useful part in the God-given mission of the church, I point out, with Moltmann,[11] that part of that mission is worship. Pentecostals can find themselves in the position of loving God dearly but taking too little notice of what God is like. However, it is appropriate to get to know the one we love. Furthermore, and turning from worship to works, it is surely the case that "the people that do know their God shall be strong, and do exploits" (Dan 11:32, KJV). If one tries to determine what was the key to Jesus' success in ministry, as depicted in the Gospels, one might highlight, among other factors, his clear and close knowledge of his divine Father's heart and mind. I believe that meditation on the nature of the Trinity can in fact enhance one's mission to the church and the world, through being encouraged, challenged, and informed.

That this claim may be true is attested by the ways in which the revival of interest in trinitarianism that has occurred in the last couple of generations is not only theoretical. It has been matched by a concern to *apply* trinitarian thinking to Christian *practice*—and no doubt to consider

9. Note the concerns expressed by Parry, *Worshipping Trinity*, e.g., 1–3.

10. Moltmann, *Trinity and Kingdom*, 5–7.

11. Ibid., 7–9.

ways in which Christian experience and practice might illumine trinitarian doctrine, for gone are the days when the flow of thought between theory and practice has been regarded as all moving in one direction.[12] In all this, I trust that the book will be informative and useful for Pentecostals, but I do not see why it might not also be just as useful to anyone who has not thought through trinitarianism to any serious extent or considered ways in which relating to God and people impacts and is impacted by how we understand God as Trinity.

The "Unitarian" Challenge

I place the word "unitarian" in inverted commas because Oneness Pentecostalism is far removed from versions of unitarianism that deny the deity of Christ.[13] In fact, in terms of its view of Jesus it could not be further removed. Nonetheless, I use the term to indicate that Oneness Pentecostalism firmly upholds what its observer David Reed calls on its behalf "the singular nature of God's being."[14] As Oneness exponents declare, "God is absolutely one (Isa. 44:6, 8, 24)—that is, one without distinctions of persons. There are no distinctions in God's eternal being."[15] Oneness Pentecostalism thus has an avowedly "unitarian" theology centered on the deity of Jesus Christ.

In my experience, many trinitarian Pentecostals are simply unaware of Oneness Pentecostalism, though a few will have heard of the term "Jesus-only" and will perhaps be aware that there is some controversy in Pentecostal circles over whether water-baptism should be performed in the name of the Father, Son, and Holy Spirit (following Matt 28:19) or in the name of Jesus Christ (following Acts 2:38). I do not recall being taught

12. For instance, Lartey writes of contextual theology in general and pastoral theology in particular that it "is a 'praxeological' discipline—one in which practical action and theory are held in creative tension. Here, theory critiques action and action critiques theory. . . . Theory provides rationale and method for practice. Practice shapes, informs and offers critical tools for theory" (*Pastoral Theology in an Intercultural World*, 24–25). For comment on this two-way traffic in relation to trinitarianism, see Parry, *Worshipping Trinity*, 11; Volf, *After Our Likeness*, 194.

13. See Lederle, *Theology with Spirit*, 80; Yong, *Spirit Poured Out*, 205–6, 227.

14. Reed, *"In Jesus' Name,"* 248. Reed observes that some Oneness Pentecostals, in order to distance themselves from trinitarianism, refer to themselves as "Christian monotheists" (*"In Jesus' Name,"* 253).

15. Society for Pentecostal Studies, "Oneness-Trinitarian Pentecostal Final Report," 214.

about the Oneness version of Pentecostalism when I was a student at a Pentecostal Bible college, and my first exposure to such teaching occurred when it emerged that its adherents were standing outside the building of the London church where I was serving at the time, apparently seeking to persuade our own dear Pentecostal congregants to convert to their view, on the basis that, as our people were baptized in the name of the Trinity rather than Jesus, they were not yet saved. This "evangelism" caused some consternation in our church, as can easily be imagined!

This widespread ignorance of Oneness Pentecostalism is despite the facts that it is nearly as old as trinitarian Pentecostalism and that it comprises many organizational groups and several millions of individuals. In 1992, Gregory Boyd estimated that there were at the time over five million Oneness Pentecostals worldwide.[16] Reed refers to a 1999 work that puts the figure at fourteen to twenty million.[17] Although this is a small percentage[18] of the roughly half billion Pentecostals, charismatics, and renewal Christians estimated to have inhabited this globe in 2000,[19] it is still a high figure, representing a force to be reckoned with.

Oneness Pentecostalism can be traced back to 1914, in the United States. A superficial reading of Reed's history would suggest that the "New Issue," as it was called at the time, split the Assemblies of God in the US just three days after the denomination was formed! This would in fact be a simplistic reading, for Oneness advocates were not expelled until 1916, but it is clear that the Oneness controversy was a thorn in the side of the Assemblies from their very earliest days.[20] In fact, the statement of beliefs that the US Assemblies of God formed in 1916 was created "mainly to counter the threat posed by the 'New Issue.'"[21]

---

16. Boyd, *Oneness Pentecostals*, 227.

17. Reed, "*In Jesus' Name*," 339.

18. Anderson's estimate that Oneness adherents may make up a quarter of the world's classical Pentecostals seems stretched (Anderson, *Introduction to Pentecostalism*, 49).

19. Barrett's figure, though presumably something of a "guesstimate," is widely quoted. See, e.g., Warrington, *Pentecostal Theology*, 12; Cartledge, *Testimony in the Spirit*, 2. Lederle offers the estimate of 600 million for 2006 (Lederle, *Theology with Spirit*, 2).

20. Reed, "*In Jesus' Name*," e.g., 362, 351.

21. Yong, *Spirit Poured Out*, 205. The British Assemblies of God did not form or develop its statement of beliefs until 1924. Its statement of beliefs was altered in 2004 in a way that highlighted its commitment to trinitarianism, "probably reflecting a greater awareness of the dispute with the oneness Pentecostal tradition, especially from the USA" (Cartledge, *Testimony in the Spirit*, 4–5, 191, quotation from 5).

Oneness beliefs about God commence with two basic premises: there is only one God; and this God is Jesus Christ. Concerning the first premise, the unity of God, Oneness belief regards this unity as indivisible. It is a simple, rigorous monotheism. Concerning the second premise, the deity of Christ, this must be allowed, from a Oneness perspective, its full force: there must be no hint that Jesus was only a "part" of God. A key text in this regard is Colossians 2:9. Logical deductions are then drawn from this pair of premises. God can be called Father to express divine transcendence. This Father—God—became incarnate—Jesus—and the humanity thus "formed" can be called the Son. "Son" thereby refers to humanity, and "Father" to divinity. God's Spirit is not a separable "person" but is another way of speaking about God, who is spirit. In summary, Oneness Pentecostalism can be regarded as a modern form of modalism, although it is clearly distinct from ancient Sabellian modalism.[22] Its view of trinitarianism is that the latter fails fully to honor Jesus, who is only somehow a part of God rather than fully God in entirety, and that it is a mild form of tritheism.[23]

While unbending polemics like that of Boyd have been aimed at Oneness beliefs,[24] there is a current trend towards more sympathetic portrayals of the system by trinitarians and towards dialogue between unitarian and trinitarian Pentecostals. Reed's detailed analysis aims for understanding and dialogue.[25] Yong especially calls for rapprochement.[26] The Society for Pentecostal Studies has been at the forefront of spurring fruitful discussions.[27] Indeed, Oneness Pentecostalism is not without its trinitarian sympathizers. Yong suggests three strengths of Oneness doctrine, which are worth quoting verbatim:

> First, Oneness Pentecostalism reminds trinitarians that Christianity is a monotheistic faith. The doctrine of the Trinity is not about

22. "Oneness theology does not fit neatly into the mold of classical modalism on two counts: its radical christocentric orientation, and its theology of the Name which particularizes and personalizes the revelation of God in the name of Jesus as God's 'proper' name for this dispensation" (Reed, "*In Jesus' Name*," 272).

23. For further details of Oneness doctrine see Reed, "*In Jesus' Name*," part III; and more briefly Boyd, *Oneness Pentecostals*, chapter 1.

24. Boyd, *Oneness Pentecostals*.

25. Reed, "*In Jesus' Name*," e.g., 260.

26. Yong, *Spirit Poured Out*, 224–34.

27. See, e.g., Society for Pentecostal Studies, "Oneness-Trinitarian Pentecostal Final Report."

three gods but, rather, about the God who transcends merely numerical oneness or threeness.

Second, the Oneness means of articulating the divine unity . . . includes a robust incarnational christology that defends the divinity of the historical Jesus Christ.

Third [we find an] . . . unexpected but important contribution of Oneness Pentecostalism for Christian theology in the world context: the bridges it affords to the Christian-Jewish and Christian-Muslim encounters . . . the potential Oneness pentecostal contribution toward the interreligious conversation should not be underestimated.[28]

Despite such sympathy and respect, criticism is offered. Reed voices several concerns. Among these is his comment that the three manifestations of the one God, as Oneness theology presents the matter, lack "permanence and personality." Furthermore, since God's threefold revelation is not a precise reflection of God's radical unity, there is "the possibility that God is not just more than but is explicitly *other* than what he is in his self-revelation." Also, "the identity and role of the humanity of Jesus is underdeveloped": "It is in the life and ministry of Jesus that the Oneness view of the dual nature of Christ begins to show its inherent weakness . . . the relationship appears more like a loose affiliation than a union."[29]

It is not my intention to offer a detailed analysis and critique of Oneness beliefs. My point here is rather that the very existence of Oneness Pentecostalism, let alone its size, spread, or influence, presents a challenge to trinitarian Pentecostalism: can the latter articulate its trinitarianism in a cogent and convincing way? Can it do so in a way that listens carefully to the history of Christian thought on the subject but which is faithful to Pentecostalism's general attitude to Scripture? In other words, can a Pentecostal trinitarianism be developed that listens first and foremost to the Christian Scriptures? Also, can this be done in a way that takes account of Pentecostalism's corporate experience of the Spirit and its sense that this experience mirrors those of many in the New Testament?

28. Yong, *Spirit Poured Out*, 227–8.

29. Reed, "*In Jesus' Name*," 268, 271, 280, 296; italics original. Some disagreement between Yong and Reed concerning the robustness of Oneness' incarnational christology is of course detectable here. Reed seems on firmer ground.

The "Binitarian" Challenge

While the word "unitarian" is a part of common parlance, "binitarianism" is reserved to theological discourse. It refers, of course, to a view of God that sees two persons. Usually, these are the Father and the Son: the Spirit is omitted. Binitarianism has sometimes been expressed formally.[30] However, the problem is much more often an informal one: many commentators have noted the relative ignoring or belittling of the Spirit's being and activities in the church's discussion of the Trinity, a belittling that is especially prevalent in Western churches. It is not surprising to find this noted by Pentecostals. Thus, for instance, Frank Macchia writes about "the fact that in the Western church, theologians have all but forgotten or abandoned the doctrine of the Holy Spirit."[31] However, the same observation is offered from other perspectives. Sometimes, it is offered with explanation. So Colin Gunton, for example, blames the *filioque* clause.[32] Moltmann takes the matter back to Augustine, and indicates how Karl Barth "fell into the same trap."[33]

Functional binitarianism overflows too easily into Christian discourse and practice. The people who told me, in my teens, the good news of God in Christ were, it might be fair to suggest, operating as functional binitarians. A memory I retain from those days was of asking them, in effect, "I know enough of Christianity to realize that there is a Father, a Son, and a Holy Spirit. You have told me at length about the Father and the Son, but have not mentioned the Spirit. What does the Spirit do?" I received a brief reply that perhaps paid lip service to the place of the Spirit in Christian beginnings, but I had to wait two years before first encountering charismatic Christianity and really learning about the dynamic activities of God's Spirit in today's churches.[34]

Arguably, this privileging of patrology and christology over pneumatology can be traced back to the New Testament itself. As Boyd, in his arguments with Oneness advocates, implicitly concedes, there are many

30. E.g. by C. F. D. Moule, as quoted in Smail, *Giving Gift*, 42.

31. Macchia, *Baptized in the Spirit*, 112 n. 28.

32. Gunton, *Promise of trinitarian Theology*, 199. For my discussion of the *filioque* controversy, see below, later in this chapter and in chapter 4.

33. Moltmann, *Trinity and the Kingdom*, 142–43.

34. In no way do I wish to belittle the positive significance of what my friends told me. I am immensely grateful to them all for their kindness and honesty in taking an interest in me, answering all my questions, and introducing me to the person of Jesus Christ. Humanly speaking, I owe my conversion to Christianity to them.

references in the New Testament to the Father and the Son that do not mention the Spirit (e.g., Matt 11:27; 1 Cor 1:3; 2 Cor 1:2; Gal 1:3; 1 John 1:3; Rev 21:22–23).[35] And if any sort of apparent binitarianism occurs even in the pages of holy writ, then the suspicion might well arise that God's being is in some sense binitarian: the sheer self-effacingness of the Spirit might give rise to the apparent absence of the Spirit even when this entity is present and active.[36]

Furthermore, the apparent binitarianism of the New Testament might be exaggerated by its readers. Larry Hurtado is an example of someone who writes repeatedly and explicitly of the binitarian worship of the New Testament churches and their writers, even using the term in section titles.[37] Admittedly, his emphasis is engendered by his subject matter and project, which concerns the genesis of the worship of Jesus within earliest Christianity. Nevertheless, the result may be a slightly skewed reading of the New Testament.[38]

Almost whenever this binitarianism is noted, it is bemoaned. Typically, the problem that is identified is that the Holy Spirit's role in Christian lives is ignored or relegated.[39] However, some authors also point out that this downgrading of pneumatology actually leads in turn to a warped christology, "because christology which is abstracted from a discussion of the relation to it of pneumatology is not christology rooted in the actual human career of the incarnate Lord."[40] Various attempts are made to redress

35. Boyd, *Oneness Pentecostals*, 44. The texts I list are those offered by Boyd. Many other examples could be found, even in such confessionally explicit statements as 1 Cor 8:6.

36. "The Person without a Face" is the title of chapter 2 in Smail, *Giving Gift*. See also chapter 2 of this book.

37. Hurtado, e.g., *Lord Jesus Christ*, 64, 74, 78, 134–51, 592–94; Hurtado, *One God, One Lord*, 2, 6, 7, 11, 12, 32, 37, 49.

38. I do not mean to imply any wider negative assessment beyond that stated here and below. Hurtado's *Lord Jesus Christ* is, in the clarity, thoroughness, and persuasiveness of its argument, truly excellent.

39. E.g., Gunton, *Promise of Trinitarian Theology*, 199; Parry, *Worshipping Trinity*, 116–18. However, note Smail, *Giving Gift*, 31: "The comparative neglect of the doctrine of the Holy Spirit both in the New Testament and in the teaching of the early Church, to say nothing of later, is not to be thought of wholly as a failure, but as something that is rooted, at least to some extent, in the very nature of the case. The mission of the Spirit is to glorify the Son and we are honouring the Spirit when our attention is most focussed on Christ."

40. Gunton, *Promise of Trinitarian Theology*, xxx.

the balance—but Pentecostals of all people ought to be well placed to take part in such a rebalancing. Thus, this work is unashamedly presenting a pneumatologically oriented trinitarianism.

Responding to the Challenges

It is not my intention to defend trinitarianism against these challenges as such. For instance, I intend no developed critique of unitarian or binitarian ideas. Rather, my hope is to develop a trinitarianism that is attractive. I hope it might be winsome to Pentecostals who are questioning Oneness claims. I also trust that it may prove helpful to trinitarians, Pentecostal and otherwise, who are unsure of the Holy Spirit's place in the Trinity.

I also want to challenge Pentecostals with the recognition that our pneumatological distinctives and insights can play a part in a wider Pentecostal contribution to theology overall. By "theology" here I mean theology proper: the study of God. Of course, as soon as I use the word "study," I must draw back. God cannot be "objectified." God cannot be put under the microscope, so to speak. It is much more true to state that humanity is "under God's microscope." Also, to write of the study of God is perhaps to give the impression that facts about God can be discovered through diligent research and that God can be brought to light and questions answered. This impression must be treated with great caution. Much that is true of God will remain a mystery. Note for example Friedrich Schmidt's comments concerning "the consciousness that men never for a single moment have *God*, or any dealings with him, at their 'disposal', and that God is only God in so far as he remains here and now the 'Lord', the power over everything which in being revealed remains a mystery, or rather first becomes a mystery thereby."[41]

METHODS

Primary Assumptions

On the basis of carefully developed and faithfully transmitted church teaching, I assume that God is Trinity. Therefore, this book does not set out to demonstrate that God is trinitarian as opposed to unitarian, binitarian, or

41. Schmidt, "Christian Revelation and Dogmatic Theology," 58; italics original.

any other "-arian." Rather, on the assumption that God is Trinity, I ask what this *means*. What sort of Trinity is God? What is the nature of the being and relations of the Father, the Son, and the Spirit? Similarly, I assume rather than argue the position of Christian theism that this God is eternal, all-powerful, and loving. God cares for creation. God has ultimately expressed love for humanity in the life, deeds, teaching, death, and resurrection of Jesus Christ. Herein lies the salvation of humanity. Furthermore, I adhere to a traditional incarnational christology, as expressed in the general creeds of the early church (even if I depart from some of the nuances and emphases of the discussion that surrounded these creeds at the time). I see the merits and attractions of what, to take one example, the "parabolic christology" of Sally McFague declares about Jesus—he is a parable of God—but cannot agree with what she denies about him. Jesus is indeed the parable of God, but God has spoken in many ways, not just in parables, and Jesus is the very impress of God's being (Heb 1:3), as well as a parable. I take Jesus "literally," not just metaphorically.[42] I also assume, along with the vast majority of my fellow Pentecostals, that God has granted humanity the Bible, of course through human intermediaries, as the primary, most reliable witness to God and the revelation of God in Christ. So again, this book will not seek to demonstrate that the Bible is a good place to begin when seeking to characterize the Trinity but will take this position for granted. Of course, I do not thereby suggest that fully developed trinitarianism is to be found there, but I do mean that if our trinitarianism contradicts the testimonies of Scripture, it is our trinitarianism that must change.

My Approach to Experience

All of our knowing begins, obviously enough, with directly perceived experiences, even intuitive ones.[43] We Pentecostals are great valuers of experience. We frequently give time and attention to our testimonies of individual

---

42. McFague, *Metaphorical Theology*, especially 18–19, 48–54. For brief comments on functional christologies in general, see Smail, *Forgotten Father*, 94–101.

43. I acknowledge that experience "is conditioned by theory in a vicious circle" (Duce, *Reading the Mind of God*, 114, referring to J. S. Feinberg) but trust that by God's grace the "vicious circle" can be, rather, a virtuous spiral. (See also Rabens, "Power from In Between," 138–50. For discussion concerning whether religious experiences can justify religious beliefs, see Peterson et al., *Reason and Religious Belief*, chapter 2: "Religious Experience.")

and corporate experiences.[44] We are also pragmatists, in the sense that this term is used in common parlance. We want to know whether something will *work*. We have succumbed to what Moltmann criticizes with the words, "What does not turn into act has no value."[45] Our concerns over church buildings, to take a concrete example (yes, the pun is deliberate), have more to do with whether there are sufficient catering and toilet facilities than over the beauty or symbolism of the architecture.

But our pragmatism is not something to be entirely ashamed of, despite Moltmann's criticisms. I owe to Yong's discussion of the work of Charles Sanders Peirce, "the founder of American pragmatism,"[46] the insight that Jesus' statement "by their fruit shall you know them" is an expression of pragmatic logic. As Peirce put it in his Pragmatic Maxim, "Consider what effects . . . we conceive the object of our conception to have. Then, our conception of these effects is the whole of our conception of the object."[47] In Yong's words, "If effects are inconceivable for any thing, such a 'thing' is probably meaningless and, as such, neither true nor false."[48] So the effects—practical ones—of my Christianity on my own self seem a good starting point for my trinitarian exploration. But how might I translate these perceived effects that come through my experiences into theological theorization? The brute objectivity of empiricism will not suffice, for it does not acknowledge sufficiently the subjective place of the "knower." Neither will individually subjective postmodern relativism do, for ideas then gleaned may be "true for me" but will have no value in persuading others.

Yong develops Peirce's appeal to the inferences drawn from perceptions, unconsciously and consciously, uncontrollably and controllably, in the process of forming beliefs. There is not merely logical induction from evidence or deduction from principles: there is "abduction"—the inference drawn by the individual that depends on the interplay of the experiences gained and the beliefs already held by the person doing the thinking.[49] In the development of a worldview—"worldmaking"—this process of inference and abduction involves: classifying experiences; weighing them for

---

44. See Cartledge, *Testimony in the Spirit*, 17.

45. Moltmann, *Trinity and Kingdom*, 5–6.

46. Yong, *Spirit-Word-Community*, 91.

47. Peirce, quoted in ibid., 155.

48. Ibid., 155.

49. Ibid., 152–53. The terms "adduction" and "retroduction" are used by some; see Duce, *Reading the Mind of God*, 107.

relevance, value, and so forth; ordering them; adding and deleting to fill in gaps and leave out trivia; and "deformation" in which perceptions are revised imaginatively, "since not all data are taken in solely on their own terms."[50] This last element is instructive: to take the raw data of perceived experience and build a worldview from them, be it Christian or secular, requires imagination.

Yong appeals for the use in this context of the "pneumatological imagination." He makes three important points about this form of imagination. He offers them as indicatives: "the pneumatological imagination is . . ." However, I wish to offer these points as imperatives: "in order to be useful, the pneumatological imagination *ought to be* . . ." The three points are as follows. First, the pneumatological imagination ought to be powerfully charismatic in both a passive and active sense, recognizing that all human capacity for thought is a gift from a powerful God and then deliberately applying that thinking in an empowered way to the task in hand. Second, this form of imagination must be Christ-centered. The Spirit and the word must cohere. The imagination ought not to run wild but must be hemmed in by the concrete reality of the Christ-event. Thirdly, the pneumatological imagination must be value-driven. It will not suffice to take a value-free approach to phenomena and especially to powers that are evidently at work in the world. There are good powers and there are evil powers. This imagination must be discerning; it must be critical.[51]

The pneumatological imagination will be at play in this book. I will repeatedly make use of *imaginative analogy* between what we and our forebears experience of God and what God essentially is.[52] I will "read back," imaginatively and analogically, from our perceptions of God to what God may actually be. In line with the three features of pneumatological imagination that Yong delineates, this process of imaginative analogy will be charismatic, christological, and critical. I will implicitly be appealing to a *charismatic* element to knowing God. While I am placing the starting

50. Yong, *Spirit-Word-Community*, 144, with reference to the work of Goodman. For discussion of the role of personal judgment in scientific and theological thinking, see Polkinghorne, *One World*, 12, 16.

51. Yong, *Spirit-Word-Community*, 134.

52. By "analogy" I mean "an observed or inferred similarity between two situations which have some properties, forms, or functions in common, although others may be different" (Jeeves and Berry, *Science, Life and Christian Belief*, 82–83; see also Duce, *Reading the Mind of God*, 121; Gunton, *Actuality of Atonement*, chapter 2. For brief discussion of Aquinas' theory of analogy, see Peterson et al., *Reason and Religious Belief*, 168–71).

point in the order by which we know things in our experience, I acknowledge that this experience is itself given by the Spirit and that any successful derivations of ideas from this experience will be enabled by the wisdom of the Spirit. I will seek constantly to be *christological*, in the sense of focusing on Christ, recognizing that his arrival in our world is the central point in God's self-revelation to this world. I will be *critical* in the sense of discerning: operating judgments that are not value-free and recognizing that ultimately all judgment is in the hands of God the Father, so that if we are to think in ways that mirror God's mind we must be discerning and selective. Part of the process will undoubtedly involve speculation. It is to be hoped, however, that centeredness on the Christ-event and openness to the views of the Christian community will save me from empty speculation. I hope the result of my labor is, to quote Yong again, "not simply speculative abstraction (though there is certainly plenty of that), but deeper spiritual and moral living."[53]

Discussion of analogy leads naturally to a comment about models. The value of imaginatively created models for the development of understanding is well recognized in the world of the physical sciences. So too does theology depend on the use of models that are related to reality, though those who advocate or use them must acknowledge that the models are not identical to the reality they portray.[54] My use of imaginative analogy will in effect create models. For instance, I will suggest that the Spirit can be viewed in terms both of impersonhood and personhood. But I will not thereby be claiming that the Spirit *actually is* both a non-person and a person. I rather wish to suggest that impersonal and personal models of the Spirit both have explanatory value in our seeking to imagine the Spirit.[55]

Experience of God, so the Bible and other witnesses tell us, is both personal and corporate. This recognition is important with respect to the dynamics that will be at work between author and readers of this book. I am writing primarily for my fellow Christians, be they Pentecostals or otherwise. Therefore the "implied reader" is Christian and has her or his own personal experience of God. At this point I have to make an assumption

---

53. Yong, *Spirit-Word-Community*, 146.

54. I thus take a "critical-realist" rather than "naive-realist" position. See Polkinghorne, *One World*, 22, 42. For discussion of models in these contexts, see Jeeves and Berry, *Science, Life and Christian Belief*, 82–87. For a wide-ranging comparison of scientific with theological models, see McFague, *Metaphorical Theology*, chapters 3–4.

55. For discussion of the value of multiple models in this context, see, e.g., McFague, *Metaphorical Theology*, 145–52.

regarding something that I cannot demonstrate. It is that my personal experience of God is, if I may for a moment address you the reader directly, in some ways analogous or similar to your personal experience of God. I work, therefore, with the hope of a "presupposition pool"[56] between us. I hope that I can presuppose some common experience of God that will enhance our conversation in two ways. First, I will be able to assume, when I record my own experiences of God, that you may have had similar ones and will understand what I mean. The second presupposition is that, like me, you will be able to use your personal experiences of God to approach the subject matter from at least a similar perspective to my own.

Finally for this section, my approach to experience takes note of the present scholarly consensus that the flow of thought between theory and practice is not all one way. I will refer on occasion to my practical experiences and activities as a Pentecostal as I seek to build up a picture of the Trinity, because these are formative for me and may resonate with the experiences and practices of readers. To take the relationship between experience and Bible reading as another example, while as a Christian I am committed to the idea that what I find in the Bible must impact my interpretation of my experiences I also recognize that these experiences impact how I interpret the Bible. This is not bad news. There is rich potential for a "hermeneutical spiral"—actually a helix—in which enhanced understanding of the text and enhanced appreciation of one's experience of God and God's world positively reinforce one another over and over again as one climbs the "spiral staircase" of understanding. And so now to the Bible I turn.

My Approach to Scripture

My authoritative source will be the protestant canon of the Christian Bible. I regard it as the trustworthy revelation of God and as the authoritative document governing Christian life. Like most Pentecostals, I am also conservative in my approach to its content and form: for example to the authorship and dating of biblical documents. However, I think that my thesis holds good even if lesser claims are adhered to. Thus, for the sake of argument, those who would regard the canonical Gospels as reliable only in their generalities concerning the history of Jesus of Nazareth, rather than in countless specifics, should not thereby be thrown off track from following

---

56. For discussion of this term, see Cotterell and Turner, *Linguistics and Biblical Interpretation*, 90–91.

the thrust of my argument. Similarly, those who reject traditional statements concerning the authorship of New Testament documents will not, I hope, on that account alone be deterred from agreeing with my points. I will use the traditional names of the biblical authors but do not intend thereby to prescribe an understanding concerning their identity. For instance, when I call the author of the Fourth Gospel "John," it will not make any difference to my argument whether he, or indeed they or she, is John the twin of James and one of the Twelve, is another otherwise unknown John, another individual altogether, or a community of writing disciples. It will be sufficient to accept the following: that Luke and Acts were written by the same person, and can therefore be viewed together to build up a composite "Lukan" view; that the Fourth Gospel and 1 John can be similarly treated, to form a "Johannine" view; and that Romans, 1 and 2 Corinthians, Galatians, Philippians, and 1 and 2 Thessalonians, taken together, offer a "Pauline" view, reflecting the writing of one man whose autobiographical comments he included in these letters are accurate, so that one can conclude that he lived during the lifetimes of personal witnesses of the life and death of Jesus of Nazareth.

While acknowledging the biblical canon, I readily recognize that I, like many readers of the Bible, operate with something of a canon-within-a-canon. To some extent, of course, a study of this sort demands that far more attention be given to certain texts than to others. But beyond this necessary process of selection, I acknowledge that I, like many other Pentecostals, warm especially to Luke-Acts. James Dunn may well have a typical Pentecostal in mind at the close of the following: someone finds "Paul most congenial, while another recoils from Paul and relaxes with John, while yet another turns in puzzlement from both to the simplicities of Acts."[57] I hope that my interest in Acts, expressed in this book as well as elsewhere, is not occasioned merely by the fact that I find Paul and John overly complex. Rather, we Pentecostals have various reasons for listening especially carefully to Luke-Acts.[58] For a start, with the exception of one inconsequential reference in Paul's letters, only Acts mentions Pentecost. I recognize the danger that I may arrive at a picture of the Trinity that has an unduly Lukan hue. Nevertheless, I can only appeal to the uniqueness of Luke's witness in the New Testament. I seek to listen carefully to other New Testament

57. Dunn, *Unity and Diversity*, 375.
58. See Mittelstadt, *Reading Luke-Acts*, throughout.

voices, but admit that on some of the matters I discuss, Luke is nearest to the microphone.

More broadly, my canon-within-a-canon will be the New Testament. As replete as the Old Testament may be with presages of the Trinity, one must acknowledge that it was only with the arrival of the Christ-event that worshippers of the God of Abraham, Isaac, and Jacob had to grapple with a rapid reconfiguring of their monotheism.[59] Certain events occurring within and soon after the earthly life of Jesus of Nazareth were the clear cause of an explosion of new theological investigations that led eventually to the development of a Christianity that could be clearly distinguished from the Judaism(s) of the day.[60]

My approach to the New Testament will be partly historical and partly theological. I will examine the religious experiences, as far as we can glean what these were, of the first people who came to call themselves Christians. I will also consider in detail their theological interpretations of those experiences, as presented to us through the words of their key spokespeople whose works have been preserved in the New Testament. Of course, all recorded experience is interpreted experience and so there will necessarily be a considerable degree of overlap between these two investigative procedures.

In examining these ancient religious experiences, I recognize that I am departing from the emphases of much New Testament scholarship. Johnson helpfully explores the widespread ignoring by this scholarship of New Testament experience.[61] He acknowledges several reasons for this avoidance: New Testament history "focuses on definable events in time and space"; the "raw language of religious experience" is "too embarrassing"; some New Testament studies are laden with theories that demand "that language of religious experience is either meaningless or manipulative"; and experience is too "individual, psychosomatic, interior, subjective, and interpretive" for scientific study.[62] Nevertheless, Johnson rightly calls for a reversal of this approach, pointing out that "to ignore the language of religious experience in early Christian writings is to neglect the specific historical character of this movement and thereby to make its historical continuation and success

---

59. For a strong defense of the belief that post-exilic Judaism maintained its monotheism, see Hurtado, *One God, One Lord*, throughout.

60. See Dunn, *Partings of the Ways*, throughout.

61. Johnson, *Religious Experience in Earliest Christianity*, chapters 1 and 2.

62. Ibid., 12–13, 41, 51.

all the more difficult to understand."[63] He admits the difficulties involved in listening to New Testament reports and interpretations of experience but calls for ears attentive to this feature of early Christian life. I will seek to answer this call.

My Approach to Tradition

My approach to Christian tradition will concentrate far more on beliefs handed down than on practices handed down. As is well known, massive developments occurred in beliefs concerning the Trinity during the third and fourth centuries of the Christian era. I will consider some of these developments, although I will tend to do so only through the interpretive lenses of late twentieth- and early twenty-first-century writers, for there has been another veritable explosion of interest in the Trinity in recent decades that has picked up and further developed the beliefs of the early centuries. The new interest has been widely observed. For example, Colin Gunton's second sentence in his 1991 *Promise of Trinitarian Theology* referred to "renewed interest and debate" concerning the Trinity, but by the time he wrote the preface to the 1997 second edition, he began with the words, "Suddenly we are all trinitarians, or so it would seem. As the result of a number of influences, both churchly and secular, the doctrine of the Trinity is now discussed in places where even a short time ago it would have been regarded as an irrelevance."[64] Alister McGrath notes that the genesis of this renewed interest is widely ascribed to the creativity of Karl Barth, expressed in his massive *Church Dogmatics*.[65] Thus the trinitarianism of some who have built on Barth's work, for instance, Jürgen Moltmann and Tom Smail among the Protestants and Hans Urs von Balthasar among Catholics, will gain my attention, as will the trinitarian thinking of Pentecostals such as Frank Macchia and Amos Yong.

Some fellow Pentecostals may be surprised to find me listening to Christian tradition. The question may be asked, "Is not the Bible sufficient?" But for me to imagine myself as the only reader of the Bible would be absurd. Others have read it before me. To "reinvent the wheel" in this respect would be not only unnecessary but also potentially dangerous. Also, reading the Bible insulated from previous readings is in fact impossible. I

63. Ibid., 36.

64. Gunton, *Promise of Trinitarian Theology*, 1, xv.

65. McGrath, *Theology: The Basics*, 101.

am informed by my own Pentecostal tradition, if nothing else. And Pentecostalism rests not only on scriptural teaching but also on the traditions of nineteenth-century holiness and healing movements out of which it grew, whether it cares to acknowledge this theological dependence or not. Certainly, observers of Pentecostalism are aware of its theological links with the wider Christian world, past and present. J. C. O'Neill remarks:

> The shrewd pentecostalist preacher who commands his millions of devoted followers might insist it is his continued supernaturalist theology that does it, but what keeps the show on the road is the belief he imbibed from his Bible College teachers, which they in turn got from conservative German scholarship, that knew to drink from the same fountain as their radical colleagues, that the Bible gives anyone who reads it the clue to the history of the world.[66]

Historical links and concomitant theological indebtedness are not only identifiable: they are useful. T. F. Torrance offers the following assessment of tradition's value in theological enquiry:

> The immense value of church history and of the history of doctrine is the dimension of historical depth it gives to one's understanding of the faith, and the balance it brings into one's judgments. . . . [N]o constructive thinking that is worth while [sic] can be undertaken that sets at naught the intellectual labours of the centuries that are enshrined in tradition, or be undertaken on the arrogant assumption that everything must be thought through *de novo* as if nothing true had already been done or said.[67]

Note too the positive assessment of R. C. Hanson:

> [I]t is in fact impossible, not to say undesirable, to move from the period of the Old and the New Testaments directly to our own day, to "confront" the men [sic] of the twentieth century with the Bible, as if nothing had happened to the Christian religion between the first and the twentieth centuries. Christianity is "the religion of a book," but the religion is not the book. . . . We regard one particular period of history as normative, but all Christian history must be illustrative. . . . It must first be recognized that no group of Christians in the whole history of Christianity has ever succeeded in confining its doctrine to the Bible and the Bible alone. . . . [This]

66. O'Neill, *The Bible's Authority*, 3.

67. Torrance, *Theology in Reconstruction*, 23, 24.

is a self-evidently impossible principle. In the first place, no institution can exist in history without creating a tradition, be it a cricket club, a bird-watching society, a parliament, a police force or a literary clique. Those institutions which attempt to reject tradition merely succeed in establishing a tradition of rejecting tradition. . . . In the second place, every intelligent person ought to realize that the Bible does not interpret itself. This is meant in the simplest and directest way. If any reader were to take a modern printed copy of the Bible and place it, open, in Trafalgar Square, it would not begin either to read itself aloud or to preach itself. . . . No believing Christian ever believes nakedly the Bible and nothing but the Bible without any interposition of an interpreting Church, even though he may think he does.[68]

I intend to follow the good advice of these authors and listen carefully to the great thinkers on the Trinity who have emerged over the centuries. I cannot possibly hope to interact with them all and will tend to interact with more authors who hail from Western Protestantism than from Roman Catholicism or Eastern Orthodoxy. Nevertheless, chief voices from these other traditions will not be ignored and at times I will side with them rather than with Protestant ones.

My Approach to Pentecost

I decided to title this book *Trinity After Pentecost* for two reasons, quite apart from the fact that Trinity Sunday follows a week after Pentecost Sunday in the church year. The first reason is that as a Pentecostal interested in theology, I should be able to write an account of the Trinity that follows from my Pentecostal position with its various attendant experiences, beliefs, and practices. In my case, the dependence is not chronological: I was a trinitarian *before* I was a Pentecostal. Nevertheless, if my Pentecostal views have theological as well as practical value, they should be formative of my trinitarianism (I do not deny that the process should also be true *vice versa* and that my trinitarianism should creatively inform my Pentecostalism). The second reason for my choice of book title is that as far as I can see, Pentecost occupies a key place in the history of trinitarian reflection. While Luke's testimony is perhaps weightiest in supporting this point, I do not believe that my case collapses if Luke-Acts is put to one side. At some

---

68. Hanson, "Introduction," 9–13.

point soon after Jesus' death, his immediate followers experienced an influx of God's Spirit in a way that caused them both to link God's Spirit now with Jesus—intimately—and to develop their understanding of links between Jesus and God. Both developments were foundational to the trinitarianism that gradually emerged. I will explore each of these convictions in turn.

First, I turn to my own Pentecostalism. To put it another way, I turn to my Christian experience, flavored as it is with a rich vein of pneumatic activity and concern. I dare to claim that I have experienced the Spirit. Put on paper, this sounds an arrogant statement but it is no more than many or all Christians would claim. I also believe that by way of this Spirit, I experience Jesus. By way of Jesus, as portrayed by the Gospel writers and as mediated by the Spirit, I experience the Father. Some Pentecostals, and I am sure many other Christians as well, are familiar with a hymn that ponders, "You ask me how I know He lives: He lives within my heart."[69] This simple song encapsulates theology of the most profound type. Like the readers of 1 Peter 1:8, our generation and many generations past have not seen the physical Jesus. We have not seen the empty tomb. We have not seen Christ in the resurrection appearances. Though we may be convinced by intellectual argument, our actual subjective experience of God, such as it is, has one and only one source: it is the experience of the Holy Spirit deep within. Thus it is entirely appropriate that reflection on the nature of God should commence with human experience of the Spirit of Christ within, an experience that began at Pentecost.[70]

So I turn from my own Pentecostalism to the historical Pentecost. First, I must offer a comment about that word "historical." Of course, only Luke mentions a link between the day of Pentecost and the arrival of the Spirit—and many scholars doubt the historicity of Acts. Thus, for many, Pentecost as such is unhistorical. I do not share such historical skepticism. But the history to which I primarily refer does not stand or fall on the stumbling block of Lukan historicity. What is beyond historical doubt is that the first generations of Christians, as represented by their spokespeople writing in the New Testament, believed that they had experienced the Spirit as, in some way to be explored, the Spirit of Christ. Given that this claim was not made by surrounding or preceding Judaism, this explosion of experienced

69. Ackley, "He Lives! He Lives! Christ Jesus Lives Today."

70. Of course, experience of the Spirit did not begin at Pentecost. However, experience of God's Spirit *as the Spirit of Christ* began then, even if with hindsight 1 Peter 1:11 can call the Spirit experienced by Old Testament prophets the "Spirit of Christ."

Spirit-activity may be labeled "Pentecost" without concern about the historicity of the precise details Luke recorded. So, with this somewhat broader concept of Pentecost in place, I turn to consider its implications for the Trinity.

While the eschatological implications of Pentecost are vitally important, I wish to focus on the christological aspects of this development. It was the experience of the Spirit in the lives of these early Christians that first led to the realization that Jesus of Nazareth was the Lord of glory, in a way that did not destroy their strict Jewish monotheism. In more general terms, their religious experience informed their attitude to Jesus, enabling them to offer him cultic worship—"official" worship—and initiating a process of theological reflection and development that led to trinitarian belief.

Expressed in these general terms, I have simply repeated the position espoused by Larry Hurtado. Hurtado's contribution to the historical study of the beginnings of Christ-devotion is superb. He sets out to explain what the key factors were that led so early to an intense and widespread devotion to Christ as to God, and finds four. They were: *Jewish monotheism*, which was strict despite the veneration in some circles of senior angels and exalted historical figures such as Moses; the *impact of Jesus'* human history on those around him, which had the effect of polarizing people for or against him so that while some had him executed, others devoted their lives to him; *religious experiences* gained soon after this execution, which created the conviction that this Jesus was, among other things, enthroned alongside the one God in heaven; and the turbulent *religious environment* in which Christianity was born, which was often hostile to the first Christians, thus forcing them to clarify and declare their devotion to Jesus. Undoubtedly, Hurtado's case is strong. He neatly cuts away the ground beneath numerous counter-arguments and contrary positions. His landmark work will surely stand the test of time.[71]

However, it suffers from a weakness that is relevant to my thesis. In a book that focuses in a sustained manner on what he calls the binitarian worship of the early churches, he consistently fails to offer any possible distinctions between the religious experiences he describes as resurrection appearances and the religious experiences—which he hardly ever mentions—that he accurately points out were regarded at the time as being mediated by the Spirit or involved what was called receiving the Spirit.[72]

71. Hurtado, *Lord Jesus Christ*, e.g., chapter 1.

72. Turner makes a similar criticism of Hurtado's earlier, briefer book, *One God, One Lord* (Turner, "Spirit of Christ," 416).

His coalescing of these two sets of experiences is not true to the two foremost New Testament authors on the subject: Luke and Paul. Admittedly, John draws no cast-iron distinction between resurrection appearances and reception of the Spirit (John 20:22). However, the same cannot be said for Luke—of course—and even for Paul. In the case of Luke, the argument is obvious. Luke presented a time lapse between the resurrection appearances being brought to a distinct end by Christ's ascension and the arrival of the Spirit on the Day of Pentecost. Resurrection appearances were pre-ascension; Pentecost was post-ascension. The ascension is absent as a concept from Paul's letters, admittedly. Thus, Paul's position on the matter is more obscure. But it is visible in 1 Corinthians 15. Here, Paul limited resurrection appearances to a relatively small number of individuals, none of whom were in Corinth at the time (or he would presumably have declared so). On the other hand, he indicated that *all* the Corinthians had received the Spirit "to drink" (1 Cor 12:13). Thus he drew a clear conceptual distinction between experiencing a resurrection appearance and experiencing the Spirit. While he offered no account of Christ's ascension, Paul clearly regarded the resurrection appearances as occurring during a limited period of time that, by the time he wrote 1 Corinthians, *was over*. This is clear from his testimony concerning his own encounter, as he understood it, with the risen Christ. While some scholars regard this as a spiritual experience—Hurtado calls it a vision[73]—Paul saw otherwise. This is precisely why he called himself one abnormally born and particularly why he described his experience as "last of all" (1 Cor 15:8). It was not to be repeated. God had graciously joined him onto the end of the line of those who saw the resurrected Christ with their eyes. This was his implication. Resurrection appearances were now over. Spirit-reception was still available for all to enjoy. It is, admittedly, far less clear that Paul regarded the Spirit's arrival rather than resurrection appearances as the religious experience that offered evidence to him and his audiences that Jesus was Lord. Nevertheless,

---

73. Hurtado, *Lord Jesus Christ*, 71 n. 127. Hurtado is content to regard "appearance" in this context and "vision" interchangeably, as "visual experiences which the recipients described as specially given to them by God and, as such, distinguishable from everyday and public visual experiences understood as resulting from encounter with objects and events that are freely visible to anyone on site at the time." This understanding does not seem to tally with Paul's focus on the fact that Christ, in a resurrection appearance, could be seen by 500 people at once (1 Cor 15:6). Paul's implication seems to be that anyone there would have seen Christ.

this case is hinted in 1 Corinthians 12:3 and in Romans 1:4. I will consider these texts in detail in chapter 2.

In conclusion, most clearly in Luke but implied in Paul—though absent from John—we find a distinction drawn between resurrection appearances and the Spirit's arrival. It was the *latter experience, not the former* which led to the early Christians' devotion to Jesus in the many ways expressed in the New Testament and recognized by Hurtado and which in turn led to the earliest forms of proto-trinitarian thinking. This makes sense. Jesus' followers knew of others who had been raised from the dead: their Scriptures contained such accounts. According to the Gospels, such remarkable events had occurred as the result of Jesus' miraculous ministry. For Jesus to be raised by the power of God would not in itself suggest that he was more than a man favored by God. Even for someone to be enthroned in heaven did not, in their worldview, necessarily entail that this person was in some sense divine. As Hurtado acknowledges, Jewish writings of the time referred to people who after their successful earthly lives were offered a throne in heaven beside God's, as a reward.[74] No, what really persuaded these first Christians that Jesus is Lord was the arrival of the Spirit as the Spirit of Jesus, the Spirit sensed as sent by Jesus and conveying the subjective experience of Jesus' presence to them. They were persuaded that Jesus is Lord by Pentecost. Only this event moved their thinking pivotally over the Rubicon, for now they had to reckon with the realization that the ascended Jesus could grant God's Spirit. This idea also dissociated the Spirit sufficiently from Jesus' Father for the Spirit's identity "within" God to emerge. Only after Pentecost was the scene set for the emergence of trinitarianism. It was truly Trinity after Pentecost.

My Approach to Eternity

By "eternity" I mean the environment in which God dwells, conceived meta-chronologically rather than meta-spatially. The process of imaginative analogy that I will employ seeks above all to form a bridge between what we know through experience in time and what we believe by faith about eternity. As soon as we begin to think about eternity we face a problem, for we humans in this world must all acknowledge that we do not really know what eternity is. I suggest we might not know it existed if this was not

---

74. Hurtado, *Lord Jesus Christ*, 360. For example, concerning Jewish ideas about a heavenly enthronement of Moses, see Hurtado, *One God, One Lord*, 56–63.

revealed to us by the eternal God. When we try to imagine what eternity is, all we can do is gaze from afar and employ analogies that arise from our experience of time as a series of changes. On this analogical basis, eternity can be viewed either as an unendingly long period of time—an unending series of changes; or as an unchanging state—a stasis in which nothing happens at all. While none of us, I guess, would wish to experience the latter, traditional classical theism has rather cruelly confined God to it: the perfect God cannot change from perfection or merely have the potential to change to perfection. Thus God cannot change: God is immutable.

Two considerations should make us cautious about following classical theology at this point. The first is the recognition that the authors of the Bible sometimes seemed to present eternity as an unendingly long time (e.g., note the contrast with "momentary" in 2 Cor 4:17). The second is the valuable thinking of twentieth-century theologians on the subject. They suggest that we must avoid too great a distinction—a sort of "dualism"—between time and eternity.[75] They have Scripture on their side, for it declares that those who know God in Christ enjoy eternal life, if proleptically, while still living in this time-bound world: eternity has broken into time in the incarnation and the salvation for humanity that flows from it. So one does not need to accept all the tenets of open theism to agree with Clark Pinnock that God does not simply exist *outside* time. As Pinnock observes, "if God did not experience events as they transpire, he would not experience or know the world as it actually is."[76] I agree with Pinnock's suggestion that "God's eternity embraces time and takes temporal events into the divine life" while at the same time valuing his caveat: "When I say that God is in time, I do not mean that God is exhaustively in time. Even in human experience, we partially transcend time through memory, imagination and reason. God's transcendence over time is vastly more perfect than is ours."[77] Thus it is unwise to see eternity, and God's place in it, as a polar opposite from time—an unchanging state lying outside time. Eternity relates to time in some mysterious way that we probably cannot imagine. Perhaps we are on the right lines to speculate that eternity includes time but is also far more than it. The relevance that this discussion has to the Trinity lies in a traditional distinction that follows the dualism between changing time and an unchanging eternity.

75. E.g., Gunton, *Promise of Trinitarian Theology*, 172; Yong, *Spirit Poured Out*, 210.

76. Pinnock, *Openness of God*, 120.

77. Ibid., 121; see also Pinnock, *Most Moved Mover*, 32, 96–99.

The classical doctrine of the Trinity grew up in an age when Christian ideas were being expressed in a context of Greek philosophy. Certain ideas found in the Bible were stripped of their paradoxical mystery and expressed as rigid formulae in the emerging classical theism of the day. In particular for our purposes, the biblical declaration that the eternal God does not change, which in Scripture was held in paradoxical tension with such time-bound statements as "the Word became flesh," was torn from that context and turned into the rigid statement, referred to above, that God is incapable of change. The Trinity presents a problem to this doctrine of God's immutability, because the activities of the Trinity in God's created order—the cosmos—seem to imply change in God and indeed some measure of dependence on the cosmos. Thus, for instance, the Word not only became flesh but was killed by people. The Word changed and was dependent on the cosmos for its destiny. If the Word is the second person of the Trinity, a contradiction is formed between statements concerning the immutable trinitarian God and the trinitarian God who actually relates to the cosmos.[78]

The classic answer was in effect to posit two Trinities. The first was the Trinity as God is in all eternity, self-contained and, so to speak, divorced from all that lies beyond: God as God is *within*. This is often called the *immanent* Trinity. The second is the Trinity that actually deals with everything else—everything that lies outside God: often termed the *economic* Trinity. There is some warrant for maintaining a paradoxical tension between these ideas of the Trinity. As Balthasar wrote, "the process of establishing and experiencing the world" must remain for God "a perfectly free decision."[79] In other words, for God to be God and Lord, there has to be a sense in which the Trinity is not contingent upon the vicissitudes of the cosmos' history. However, to stretch this point too far so that one ends up with two disparate Trinities is hardly a position to which the Bible, for instance, lends itself. So recent scholars have by and large tended to side with Karl Rahner, who famously wrote that "The 'economic' Trinity is the 'immanent' Trinity and the 'immanent' Trinity is the 'economic' Trinity."[80] This is not without its difficulties but it presents a far more coherent picture of God's self-revelation in and through the persons of the Trinity.[81]

78. See, e.g., Moltmann, *Trinity and Kingdom*, 160.

79. Balthasar, *Mysterium Paschale*, 35.

80. Rahner, *Trinity*, 22; italics removed.

81. For robust statements distinguishing between economic Trinity and immanent Trinity, see Lossky, *Mystical Theology*, 138, 158.

In Rahner's favor is the realization that, unless God presents untruths, the God who is revealed through the time-bound human history of Jesus of Nazareth is the *same* God who exists in eternity. This book proceeds on such a premise: God does not set out to deceive and therefore all that is genuinely revealed about God is consistent with God's actual being. What Rahner's position lacks is an overt recognition that the immanent Trinity might be much *more* than the economic Trinity. The economic Trinity is limited by the economy. For example, the economic Trinity is expressed in a finite number of acts that God performs in this finite created order—even though this number is incalculably huge. The finitude is introduced here not by limitation in God but by limitations in this created order. On the other hand, the immanent Trinity is unlimited. God is not limited to those aspects that are revealed. God is not obligated to reveal all that God is, and it would be unreasonable to suppose that finite humans could, if all were revealed, grasp all that is characteristic of this infinite God. God can, so to speak, keep secrets and so the God who *is* can be more than the God we find *revealed* in this history.[82]

Despite this awareness that the immanent Trinity is more than the economic Trinity, we may say that all that can be known about the economic Trinity—that which is revealed to us—is true of the immanent Trinity. Thus the choice to use one's pneumatological imagination to "read back" analogically from God's activities in the economy to the inner world of the immanent Trinity is valid.[83] One does not thereby probe all that is true of God; but what one discovers, if this pneumatological imagination has been put to good use, is indicative of truths about God.

---

82. Moltmann offers the useful observation that the relationship between the immanent Trinity and economic Trinity is not only that of analogy "from below," in which divine, trinitarian acts towards the economy reveal aspects of God's "prior" immanent trinitarian life. It is also the case that such outward acts play their part in fashioning God's own trinitarian life. So, for example, the dreadful dynamics of the cross play their part in the very eternal relationship between the Father and the Son (Moltmann, *Trinity and Kingdom*, 159).

83. Rahner denied that the economic Trinity is "merely . . . an analogy of the inner Trinity" (*Trinity*, 35). I do not disagree with this. My point is that our *experience* of the economic Trinity offers us a model, by way of *analogy*, for contemplating the immanent Trinity. For further defenses of the claim that one can see the immanent Trinity "through the window" of the economic Trinity, see Smail, *Forgotten Father*, 24; Smail, *Giving Gift*, 164; Smail, *Like Father, Like Son*, 160; Volf, "Being As God Is," 4–5.

My Approach to Personhood

Trinitarians declare, some with more reservations than others, that there is one God and this God is three "persons." This word "person," it is often immediately pointed out, is being used in a distinct, technical, analogous sense and should not be understood to indicate what we might otherwise call "people." But if this is so, what does the word mean in this context and is it in fact helpful to hedge the word about with such qualifiers as "distinct," "technical," or "analogous"? Volf is an example of this tendency. He writes that "person" used with reference to God can only be understood by way of *analogy* with "person" used with reference to humans.[84] I am not sure this is helpful. If "person" used of God means something different, even though analogous, to person used of, say, me, then how can we know what the word "person" means when applied to its divine form? It might be more useful to start this discussion with the assumption that in trinitarian discussion "person" can be used in what I will call a "normal straightforward" sense. Thereafter it might become possible to see whether this "naive" view of personhood can fit with all we say about God, or whether there are *impersonal* ways that we also need to conceptualize the being of God and each "mode of being" or "member" of the Trinity.[85] If we decide that there are both personal and impersonal ways of speaking of God, then we need not use the *word* "person" in a distinct, technical sense. Rather, we can conclude that "personhood," straightforwardly understood, must be combined with "impersonhood" in speaking of the Trinity.

When proto-trinitarian reflection was first shared aloud and in writing, this occurred in the Greek language. More mature trinitarian definition occurred in both Greek and Latin. It was the Latin language that provided the word *persona*, from the pen of Tertullian.[86] The word was taken from the theater, where the role an actor performed was termed *persona* (originally, the word referred to the mask an actor held up before the face, to help the audience know which character in the performance was being played).[87]

84. Volf, *After Our Likeness*, 199.

85. "Mode of being" was Barth's preferred term (e.g., *Church Dogmatics*, 1/1, 359); "member" is used by Alan Torrance (e.g., *Persons in Communion*, 225, 227, 237).

86. Kelly, *Early Christian Doctrines*, 112. According to Kelly (ibid., 115), "as employed by Tertullian it [*persona*] connoted the concrete presentation of an individual as such." However, any connotation of self-consciousness, which I will discuss presently, was not "at all prominent."

87. See, e.g., Lossky, *Mystical Theology*, 51.

This use lives on in the compound term, *dramatis personae*, and in the relatively uncommon use of the word *persona* alone with this ancient sense.

In this case as in so many, language has evolved, as can be seen from the simple observation that we trinitarians do *not* in fact refer to "one God; three *people*"—the general modern plural of "person." But ideas as well as terms evolve. As Welker observes, "with different social and cultural contexts, the definition of 'person' and of the essence of personhood changes."[88] It is important to consider how to respond to this conceptual and linguistic evolution. There are three main options. First, the term can continue to be used of the Trinity with the appeal constantly repeated that it is a technical term bearing little or no direct relation in this context to its senses in other uses.[89] This is a common strategy but runs the risk that the word will be understood, by any other than the carefully initiated, in ways that reflect neither its earlier meaning nor the current author's intention. Secondly, the word "person" can be excised from this context on the ground that it is a misleading term that should be abandoned.[90] This has been attempted but has not found favor. The word "person" is still standard issue when the Trinity is discussed. Thirdly, its continued use can be maintained with recognition that any evolution in meaning of the term has been at least to some extent paralleled by evolution in understanding of the trinitarian persons, whatever the nature of the masks worn by ancient Latin actors. The word can be infused with "new" meaning.[91] Current discussion concerning meanings of the word "person" in trinitarian thought have usually centered on its link to relationships and relationality.[92] To state that someone or something is "personal" is to imply that this entity can relate. Thus when I use the word "person" in this book I will refer to some*one with, at least potentially, a sense of self and an ability to relate to non-self as "other."*[93]

88. Welker, "The Autonomous Person?" 99.

89. Such is the reluctant advice of Rahner, *Trinity*, 44.

90. Barth was a leading proponent of the word's demise: see, e.g., *Church Dogmatics*, 1/1, 355.

91. This is in effect the approach taken by Moltmann, in, e.g., *Trinity and Kingdom*, 145, 155–57. According to Lossky, the situation is complicated by the fact that twentieth-century ideas of personhood have themselves been informed by *theological* understandings of "person," which have evolved over the centuries (*Mystical Theology*, 53).

92. However, this should not imply that a person is no more than a web of relationships. See Gunton, *Promise*, 92, 200; Volf, *After Our Likeness*, 67–69: "Pure relations can neither speak nor hear" (69).

93. Compare Hefner's discussion, "Imago Dei," 84.

It is immediately apparent that the working definition I am offering is a psychological and sociological one rather than a theological one.[94] This is because I want to use the term in a way that is applicable primarily to the relationship between Jesus of Nazareth and his Father God, as portrayed in the Gospels. This is the Jesus who, according to Luke, poured out the promised Spirit. I do not begin with speculative theories about the eternal essence and roles of three divine "members." Rather, the data forming a starting point are those referring to Jesus' prayer life, in which he clearly related to another as "non-self"—in other words as "you" as opposed to "I." He talked and listened to this Other in ways that seem analogous to the ways in which he related to his human companions, or perhaps more particularly in ways analogous to how they related to him: receiving instructions and encouragement, for instance.

One particular aspect of this capacity to relate that will be key for the development of this book's themes is the capacity to love another person (though no doubt a capacity to hate may by this definition be just as personal). We know that God's love is self-giving. When we look at the love expressed on the cross we see as well that this love is willing to be emptied of all and to be brought utterly low so that the personal objects of this love might be lifted up and fulfilled. Such love is *kenotic* (self-emptying) in that it gives away everything—that as a result, so to speak, there is nothing left. It allows itself to be brought unimaginably low. It gives away. The beloved is lifted up. The beloved is filled. This love *exalts* its object. Where we find such love being expressed, we find it being expressed *by a person.*

My working definition of "person" includes the word "potentially." A person is someone with, at least *potentially,* a sense of self and an ability to relate to non-self as "other." I include this word as I do not want to suggest that a human infant should be considered a non-person, prior to the postulated stage in development when it develops a sense of self. Neither would I wish to suggest that personhood is absent from someone whose sense of self or capacity to relate is compromised through severe neurological malformation, mental illness, physical trauma, or physiological degeneration.

---

94. There has been much study concerning definitions of "person," for instance in the fields of bioethics and medical ethics. Harris highlights as part of personhood "the capacity to value existence," by which "existence" he means life (Harris, "Four Legs Good, Personhood Better!" 52). Others include, for instance, the capacity to make creative choices (see Jones, *Valuing People,* especially chapter 5). Yet others present what is arguably a sceptical view, that all notions of personhood and self are socially constructed (e.g., Teske, "Social Construction").

Also, my definition clearly allows non-humans to be regarded as persons. Again, therefore, the word "potentially" is important, for it allows me to assume personhood, or postulate a degree of personhood, in those beings from which empirical data concerning the capacity to relate to non-self are not available. In the heavenly sphere, for instance, I assume that angels are persons, though I can offer no empirical data that verify their capacity to sense self and non-self in relational terms. Clearly, they are presented in the Scriptures as having the capacity to reveal themselves to humans relationally, and it may be a reasonable assumption that these revelations are of angels as they are in themselves, but such a thought must remain an assumption.[95]

These considerations about angels are, however, secondary to my present purpose. The key point that I wish to emphasize here is that a person is in relationships that are undergirded by a sense of self as distinct from others. From this follows a moral consequence, for such relationships, at least as we humans experience them, throw up constant choices: do I advance the good of my *self*, or do I put the *other* ahead of self's interests? In other words, will I be *selfish* or *selfless*? We can express this moral choice in terms of love: will I be unloving or loving? I will, however, be expressing this more often in terms of *kenosis*: will I make the loving choice whereby I empty self in order to fulfill or otherwise advance the other? I will explore this idea in more detail in the following section but for now want to hammer home the concept that where we find the subject of voluntary kenosis we are dealing with a *person*: *someone*, not *something*, chooses to put aside self's interests in order to advance the interests of the other.[96]

95. In the non-human earthly sphere, my definition includes those animals that can relate in the ways I have been describing. I do not imagine that pet-owners are resorting to undue anthropomorphism when they describe, say, their dogs in personal terms. Pet dogs genuinely exhibit the apparent capacity, for instance, to miss their owners when they are away from home, to welcome these owners enthusiastically on arrival, and in other ways to show what looks like genuine affection. The degree to which, however, these relationships are founded upon a genuine sense of self is perhaps not open to empirical research. Whether a dove alighting on a man—choosing which person to land on—should be regarded as acting "personally" is, I suggest, moot.

96. One might go further still. Lossky goes so far as to state, "the perfection of the person consists in self-abandonment: the person expresses itself most truly in that it renounces to exist for itself" (*Mystical Theology*, 144).

RESULTS

It may seem odd to state a book's conclusions in its introduction but it will be helpful to know where this book is heading. Here I indicate something of the process that emerges as the book progresses and something of the findings I glean from this process.

Personhood and Impersonhood

Readers who have looked ahead will already have seen that my next chapter is not about the Father but about the Spirit. I set out there my reasons for my choice of chapter order but suffice it to say at this point that this ordering fits with my desire to develop a *pneumatological* trinitarianism. Early consideration of the Spirit informs the picture of the Trinity that emerges. I quickly proceed to discussion about the Spirit as a person. I conclude that the Spirit can be seen three ways, all of which have scriptural support and all of which are useful in trinitarian thought. The first of these ways is that the Spirit can be viewed functionally or instrumentally. The Spirit is the means by which or the mode in which God acts. The Spirit is the "hand" God uses to perform and the "breath" God employs to speak. The second way of seeing the Spirit is as an entity but not a person. Common biblical metaphors that help with this conceptualization are oil and water. The third way to regard the Spirit, least supported in the Bible, is as a person in the sense explored above.

These three ways of seeing the Spirit, in turn, open up three ways of regarding the Trinity. Put another way, the three aspects lend themselves to three *models* for conceptualizing the Trinity. These are an instrumental model, a substantial model, and a relational model. Secondly, the first two ways of viewing the Spirit—functional on the one hand and ontological but impersonal on the other—become important considerations when the unity of this trinitarian God is discussed. Thirdly, the final way of seeing the Spirit—as a person—opens up the idea of kenosis that is woven throughout the book. It also highlights another important consideration: the dynamic rather than static being of God.

A Dynamic Trinity

The Trinity as presented in this book is dynamic, not static. There is an eternal mutual movement in which each person empties the self of self in order to elevate the other. Put in different terms, each voluntarily experiences "kenosis" so as to produce the exaltation of the other. This dynamism within the life of God is vital. God is eternal and yet God is also becoming. The Trinity is eternal but also eschatological. The ultimate position in the process is no doubt expressed in the eternal being of the immanent Trinity but has not yet been fully expressed in the time-bound activity of the economic Trinity.

This Pentecostal trinitarianism, like all others, has its dangers. Its very dynamism leads to those dangers. It carries the danger of suggesting that there is more than one God, in dynamic relations with (an)other God(s). The danger could be of a ditheism of the Father and the Son or a frank tritheism. I will be seeking to avert this danger not by appeal to some ontologically prior, underlying "divine essence" in which all three persons have their being but by recognition of the monarchy of the Father to which the Son and the Spirit, in kenosis, submit. To state that this Pentecostal trinitarianism is saved from ditheism or tritheism by a strong commitment to the monarchy of the Father brings us to its next danger. This dynamic trinitarianism carries with it the danger of subordinationism. In other words, if the Father is the monarch and sole cause, the Son and the Spirit might be regarded as less than God. It is protected from this not so much by appeal to a doctrine of eternal "co-equality," as true as this doctrine is, but by reciprocity. The Son would indeed be subordinated to the Father in the sense of being subjugated by him if it were not for the fact the Father reciprocally abases himself kenotically in utter love by exalting and filling the Son. Insofar as the Spirit can be viewed personally and relationally, similar comments can be made regarding the reciprocity of the Spirit's relationships with the Father and the Son.

I have mentioned kenosis twice in this brief section. So to this central theme I now turn.

Kenosis and Exaltation

Starting from Pentecost, this book finds the inner dynamic of the relationships within the Trinity to be a loving mutuality of what I will be referring to as "kenosis" and "exaltation." By kenosis I refer to *self-emptying*. There would be poetic symmetry if I partnered this term with *"plerosis,"* to refer to the *filling of another*. However, I find that the biblical picture, most overtly in Philippians 2:7–9, is of self-emptying followed by exaltation. Thus, I have chosen to "partner" kenosis with exaltation, even though the same sense of poetic symmetry might suggest that *exaltation of the other* should have been placed in contrast to *abasement of the self*. This pair of loving activities is a key focus of this book, for it forms the heart of the relations between the trinitarian persons that I will explore. From this flows all else, including the eternal generation of the Son and the eternal procession of the Spirit. I am not the first to have made such points. Lossky, with reference to Cyril of Alexandria, states, "this renunciation of His [the Son's] own will is not a choice, or an act, but is so to speak the very being of the Persons of the Trinity."[97] Balthasar declares that it is necessary to think of God in a way "which relates the event of the Kenosis of the Son of God to what one can, by analogy, designate as the eternal 'event' of the divine processions."[98] I too will relate the kenosis of the Son to the relationships of the trinitarian persons, but I will also explore in detail the kenosis of the other persons, and will discuss their concomitant exaltation of one another.

I am not claiming that the picture of the Trinity that emerges in this book is a definitive statement about the actual being of the Trinity (far from it) but I am suggesting that Pentecost provides a model—a kenosis/exaltation model—that helps us to think constructively about the Trinity. It is widely recognized—is perhaps a truism—that the relationships between the persons of the Trinity are loving. My approach offers a window into the nature of that love, as it is expressed in our world and therefore visibly to the eyes of faith, and as it is, I suggest, expressed within the invisible realm of the immanent Trinity.

The Unity of God

Starting trinitarian discussion with the Spirit is really helpful when it comes to considering the unity of God. How is it that this trinitarian God is but one God and not three Gods? All three views of the Spirit offer answers. The instrumental view, allied to an instrumental view of the Son, points to the being of God as one person with two hands or using breath to speak the

97. Lossky, *Mystical Theology*, 144.

98. Balthasar, *Mysterium Paschale*, viii.

word. The other, ontological, ways of viewing the Spirit help with understanding the technical idea of *perichoresis*.

Traditional doctrines of the Trinity explain the unity of the three persons in terms of *perichoresis*, by which term is meant the mutual interpenetration of each divine person with the others. They belong to one another and share each other's "personal space." Current trinitarian thinking often highlights the social, relational aspects of the Trinity. With this in view, thinking about *perichoresis* often uses the metaphor of dance to focus on the dynamic relational ways in which the persons of the Trinity relate to each other. However, this view of *perichoresis* on its own does not offer a strong presentation of the unity of God. The trinitarian persons, as partners in a dance, can look too much like *separate* beings. The views of the Spirit I develop allow one to see perichoresis as both *relational* and *pervasive*. The idea of the Spirit as an impersonal being pervading all that is allows for the idea of the Spirit as the being pervading all that God is (God is spirit). The Spirit is the divine "adhesive" ensuring the unity of God. This pervasive view of *perichoresis* is an important balancing concept to the one that develops from seeing the Spirit, like the Father and the Son, as a person in relationship.

Trinitarian Models

The Trinity has been characterized in numerous ways. Some portrayals have tended towards "modalism," seeing the persons as *modes* of God's eternal and internal being. Thus one can speak of modalistic or modal trinitarianism. Its danger is that it can stray from trinitarianism into a unitarian modalism. On the other hand, some have stressed the personal aspects of the Trinity to the point where their portrayals are best characterized as *social* trinitarianism. The danger here is that without due care, this form of trinitarianism drifts into tritheism.

As I have already begun to indicate earlier in this chapter, the picture of the Trinity that emerges through the course of this study can be considered as *both* modal *and* social (though I will offer different terms: instrumental and relational). However, I not only consider these two models but also wish to suggest a third: a substantial. By "substantial" I do not mean to suggest that the Trinity is a physical substance, but that there are ontological questions that can be answered without resorting to discussions of personhood. Insofar as three models emerge, the question will arise about how they may fit together. Two answers will be given. First, they must sit in paradoxical tension with one another. The other answer is that these three models can work together in "perichoretic" unity. Like the perichoresis in the Trinity, the perichoresis of these three models is both relational and pervasive. The models are in *relation* to one another analogically, for they all refer to the Father, Son, and Spirit, and are in a sense metaphors of each other. They belong together. But these models must also *pervade* one another, so that none must be allowed to develop at the expense of the others. In this combination they are helpful ways for us to conceive of the Trinity.

Having said that I will work with three models of the Trinity, it will become clear that of these, the relational model is my primary one. It cannot function as the sole one but, overall, it does have more explanatory power than the instrumental or substantial models and, in particular, coheres with all that I will be saying about kenosis. The social, personal aspects of the Trinity will be seen most clearly in the relations between the Father and the Son. Their personal relations with one another can easily be conceptualized. The instrumental and substantial aspects will be clearest in the interactions between the Father and Son on the one hand, and the Spirit on the other. The Spirit occupies the least personal position in the Trinity. Much that can accurately be stated about the Spirit can be stated in entirely impersonal terms. Only the briefest hints lay open the possibility—though it is a real possibility—of conceiving of the Spirit in personal terms. This is not to suggest that God or one aspect of God is less than personal. It is to suggest that God can be more than personal because God can be other than personal as well as being personal. That I conceive of the Trinity in relational, instrumental, and substantial terms does not suggest to me that there is contradiction at the heart of the Trinity. Rather, it suggests that three models that can be imaginatively created in thinking about the Trinity all have explanatory power that, by way of analogy, helps to clarify different aspects of the nature of God.

CHAPTER SUMMARY

This introductory chapter has set out my position in advance of more detailed discussion about the persons of the Trinity and their relations with each other. First, I identified challenges that suggest the need for an articulated Pentecostal trinitarianism to be available. These are: the "trinitarian" challenge—that Pentecostals ignore or misunderstand the Trinity; the "unitarian" challenge—presented by the existence and growth of Oneness Pentecostalism; and the "binitarian" challenge—expressed in the widespread ignoring or underplaying of the Spirit and the Spirit's roles in theological writing and church practice.

Next, this chapter discussed the methods this book will employ. It considered the basic assumptions that underlie its development, and its approaches to experience, Scripture, and tradition, before proceeding to unpack its attitude to Pentecost, both in terms of my being a Pentecostal and in terms of the historical datum of Pentecost, understood as the explosion of the Spirit's activity in the lives of the first Christians. Later in this section, it considered eternity and its relation to any possible distinctions that can be drawn between the economic Trinity and the immanent Trinity, before discussing meanings of "person."

Finally, this chapter perhaps precipitately provided the results of my deliberations before presenting their reasoning, which will of course follow in the chapters to come. The Pentecostal trinitarianism that I will be offering is characterized centrally by kenosis and exaltation, which processes form the basis of the Trinity's eternal immanent dynamic relations. The Pentecostal trinitarianism I advocate is primarily relational but also instrumental and substantial. These three models interplay in paradoxical and perichoretic unity.

2

Pentecost and the Spirit

INTRODUCTION

THE TRADITIONAL TRINITARIAN FORMULA begins with the Father: Father, Son, and Holy Spirit. One might naturally think that trinitarian discussion is best served if the same order is followed. If one were to develop a trinitarianism "from above," starting not with human experience but with the being of God, then one might well begin with the Father, for as the term "Father" suggests, in traditional trinitarianism the Father is the primordial person of the Trinity and the eternal source of the other two. However, in a Pentecostal trinitarianism that begins with human experience of God and seeks by way of imaginative analogy to trace back from this to God's own being, then it seems sensible to begin with the Spirit. This policy, it is worth noting, forms the basis of the chapter order as well as the logical order of Yong's trinitarian hermeneutic, *Spirit-Word-Community*.[1] And there is good reason to begin with the Spirit. All our experience of God is, most directly, of the Spirit. In a way this is to state the obvious or to offer a circular argument, for by Spirit we may simply mean God's immanence—God's "with-us-ness."[2] But this observation does not make the statement untrue.

---

1. Yong, *Spirit-Word-Community*, especially 7, 14, 27; and the order of the chapters.

2. I make no further attempt to define the terms "Spirit" and "spirit," other than to indicate that I use "Spirit" to refer to the third person of the Trinity and "spirit," when God is the focus of my discussion, to refer to the mysterious and incorporeal nature of God as suggested in John 3:8; 4:24.

It might be argued that a Christian's most immediate religious experience is of Jesus or the Father or a set of propositions called the gospel. To take my own Christian story as an example, I am a convert to committed Christianity. The message that was shared with me by concerned friends was about God as Father and about Jesus, not about the Spirit. So surely my first acquaintance, mediated through this message, was with the Father or Jesus? But I can only appeal to the work of the Spirit as a meaningful explanation for how I first came to *experience* God. The occasion, in late 1976, when I accepted the Christian gospel and committed my life to God was not the first time I had heard the gospel. Earlier in my teens I had been offered the same message by one or two other school friends. But on these earlier occasions, the message had not sunk in. I had somehow shrugged it off. I can offer no explanation as to how the message eluded me in earlier years but reached me on this subsequent occasion. That it did finally sink in I can only ascribe to the influence of the Spirit. The message had not changed. I doubt whether I had changed significantly over the course of a year or so. But somehow on this latter occasion the Spirit opened my life to the truth and significance of what I was hearing. I suggest I am not alone in this. Human relationship with God starts with the Spirit.

In the rest of this chapter, I explore first the Spirit's distinctions, considering first both the commonality and the differences between the Spirit and the Father. After passing briefly over the commonality and differences between the Spirit and the Son, for I will cover that in detail in chapter 3, I attend to the same topic concerning the Spirit and created intermediaries. In the subsequent section, I consider both the impersonhood and the personhood of the Spirit. The section thereafter is about the Spirit's kenosis. Finally, I explore the various roles of the Spirit in the life of the Son, before bringing the chapter to a conclusion.

THE SPIRIT'S DISTINCTIONS

I suggested in the introduction to this chapter that my experience of the Spirit convinced me of the fatherhood of God and the lordship of Christ.[3] However, we need to acknowledge that this sort of experience, which many

---

3. In this book I am not focusing on any distinction between receiving the Spirit in the context of conversion and receiving the Spirit—a baptism in the Spirit, as we Pentecostals tend to call it—in the context of empowerment. For my thoughts on this subject, see my *Baptism in the Spirit*, throughout.

have shared, is not in itself sufficient to persuade all such recipients that the Spirit is distinguishable from the Father whose fatherhood the Spirit declares or from the Son whose lordship the Spirit declares.[4] After all, Oneness Pentecostals seem to have the same experience of the Spirit but reach different conclusions about the Trinity. Thus our own experience alone is not sufficient in determining the relationship between the Spirit and the Father—or indeed the Son. We must turn to the shared experiences and testimonies of the wider community: and the place to turn first is to that witness which emerged closest to the original Christian action—the New Testament—for whatever view we hold on whether the New Testament and the Old Testament are inspired in some way—and I believe they are—we cannot deny that the New Testament contains voices far closer to the events central to the gospel than our own.

It is first important to consider whether the New Testament's primary witnesses made any distinctions between the Spirit and the Father and to explore the degree of common ground they found between the two. Thereafter it will be useful as well to discuss whether the Spirit is a created intermediary or truly God. I will not discuss distinctions between the Son and the Spirit until chapter 3, and consider questions about the Father and the Son in chapter 4, so that each chapter contains one aspect of this triad of distinctions.

The Spirit and the Father

It is first important to consider whether the New Testament's main writers on the Spirit made any distinctions between the Spirit and the Father. It might turn out to be the case, for instance, that every reference to the Spirit is simply shorthand for "God the Father by the Spirit." If so, another shorthand term, such as "God," might be exchangeable in a given text without any significant shift in meaning. Certainly, such a substitution could be suggested in many New Testament instances. To offer one such example, "the Holy Spirit said, 'Separate for me Barnabas and Saul'" (Acts 13:2) might have been written, perhaps without undue change in meaning, "God said, 'Separate for me . . . ,'" or even, "the Father said, 'Separate for me . . .'"

---

4. This is despite Smail's cogent argument that our human but divinely enabled freedom to declare the lordship of Christ is evidence of real distinction between the Spirit in us who enables the declaration, and the Son whose lordship is thus declared (Smail, *Giving Gift*, 68–69). For my discussion of 1 Cor 12:3, see below, pages 90–91.

(cf. Mark 12:26; Acts 7:3, 6; 2 Cor 4:6; 6:16; Heb 5:5). With this observation in mind, clear evidence for distinctions must be sought.

I commence this study with Luke's account of Pentecost. Certainly Luke's explanation of Pentecost, offered through the preaching of Peter, provides no opportunity to confuse the Spirit and the Father.[5] According to Acts 2:33 the Spirit is a promised gift that can be handed by the Father to the Son and then poured out on Christ's followers. This coheres with the content of Joel's prophecy that Peter had just quoted: the Spirit is not so much God's self as something God pours out on all flesh (Acts 2:17). The picture is confirmed elsewhere in the Lukan literature. At Jesus' baptism, after the Spirit descended *to earth* in dove-like manner, the sound was heard of the Father's voice *from heaven* (Luke 3:22). And according to Jesus' promise, the Holy Spirit, or good Spirit, is to be given *by the Father* in divine response to trusting prayer (Luke 11:13).

Yet the picture is not as clear-cut as the evidence presented in the previous paragraph might suggest. Acts 10:38, while stating that God granted anointing to Jesus, also firmly links that *Spirit*-anointing with God *the Father*'s presence.[6] Acts 2:22 indicates that it was *God* who performed signs and wonders through the Jesus who had appealed to his powerful *Spirit*-anointing for his capacity to heal for instance the blind (Luke 4:18; cf. 4:14; 5:17). The *filling of the Spirit* was God's answer to the disciples' prayer that the *Father* would stretch out a hand to heal (Acts 4:30–31). Thus the Lukan picture is somewhat mixed: the Spirit is indeed distinguished from the Father on significant occasions, while at other times, though never so explicitly, the Spirit is closely related to the Father in ways that almost seem to merge their identity.

In Paul's letters a similarly dual picture emerges. One needs to look no further than 1 Corinthians 2:10–11 where, as illustrated by analogy with a human's spirit, God's Spirit is understood as the *only* competent reader of God's innermost being—God's "depths." God's Spirit and God's Spirit alone can trace God's deepest thoughts. The Spirit is not a creature from whom or from which such mysteries remain forever hidden, or hidden until revealed.

---

5. For discussion concerning why such religious experiences as those described in Acts 2 should have been interpreted as experiences *of the Spirit at all*, see Rabens, "Power from In Between," 146–49.

6. With the frequent exception of Jesus' own reported use of the term, neither Luke as narrator nor Luke's characters except Peter in Acts 2:33 called God "Father." However, the God who was with Jesus according to Acts 10:38 was the obviously the God whom the Lukan Jesus constantly addressed as "Father."

Thus this Spirit appears to be as innately involved in the being of God as a human spirit is in that human's being. (This heavenly mind reading is reciprocated in Rom 8:27.) Nevertheless, the Spirit can be distinguished from "God"—as also the human spirit can here be distinguished from the human being. The Spirit is the means by which God has acted (2:10—in this case, the action being that of revealing), and can be given to humans such that the Spirit received is the Spirit *from* God (2:12; 6:19).

In Johannine material, too, the Spirit is divinely given (John 3:34; 7:39; 1 John 4:13). In John 14:16–17, it is clearly the Father who gives the Spirit of truth. That the Spirit is thereby distinguished from the Father is made all the clearer in John 14:26, with its use of the verb "send." This Spirit thus "proceeds out from" the Father (John 15:26) and this Paraclete will thereafter have come among Jesus' hearers (John 16:7, 13) while the Father remains in an invisible realm to which Jesus will disappear (John 16:10). Finally, in 1 John 4:2, the Spirit that acknowledges the incarnate Christ is "from" God. The Spirit is thus clearly distinguished from the Father.

However, as with Luke and Paul, the whole story has not yet been told. It would be naive to conclude from John 4:24 ("God is spirit") that in Johannine portrayal the Father equals the Spirit.[7] Nevertheless, some degree of identity is implied elsewhere. John 3:34 has already been referred to. Burge considers whether in this text the Spirit is given by the Father or the Son, and concludes that the former is more likely, with the Son the recipient of the measureless Spirit.[8] If this is so, then the Son's capacity to speak the Father's words is attributed to the Son's reception *of the Spirit*. And yet Jesus' constant testimony was that he spoke as he heard *his Father* speak—and acted as he saw *his Father* act (e.g., John 5:19, 30; 8:28). So some intimate connection between the Spirit and the Father is at least tangentially implied here.

Both these New Testament portrayals—of the Spirit as representing the inner recesses of the Father's being and of the Spirit as distinguishable from the Father, sent out into God's world and people—are in line with the dual understanding we find in the OT. It related the Spirit to God's presence and to God's face (Ps 51:11; 139:7; Ezek 39:29). This suggests the "God-ness" of the Spirit. But it also related the Spirit to God's hand and arm (e.g., Isa 63:11–12; Ezek 8:3; 37:1). These texts evoke much more the distinction

---

7. See Burge, *Anointed Community*, 192.

8. Ibid., 83–84. So too, more briefly, Beasley-Murray, *John*, 54; Turner, *Holy Spirit and Spiritual Gifts*, 59.

to be drawn between God and the Spirit, which was an "extension" of God, representing divine activity in God's world and people.[9]

A further possible piece of evidence for a New Testament distinction (at least after Pentecost) between the Spirit and the Father emerges in the writing of Turner on the subject. Turner points out that as the Pentecostal sending of the Spirit was delegated to the Son (e.g., Acts 2:33), the Son had become "Lord of the Spirit," invested with the authority to grant the Spirit to others. Turner therefore suggests that here the Spirit must be differentiated from the Father, for otherwise these New Testament texts declare that Jesus poured out the Father, which in Turner's view would be a blasphemy.[10]

In conclusion to this section, the New Testament offers a dual presentation of the Spirit: as distinguishable from the Father, most particularly in being given by the Father; and yet also intimately tied to the being of the Father, knowing the Father's mind and conveying the Father's presence. Different models of the Trinity cohere with these two presentations. The presentation that identifies the Spirit with the Father suggests a functional model—an *instrumental* one. The Spirit is an *instrument* of the Father's actions. The Father *functions* by means of the Spirit. On the other hand, the presentation that distinguishes the Spirit from the Father allows for either a social or substantial model: the Spirit is *someone* or *something* distinguishable ontologically from the Father. One can validly speak of the Father's being *and* the Spirit's being, not just of the Father acting *by means of* the Spirit. One can refer to the Spirit *ontologically* as well as *functionally*: the Spirit as an *entity*, whether that entity is a personal one or an impersonal one.

The Spirit and the Son

Again it must not simply be assumed that the New Testament writers distinguished clearly or consistently between the Spirit and the Son, any more than they did between the Spirit and the Father. Comments made in the previous section about references to the Spirit potentially being shorthand for "God the Father by the Spirit" apply as much to the Son. Thus if the example used previously, Acts 13:2, were understood to be shorthand for "Jesus by the Spirit said . . . ," then again no significant alteration in meaning might here be discerned (cf. Acts 18:9). Clearly, this is a most important

9. This continued to be the general Jewish understanding up to, including, and beyond the New Testament era. See the summary in Turner, "Spirit of Christ," 422–23.

10. Turner, *Holy Spirit and Spiritual Gifts*, 170, 176.

topic that needs careful discussion. It could appear in this chapter, or equally it could appear in the following chapter under the section title, "The Son and the Spirit." Simply for the sake of balance, I include it in chapter 3.

The Spirit and Created Intermediaries

That Paul did not regard the Spirit as a created entity has already emerged in discussion of 1 Corinthians 2:10–11, above. In apocalyptic literature, the picture was far less clear. The ways that the Spirit and creatures such as angels were portrayed means that potential confusion between them exists. In the case of Revelation, such was the apparent glory of angels that the narrator was tempted to worship one (Rev 19:10; 22:8–9). It is not entirely clear, too, whether the "seven spirits" in Revelation 1:4 were the seven angels to whom the seven letters were addressed (Rev 2:1—3:14) or whether the reference was to the Spirit of God, however understood.[11]

With Luke, the picture seems initially to be similarly confusing but on closer inspection offers a uniquely exalted pneumatology that clearly distinguishes the Spirit from such beings as angels. At times, Luke brought the function of angels and the function of the Spirit into such close narrative apposition as to suggest initially that he offered no clear conceptual distinction between them, as if for him the Spirit might simply be an angel. This suggestion is clearest in Acts 8:26–29. An *angel* of the Lord told Philip to go south (Acts 8:26) and as a consequence he met an official. The *Spirit* then told Philip to approach the man (Acts 8:29) and as a result Philip was able to speak about Christ. Here we see no apparent functional difference between the voice of an angel and the voice of the Spirit. Indeed, in isolation this passage might well suggest that the Spirit *was* the angel. While this is the clearest example, it is not the only one. Throughout Acts, both angels and the Spirit are involved in enabling, guiding, strengthening and reassuring the mission of the earliest church. In both cases, this involves their doing God's works and speaking God's words, thereby acting as God's

---

11. See discussion in Waddell, *Spirit of the Book of Revelation*, 9–21. In the second century *Vision of Isaiah*, the Spirit was repeatedly called "the angel of the Holy Spirit" (e.g., *Martyrdom and Ascension of Isaiah* 9:36, 40). However, this designation did not indicate that the Spirit was a created angel: the Spirit was *worshiped* by the heavenly gathering, *including by the angels* (*Martyrdom and Ascension of Isaiah* 9:34).

agents. The similarity is such that certain passages, heard alone, might suggest confusion of identity between the Spirit and angels.[12]

However, Luke's account indicates various ways in which he did clearly distinguish between the Spirit and created intermediaries such as angels. These distinctions emerge when consideration is given to their respective roles involving miracles, divine speech, divine apparition, human inspiration, and their relation to Christ. I will survey these aspects in turn.

There is superficial resemblance between the ministries of angels and the Spirit with regard to miracles: both performed them. However, angelic miracles, which were rare, were recorded as being performed by the angel (Luke 1:20–22; Acts 5:19; possibly 12:9–10, 23). Angels *never enabled people to perform miracles.* In contrast, the only miracles which Luke regarded as performed by the Spirit directly rather than through people were the conception of Jesus and the translation of Philip (Luke 1:35; Acts 8:39): the Spirit typically *empowered people* to perform miracles (e.g., Luke 4:18; Acts 4:30–31; 10:38; 13:9–11).[13] This suggests that the Spirit and angels are not equivalent as intermediaries between God and humanity. The agency of an angel creates a three-step procession: the God who sends; the angel who performs; and the person who benefits. The agency of the Spirit, however, creates a four-fold procession: the God who sends; the Spirit who enables; the person who performs; and the person who benefits. So an angel who performs miracles is to be more closely associated with a person who performs them than with the Spirit who enables miracles.

Turning now to Luke's depiction of divinely originated speech, the picture is similar: angels characteristically spoke, while the Spirit characteristically enabled people to speak. In fact, angels seem hardly ever to have been silent when they appeared to people: there are remarkably few records of an angel's appearance on earth in the narrative of Luke-Acts that do not involve a record of that angel's words (Luke 22:43; Acts 12:23). They acted as God's mouthpiece, bringing God's message. There is no record of angels directly enabling human speech, either by giving words or boldness, although they did occasionally offer guidance concerning future speech (Acts 5:20; 10:5, 22). In the case of the Spirit, the situation is more complex.

12. For fuller discussion, see Atkinson, "Angels and the Spirit."

13. Menzies' important thesis that the Lukan Spirit of Prophecy, like the intertestamental one, was not directly involved in miracles (*Empowered for Witness*, e.g., 102, 227) does not stand, as has been ably demonstrated by Turner (*Power from on High*, e.g., 138, 224–25, 256–64); for further discussion of this point, see my *Baptism in the Spirit*, 73–77, and the sources cited there.

As discussed above in relation to Philip, the Spirit did sometimes speak to people (Acts 8:29; 10:19; possibly 13:2; 16:7). Characteristically, however, the infilling of the Spirit enabled people themselves to become God's mouthpieces, bringing God's message (Luke 1:15–17, 41–42, 67; 2:27–28; 4:18; 10:21; 12:12; Acts 1:8; 2:4, 17; 4:8, 31; 6:10; 10:44–46; 13:9; 18:25; 19:6). These Spirit-filled people, then, rather than the Spirit, became functionally equivalent to angels as God's messengers on earth.

The next area to consider is that of divine apparition. Angels were often visible (whether in vision or "physically" was not always clear to the onlookers: e.g., Acts 12:9); the Spirit only was once or twice (Luke 3:22; [and Acts 2:3?]). The Spirit was assumed to be generally invisible. Also, while angels were sometimes thereby the objects of visions (e.g., Luke 24:23; Acts 10:3), the Spirit never was: the Spirit was the giver of visions (Acts 2:17). This places the Spirit and angels in a subject-object relationship with one another. The Spirit is the subject, regarded as acting upon angels, in that a Spirit-inspired vision might involve an angel. Angels were never presented by Luke as subjects acting upon the Spirit.[14]

In the case of human inspiration, it seems likely that Luke intended to convey the idea that those who were visited by angels and thereby guided, reassured, and informed were "inspired" as a result. The visitation itself was at least sometimes numinous enough to inspire fear or amazement (Luke 1:12, 29–30; 24:5; Acts 7:30; 10:4). However, when discussion turns to the Spirit, it is of course possible to use the word "inspiration" in a far more technical sense. The Spirit was sent by God to be in, or upon, people (Luke 1:15, 41, 67; 2:25; 4:18; Acts 1:8; 2:4; 4:8, 31; 6:3, 5; 7:55; 9:17; 10:44; 11:24; 19:6). Thus the picture is consistent: angels were external to people, whereas the Spirit was available to reside and work within.[15] The Spirit is further distinguished from angels by the widespread availability of the Spirit to be within people (Acts 2:17, 38–39). The universality of this availability implies omnipresence—a characteristic never ascribed to angels.

---

14. Whether Rev 17:3 indicates that an angel can "affect" the Spirit is moot. Various scholars see "in spirit" here, as elsewhere in the book (Rev 1:10; 4:2; 21:10), as denoting John's state of mind (what some call "ecstatic") rather than as a reference to the Spirit of God. See discussion in Waddell, *Spirit of the Book of Revelation*, 31, 138.

15. The only possible equivalents to this indwelling in Luke-Acts have to do with the realm of evil. Satan entered people (Judas—Luke 22:3; Ananias—Acts 5:3); demons were "in" people (e.g., Luke 4:33–36). However, there is no internal evidence that Luke regarded Satan or demons as part of the angelic realm, whatever the wider literary context might suggest.

Finally and most importantly, angels and the Spirit were clearly distinguished in their possible mediating of the presence of the ascended Christ. Terminologically, angels were related to God in a way that superficially mirrors the Spirit's relation to God ("angel of the Lord," "Spirit of the Lord"; "holy angel," "Holy Spirit"). When, however, their relation to the risen Christ is observed, no similarity is to be found. The coming one promised by John the Baptist was to be one who granted the Spirit (Luke 3:16). After the ascension, Jesus was indeed given the Spirit by the Father to grant (Acts 2:33). Thereafter, the Spirit could rightly be called the Spirit of Jesus (Acts 16:7), for not only could the visions the Spirit granted convey an appearing of Jesus to their recipients (Acts 7:55), but, more generally, the Spirit's whole ministry to the church offered them continuing experience of Christ. The comparison with angels is simple and clear. As Conzelmann observes, angels in Luke-Acts were never "the angel of Christ."[16] Some association (of glory) between the Son of Man and angels can be noted (Luke 9:26). However, there is no sense at all that angels appearing to people were conveying the presence of Christ. In this respect, as in the others surveyed, Luke *did not* confuse the identity of the Spirit with that of angels, and thereby did not suggest that the Spirit is a created heavenly intermediary. Rather, the contrasts that have been brought out indicate that the Spirit stands in a relationship to the created order *with* the Father and the Son.

THE SPIRIT AND PERSONHOOD

As I suggested in chapter 1, we may discover in the course of our explorations that either the Father, the Son, or the Spirit has some personal characteristics and some impersonal ones. In the case of the Spirit, we find, the impersonal seems to outweigh the personal. However, in this instance we find a further complication: the Spirit can be conceived as not even an entity, but as a function of God. I will consider each of these matters in turn, beginning with the question of ontology before moving on to consider both impersonal and personal ways of appreciating the Spirit.

16. Conzelmann, *Acts*, 41.

The Spirit Seen Functionally

In isolation, Acts 2:33 does not state what Jesus poured out, beyond characterizing it in rather puzzling fashion as "what you both see and hear." However, the context is plain: what the audience most immediately "saw and heard" and what it commented on (Acts 2:6–13) was people speaking in a wide range of human languages, declaring the glory of God. The audience did not comment on seeing any*thing* poured out at all. They referred to seeing a particular *behavior*. One is thus justified in immediately taking "poured out what you see and hear" as a functional statement, indicating metaphorically that God had so acted upon these people that they were behaving in a certain way. No *entity* may have been poured out at all. No "pouring out" as such may have occurred. But more can be said: Acts 2:3–4 declares that those whose behavior was so vividly visible and audible to the gathered crowds had just been "filled" with the Spirit, and that it was this Spirit's "arrival" that enabled their vivid behavior. Therefore one might conclude that this "Spirit" is a metaphor for the action of God that produced this behavior. Could it be, then, that there is no such thing as the Spirit?—that to say "God did such-and-such by the Spirit" is no more or less than to say that "God did such-and-such spiritually"?

Moving beyond Pentecost to the ongoing effects of the Spirit in believers' lives, many of the "actions of the Spirit" that look not only ontological but also personal at first sight can be well understood as actions of God by means of the Spirit. Turner rightly notes that "it is quite inadequate, methodologically, to build a case for the divine personhood of the Spirit in the New Testament from those places where the Spirit is said 'to teach' (Lk. 12:12); 'to give utterance' (Acts 2:4); 'to say' (Acts 8:29 . . .); 'to send' (Acts 13:4); 'to forbid' (Acts 16:16); 'to appoint as overseer' (Acts 20:28), or whatever. All these could simply be shorthand for '*God*, as Spirit (or "by his Spirit"), said, . . .' etc."[17] What Turner does not point out is that his argument here against an easy assumption that the Spirit is a person is also an argument against a similar assumption that the Spirit is any*thing* at all!

So we face an awkward question: can the word "is" be used of the Spirit? Is the Spirit an entity, or simply the mode or quality of an action or attitude of someone or something *else*? In other words, can there be an ontology of the Spirit? Smail's study of the Spirit's personhood offers only two alternatives: the Spirit is a person or the Spirit is the mode of action of

---

17. Turner, *Holy Spirit and Spiritual Gifts*, 172.

another person.[18] By this reckoning, if the Spirit is not personal then, for example, to describe the Spirit as speaking on a particular occasion is only to indicate something about the *way* God spoke then. In this framework of thought, no ontological questions can be asked of the Spirit but only functional ones. "Spirit" in this context is not really a noun but in practice an adverb.

It might be counter-argued, in reference to Acts 2:33, that a more straightforward reading of the reference to Jesus "pouring out" is that an entity was given rather than a functional, non-ontological Spirit. Only limited evidence can be offered towards this counter-argument, however. Little if any weight can be placed on the verb "pour out," for in the wider context of the New Testament, God could pour out love (Rom 5:5). Neither can much help be gained from the verb "fill." Turner notes that such phrases as "full of the Spirit" are paralleled in Luke-Acts by "full of leprosy" (Luke 5:12) and "full of anger" (Acts 19:28).[19] We are not in a position to know whether Luke thought of either leprosy or anger as a substance, however we might understand these. That Jesus received this promised Spirit from the Father does not assist: one can receive love as well as pour it out. Amassed, the language of receiving, pouring, and filling does not suggest any more than that Jesus enabled an activity at Pentecost; he "poured out" the Spirit as a function.

I offer these reflections on Acts 2 as a starting point for the suggestion that it is useful as part of one's trinitarian thinking to regard the Spirit functionally. One of the ways that I will want to characterize the Trinity is as functional or instrumental. In this picture, the unity of God is highlighted. There is one God who speaks words by means of breath out-breathed. This God is the Father. His word is the Son; his breath is the Spirit. In fact, this is not the only way in which the Trinity can be regarded functionally. I will return to this picture later, in chapter 3.

The Spirit Seen Impersonally

In the previous section I explored the possibility of conceiving of the Spirit functionally. That is not the only choice. As I remarked, Luke's presentation of Peter's speech was about Jesus pouring out "what you see and hear" and I suggested that the most immediate phenomenon that the crowd had

18. Smail, *Giving Gift*, 42.

19. Turner, *Power from on High*, 167.

seen and heard was human behavior: the disciples speaking in unlearnt languages. However, it is also possible to view what was seen and heard as including tongue-like flames and a roaring wind (Acts 2:2–3).[20] Whether these are understood as visionary phenomena or as something naturally seen and heard, the implication leans now more towards some*thing* coming "down" from heaven (however insubstantially flames and wind were understood by Luke). This impression is all the stronger in the case of the dove descending on Jesus. While Mark's account was of Jesus *seeing* (in a vision?) the heavens open and a dove come down after his baptism (Mark 1:10), Luke's account if anything heightens the physicality of the event: he wrote rather that the heaven opened and the dove came down *in bodily form* (Luke 3:21–22).[21]

More generally throughout the canon, the entity of the Spirit is referred to in metaphors that suggest a fluid, whether this is a liquid like water (rain water—Isa 32:15; flowing "river" water—John 7:38–39) or oil (anointing oil—Luke 4:18), or *possibly* a gas such as wind (John 3:8) or breath (Ezek 37:5–6, 14; John 20:22). One must be cautious: these are of course metaphors. Indeed, in the case of the last metaphor, "it is doubtful whether the Hebrew Bible conceives of the wind as a (material) substance at all."[22] Nevertheless, I want to suggest that these biblical hints at least open up for us the possibility that ontological questions can be asked—and answered—regarding the Spirit without resorting at this point to considerations of the Spirit's personhood.[23]

When I wrote at the beginning of this chapter that I experienced God's Spirit in the events surrounding my conversion to committed Christianity, I do not mean to suggest that I encountered the Spirit as a *person* to whom I spoke or who spoke to me. If anything, the person I was meeting was Jesus.

20. This is Walton's understanding ("Whose Spirit?" 47).

21. Nolland surprisingly and implausibly reads the difference between Mark and Luke the other way round, so that where "the Markan text could be taken as speaking of the Spirit 'incarnated' as a dove, Luke stands over against this possibility." If anything, to use Nolland's language, it is Luke rather than Mark who gives an impression of the Spirit "incarnated"—though reference to a "pneumatophany" might be more helpful than the use of incarnational language (Nolland, *Luke* 1:1—9:20, 161).

22. Rabens, *Holy Spirit and Ethics*, 37.

23. I do not mean to suggest that biblical authors conceived of the Spirit as a *material* entity. For discussion of the use of metaphor in this context, see Rabens, *Holy Spirit and Ethics*, 37, 43–46. For discussion of the Stoic view of a material Spirit and its contrasts with Jewish views, see Rabens, *Holy Spirit and Ethics*, 25–79; see also Levison, *Filled with the Spirit*, e.g., 138–40.

Like many a Christian, I do not regularly pray to the Spirit or sing to the Spirit. I probably make no clear semantic distinction in everyday practice between "the Spirit said" and "Jesus said." We Christians are told by the creeds that along with the Father and the Son the Spirit is to be worshiped and glorified[24] but we do not often make any attempt to relate personally to the Spirit. In the Pentecostal circles in which I move, immediate experience of the Spirit is often termed as experiencing God's anointing and is described quite often in physical terms, whether this be characterized by analogy as electricity, heat, or some other earthly phenomenon. At other times the description might be of being "urged" to prophesy or so forth.[25] I am not sure that I have ever heard anyone testify to a vision in which they have *seen* the Spirit as an otherwise apparently human person (in the way that I have heard of visions of Jesus). This experienced impersonality of the Spirit is mirrored in the New Testament. I explore the New Testament's witness to the impersonhood of the Spirit in two halves. In the latter half of this subsection I will consider the Spirit's involvement in the world and especially the living world as one way of gaining understanding of the impersonal Spirit within the Trinity. Before reaching that point, however, I will explore the Spirit's impersonal involvement specifically in the lives of Christians as a starting point for imagining the impersonal Spirit in the Trinity.

I begin this part as usual with Pentecost and its explanation centered on Acts 2:33. The Spirit is portrayed here as impersonal. A person is not poured out. People are not filled (Acts 2:4) with a person. This presentation is typical of biblical language and concepts. One must acknowledge that the biblical accounts of the Spirit's involvement in God's people are usually in terms that suggest the Spirit is impersonal. Furthermore, the ways that this Spirit affects recipients is often impersonal. This was true on the day of Pentecost. The narrative in Acts does not suggest that the disciples met a new person on that day but that they were inwardly influenced in ways that led to their unexpected behavior: some onlookers thought they were filled with an intoxicating substance, sweet wine, not with a person (Acts 2:13). And the heavenly manifestations in Luke's presentation were of flames and of wind—hardly personal!

---

24. Expanded Nicene Creed, issued by the Council of Constantinople in 381.

25. See, e.g., Dye, *Revival Phenomena*; Dixon, *Signs of Revival*; Deere, *Surprised by the Voice of God*, throughout.

These observations concerning the Spirit's relations with Christians are relevant to understanding the place of the Spirit in the Trinity, for they mirror in many ways the involvement of the Spirit in the life of the human Jesus. As, at Pentecost, the Spirit's arrival was heralded by the impersonal manifestations of fire and wind, so too, at the Jordan River, the Spirit's arrival was heralded by the possibly impersonal manifestation of a descending dove. Many of the ensuing ways in which the Spirit influenced Jesus can be understood impersonally. The fullest Synoptic testimony to the place of the Spirit in the life of Jesus is of course Luke's. There, the newly arrived Spirit was a feature of which Jesus could be "full" (Luke 4:1). This need not mean "full" as in "a full tank of water." As Turner explains, the reference can be paralleled with those to being full of anger or of joy.[26] It is nonetheless impersonal. Admittedly, Jesus was led by this Spirit (Luke 4:1) but this fits precisely with Turner's point quoted at some length in the previous section, that such a phrase could be shorthand for "God led Jesus by the Spirit." More characteristically in Luke, this Spirit was seen as the source of a remarkable power in Jesus' life (Luke 4:14, cf. 5:17; 6:19; 8:46 [reflecting Mark 5:30]) and on one occasion the source, probably, of Jesus' joy (Luke 10:21). In John's Gospel—the one where the Spirit as Paraclete was presented most personally—the Spirit on Jesus was also portrayed in impersonal ways (John 1:32; 3:34; 6:27[27]).

However, both Luke and John implied that though the Spirit on Jesus was *impersonal*, the Spirit thereby played a part in the *personal* relationship between the Father and Jesus. In Luke 10:21–22, the implication is that not only was the Spirit at this point the source of Jesus' joy but also of his knowledge of God as Father. In John 3:34–35, the implication is that not only is the Spirit part of the "all things" that the Father has placed in the Son's hand but the Spirit is perhaps *the means* by which the Father expresses love to the Son and places all in his hands. Most particularly, in all the Synoptic Gospels the descent of the dove was accompanied by a heavenly voice *affirming* paternal/filial relationship. I will discuss this further below.

Reading back now from the Spirit-enabled relationship between Jesus and his Father God to the economic—and by imaginative analogy to the immanent—Trinity, the Spirit can be seen, at least partially, in impersonal terms within the *relations of the Father and the Son*. The Spirit can be

26. Turner, *Power from on High*, 166–67; and see above, page 50.

27. See Burge, *Anointed Community*, 85 for exegesis that takes *sphragizein* (to seal) as a reference to granting the Spirit.

imagined at this point not as one of three persons engaged in both mutual and outward love but as somehow the very means of expression of that love as it is expressed by the other two persons. Augustine's exposition of the Spirit as the love between the Father and the Son is well known.[28] However, it struggled to offer a scriptural foundation and only approximates to what is being suggested here: that the Spirit is not so much the love between the Father and the Son but the means of expression of that love: the expression of love that the Father has for the Son, and *vice versa*, is an impersonal function of the Spirit.

I move now to the second half of this subsection and to the involvement of the Spirit in the wider creation. The impersonal note is often sounded here too: in many strands of the OT, there was for instance no clear conceptual distance between the S/spirit God gave creatures and the breath that entered them—impersonally—to keep them alive, as is evidenced by the repeated references in this context to nostrils (e.g., Gen 2:7; 7:22; Job 27:3). This idea goes beyond God's S/spirit in humanity. While this S/spirit in humans could be distinguished occasionally from the state of non-human creatures (e.g., Isa 31:3; Job 12:10), it is sometimes the case that non-human living creatures were described too as having this S/spirit (e.g., Gen 7:22;[29] Ps 104:29–30; Eccl 3:19, though note the uncertainty of 3:21). However, there seems to be little if any Old Testament interest in any possible relation of God's S/spirit to non-living creation, beyond the recognition that once this S/spirit had departed from a living creature, it died (e.g., Ps 104:29; Eccl 3:19). In the New Testament, while this link between God's Spirit and the natural life of all is rare, here too the non-human creation, and perhaps even non-living creation, will be brought into full eschatological existence, it seems, through the (presumably impersonal) agency of the Spirit (Rom 8:19–23, implied).

So the Bible links the Spirit to the life of all living beings and to the existence of all entities, though with far more emphasis on the former than the latter. And it does this in impersonal terms. It does not take much conceptual extrapolation, then, to conceive of the Spirit as the ongoing cause of the existence of all things. The Spirit is the substratum—the causative matrix—of all existence. If I look at a leaf I do not *need* to conceive of

---

28. For brief descriptions of Augustine's position, see, e.g., Yong, *Spirit-Word-Community*, 62–63; Gunton, *Promise of Trinitarian Theology*, 48–51; Knell, *Immanent Person of the Holy Spirit*, 113–15.

29. See Levison, *Filled with the Spirit*, 16–17.

God having a personal relationship with it but can imagine that the Spirit upholds its existence in an intimately direct though impersonal way. The related idea that God is the ground of being itself was developed famously by the German theologian Paul Tillich and popularized in England by John A. T. Robinson, then bishop of Woolwich, in his slim volume, *Honest to God*. Robinson claimed that just as modern humanity had to reject, with its rejection of a triple-decker universe, a notion of "God up there," so now too the idea of "God out there" needed to be rejected. God was to be seen as the "the ultimate depth of all our being, the creative ground and meaning of all our existence."[30] This was not actually to reject the idea that God is personal but the idea had to be reformulated drastically: "For this way of thinking, to say that 'God is personal' is to say that 'reality at its very deepest level is personal', that personality is of ultimate significance in the constitution of the universe, that in personal relationships we touch the final meaning of existence as nowhere else."[31]

It is difficult to imagine how the claim that "reality at its very deepest level is personal" could be demonstrated. It seems much easier to accept that Robinson's vision of God was actually impersonal. But was it inaccurate? Certainly, Robinson's position was seen by many commentators as a rejection of Christian theism in what it denied. C. S. Lewis, however, was wise to burst Robinson's balloon and deflate the controversial idea by agreeing with it—not in what it denied but in what it affirmed: "We have always thought of God as being not only 'in', 'above', but also 'below' us: as the depth of ground. We can imaginatively speak of 'Father in heaven' yet also of the everlasting arms that are 'beneath'. We do not understand why the Bishop is so anxious to canonize the one image and forbid the other. We admit his freedom to use which he prefers. We claim our freedom to use both."[32] Lewis' sense that God can be conceived as "the depth of ground," in other words as impersonally causing and upholding existence, has been echoed by others with specific reference to the Spirit. The Spirit is understood by several key voices to be capable of being conceptualized impersonally as the "field," for instance, of existence. This is the position adopted by Jürgen Moltmann and Wolfhart Pannenberg.[33] More recently,

30. Robinson, *Honest to God*, 47.

31. Ibid., 48–49.

32. Lewis, *Undeceptions*, 149.

33. See discussion in Bauckham, *Theology of Moltmann*, 186–87; Grenz and Olson, *20th Century Theology*, 193–94.

Yong has made a similar point: "The Spirit is not contradictory to nature, as modernity would have it; rather, the Spirit infuses the world. The vivifying breath of God provides the ontological conditions"[34] for existence. As Yong notes, this is not a departure from classical Christian theism. It has long been understood that the Spirit is "the divine source of life within which all creatures live, move, and have their being."[35]

This can be instructive for trinitarianism. If the Spirit is capable of impersonally pervading and thereby upholding the being of all that is created, then by imaginative analogy, the Spirit has the capacity, impersonally, to pervade and thereby uphold the eternal being of the uncreated: the Father and the Son. This fits with an aspect of Johannine theology: Jesus stated that God is spirit (John 4:24). As Jesus was here presented as speaking of another, not of himself, I take this to mean that the Father is spirit, though much the same could be said of the preincarnate Son. In other words, in the terms I am developing, the Father's being is so pervaded and upheld by the Spirit that the Father can genuinely be called "spirit."[36] In contrast to the created order, this does not mean that the Spirit is the cause of the Father's existence. However, it may be evidence of the Father's kenosis in relation to the Spirit that the Father allows himself to exist only in and by the Spirit. If this is the case, we also find some reciprocity here: the Spirit owes eternal existence to the Father, the fount of all, and the Father owes eternal existence to the Spirit, the pervasive matrix of divine as well as created life.

It is also worth noting that we have here a statement of "perichoresis." In other words, at least with respect to the Spirit's place in their lives, the Spirit's being, as understood impersonally, totally pervades that of the Father and the Son. In chapter 1, two ways of seeing perichoresis were introduced: relational and pervasive. Clearly, here, the aspect of perichoresis in view is the *pervasive* one, not the relational one.[37]

Finally before I complete this section a further matter needs to be raised. It concerns whether the idea of the impersonal Spirit detracts from God. If one naturally recoils from the thought of God or God's Spirit seen in impersonal terms, it is probably because one draws the inference "less

---

34. Yong, *Spirit Poured Out*, 281.

35. Yong, "Spirit and Creation," 95.

36. The material created order cannot be called "spirit," for it has a physical created existence which is other than, though owing everything to, the existence of God. Neither can the Son Jesus be called "spirit," though for a different reason: that of incarnation.

37. See further discussion in chapter 5.

than personal."[38] If God is in any sense *impersonal*, God must be *less than personal*: something that can be attributed to a person must be lacking in God. But why should this be? Surely, God could be more than personal? Surely, God might have attributes that strike us persons as "personal," *and* attributes that do not? Would that not be to magnify, rather than to diminish, God? Thus C. S. Lewis' response to John Robinson, referred to earlier in this section, also contained the observation that trinitarian doctrine allows for the idea that "'not a person' [can be] taken to mean 'a person and more.'"[39] Similarly, Otto declared:

> When we turn to the New Testament, we see that the "Pneumatology" and doctrine of Immanence in Paul and John, which give such unmistakable expression to the supra-personal aspect of the divine as the "Light" and the "Life," do not mean a sudden irruption into religion of a wholly novel and alien element, but merely the complete realization of what was all the while potential in the character of Yahweh in his essence as a numen.
>
> *
>
> Our usual prayers and hymns confine themselves to the region which I call the "rational." They lack that element which I call the non-rational or the "numinous." . . . It is a defect in our devotional poetry that it hardly knows any other image for the eternal mystery of the Godhead than those drawn from social intercourse and personal relationship, and so tends to lose sight of just the mysterious transcendent aspect of deity.[40]

Perhaps Otto was wise to use the term "*supra*-personal" rather than "*impersonal.*" I wish to suggest that to see impersonhood in God magnifies rather than diminishes God—that, as Otto put it, to focus *only* on the personal in God may be to "lose sight of the mysterious transcendent" in God.

In parallel with this thought that the Spirit might be magnified by being conceived in supra-personal ways is the idea that to have *only* personal images of God might be to diminish through "domestication." McFague writes of the Old Testament depiction of God: "nonhuman images are

---

38. Thinking of this type may be a cause of the embarrassment that some commentators seem to exhibit over the degree to which the Bible presents the Spirit in impersonal terms. This embarrassment is evident in the way these commentators have a tendency to *exaggerate* the degree to which the New Testament presents the Spirit as personal (e.g., Smail, *Giving Gift*, 34–35; Witherington and Ice, *Shadow of the Almighty*, chapter 4).

39. Lewis, *Undeceptions*, 150.

40. Otto, *The Idea of the Holy*, 200–201, 202–3.

frequent and especially powerful for intimating feelings of the sublime and mysterious as well as for balancing [personal, relational] images which domesticate." As examples she mentions "God as thunder, lion, torrent, bear, and ocean."[41] So to ascribe impersonal being to the Spirit might actually protect our view of the Spirit from a domestication that would render the Spirit, as conceived by us humans, considerably less than what or who the Spirit actually is.

At this point, my discussion turns, in contrast, to the Spirit as a person. In engaging in further discussion of the Spirit as a person, I am *not* suggesting that there are two Spirits: impersonal and personal. I am implying that there are two *ways* that the Spirit can be conceived.

The Spirit Seen Personally

When the reader of the Bible turns from seeking evidence for the impersonhood of the Spirit to seeking evidence for personhood, the material available is much sparser. However, it is present. I begin this part of the discussion not with references to the Spirit's interacting with the wider creation, but with the Spirit's relating to the Father and the Son. In particular, I turn to the Johannine material on this subject, for it is in John that this aspect of the Spirit is most explicit, even if still rare.

The passage in question is John 16:13–15.[42] The matter in question is self-giving kenotic love. As I developed in the previous chapter, I am using the word "person" of an entity with at least a potential sense of self and the capacity to relate to others. In particular, I explored the role of self-giving love that is kenotic of the self and exalting of the other. The Spirit clearly exalts Jesus (John 16:14). More than that, however, the Spirit is kenotic, speaking not the words generated by the self but those given by the Son (John 16:13). This involves the disregarding of the self and the acceptance of the other, whose words are chosen as the ones to be expressed. Just as the Son spoke the words he heard from the Father (John 8:28), kenotically laying aside his own generation of words to speak, so too the Spirit would speak those words heard from the Son, kenotically laying aside self-generated words. Implicitly, the Spirit who would thus glorify the Son would

41. McFague, *Metaphorical Theology*, 43.

42. Unlike Burge, *Anointed Community*, 142, I do not offer grammatical arguments concerning masculine and neuter pronouns in this passage. For weaknesses in Burge's approach, see Turner, *Holy Spirit and Spiritual Gifts*, 178–79.

also, thereby, glorify the Father. I explore the kenosis of the Spirit at greater length in the next section. At this stage it is simply my intention to indicate that there is kenotic glorifying of another in the Spirit's activities, and that we can understand this as evidence of personhood.

But is the Spirit here truly personal, or is it the case that the linguistic device of personification is being used here to explain a difficult concept, as Kenney argues?[43] Kenney's position rests upon several factors. First, he sees an impersonal presentation of the Spirit in the rest of the Fourth Gospel, creating a tension that would need explanation if in the farewell discourses, and only here, the presentation suddenly switches from impersonal to personal (and then back again afterwards). Secondly, the concept of ancient patron-client "brokerage," of which Kenney makes much, provides for him an interpretative key for understanding this personification. Brokers in that day were, as he puts it, "go-betweens"[44] who mediated between patrons—those with power in society—and their clients. With God pictured as the ultimate Patron, biblical accounts of human (client) relationships with this Patron included brokers, be they Abraham, Moses, David, or ultimately Jesus. According to Kenney, John was forced to personify "spirit" in order to show how Jesus' brokerage of this divine-human relationship continued after Jesus' physical departure from his followers.[45]

If the only information regarding the Spirit's role that the farewell discourses offered involved revelation to humans, Kenney's argument might carry some weight. However, as I have shown above, this is not the case. We are told of this role with respect to the other persons of God. As such the Spirit emerges as a person in relationship—kenotic relationship—with the Son (explicitly), and the Father (implicitly). Turning to the apparent inconsistency between impersonal presentations of the Spirit in most of John's Gospel and personal presentation in the farewell discourses, this would only be problematic if presentations of this nature must be fixed and monochrome. As soon as it is conceded that such use of language actually allows for rich combinations of concepts through what are sometimes metaphorical developments of models, then there is no genuine problem for the modern reader in finding both presentations of the Spirit in one gospel. Furthermore, Kenney's suggestion is unnecessary, whatever the importance of brokerage. If the Johannine Jesus had wanted to indicate that he

---

43. Kenney, *Translating H/holy S/spirit*, 45–48.

44. Ibid., 44.

45. Ibid., 47.

would continue to reveal the Father to his followers even after his physical departure, he could have said so directly. This is not a difficult concept that requires some postulated personification in order to be communicated. The Johannine Jesus was referring to another person when he said, "that one will glorify me" (John 16:14). It would not be true to the character of Jesus as presented in John for him to have meant by these words, "I, in spiritual mode, will glorify myself" (see, e.g., John 8:54).

Traditional trinitarianism has generally declared that the Spirit relates personally within the Trinity but impersonally towards all else.[46] This is a clear case of the worrying trend of the tradition to distinguish between the immanent Trinity and economic Trinity in ways that make one contradictory of the other. This is implausible, on the basis that God, being no hypocrite, reveals truths about God, even if not the whole truth. Let me suggest that if the Spirit can relate personally within the Trinity, however rarely this concept may be presented, then it will be more likely than not that the Spirit will at least in rare ways relate personally to, for instance, Christians. I explore this in the next section.

THE KENOSIS OF THE SPIRIT

As soon as it is posited that the Spirit can be viewed in personal terms, a whole new world of possibility opens up, for there are many other activities of the Spirit that can be regarded as kenotic *if they are viewed in personal terms*. I will consider kenosis of the Spirit at Pentecost, first in terms of the Spirit's relations with God's people and then in terms of the Spirit's relations with the Son.

The Spirit's Kenosis and God's People

We Pentecostals tend to think about the relations between the Spirit and God's people at Pentecost in terms of what the event meant for the people. In my experience, we ignore what this event meant for the Spirit. I want to suggest that what we often call the "descent" of the Spirit was an immensely kenotic event.[47] The word "descent" arises from the triple-decker worldview that Robinson was so quick to deride in *Honest to God*.[48] It

---

46. See, e.g., Bauckham, *Theology of Moltmann*, 169–70.

47. Lossky also calls the Spirit's "descent" a kenosis (*Mystical Theology*, 168).

48. Walton clarifies Luke's cosmology in "'The Heavens Opened.'"

has a quasi-physical connotation: as Jesus ascended through the clouds to the Father's right hand, so from there the Spirit descended to earth. But, in personal and relational terms, does not such a "descent" also speak of humbling?

Christians are entirely conversant with [*familiar with*] the thought that in becoming a baby in the womb of Mary, the eternal word—the *Logos*—was *descending* into the squalid depths of our human world and that this was an act of extraordinary self-humbling and self-emptying. Paul said as much, without using *Logos* language (Phil 2:6–8). Why should the descent of the Spirit be seen any differently? It might be argued that there is no similarity at all: that the *Logos* became a human and faced all the challenges of this existence, such as being tempted. The Spirit was "spared" all these indignities in remaining non-human. I am not so sure. The Spirit *engages* with human life in all its squalor. Take prayer as an example. Given that Paul did not consistently conflate [*combine into one*] the Son and the Spirit but offered some distinction between them,[49] Romans 8:26, 34 can be read as an account of two divine intercessors interceding in remarkably different ways. The Spirit prays "within" believers, on the human side of the divine-human divide. The Son intercedes at the Father's right hand. What a difference! The Spirit, here distinguished from God (Rom 8:27), has humbled self in "siding" with the inadequate human intercessor who hardly knows what or how to pray. This is kenosis in relation to the believer. Kenosis in relation to the believer is also evident in the oft-observed feature that the Spirit is, to quote Smail, a "person without a face."[50] The Spirit's effect on the Christian believer is to draw attention not to the Spirit's self but to the Father and the Son. The Spirit is invisible and difficult to define or characterize with precision. As indicated by John, Jesus said as much (John 3:8). I might even go so far as to suggest that, if the personhood of the Spirit is recognized, we can see the Spirit's kenosis most especially in the Spirit's willingness, as a person, to be presented so consistently in impersonal terms: the person of the Spirit is, so to speak, even prepared to go without personhood—that is true kenosis!

In the previous paragraph I have traced this kenosis of the Spirit back to Pentecost but of course the Spirit was engaged with the created order long before then. From the beginning of creation itself, the Genesis story

---

49. For fuller discussion of this point, see chapter 3.

50. Title of chapter 2, Smail, *Giving Gift*. See also Gunton, *Promise of Trinitarian Theology*, 199; Lossky, *Mystical Theology*, 159–64, 168, 172; Parry, *Worshipping Trinity*, 79; Yong, *Spirit-Word-Community*, 70, 136, 138, 161.

tells us, God's Spirit was hovering[51] over the face of the deep. I posit that this was a deeply kenotic act. God's Spirit engaged intimately with darkness and chaos so that light and order might come out of it at God's word. The Spirit, viewed as a person, has since the dawn of time related kenotically to everything that God has made.

The Spirit's Kenosis and the Son

During his earthly ministry the Son's human life and activity was dependent on the Spirit. The Spirit played a part in the Son's conception as the human Jesus, at least according to Matthew and Luke (Matt 1:18, 20; Luke 1:35). Jesus' public ministry could not begin, it seems, until the Spirit empowered him for the task (most clearly, among the Gospel writers, in Luke).[52] The ascension changed the situation. From Pentecost, the Spirit's earthly life and activity was dependent on the Son (though only at the instigation of the Father). Thereafter, the Son sends the Spirit and is, so to speak, "in charge" of the Spirit's activity. To put this in overly blunt terms, Pentecost marked the end of the Spirit's "rule" over Jesus and the initiation of the exalted Jesus' "rule" over the Spirit. As Turner repeatedly puts it, the exalted Christ is now "Lord" of the Spirit.[53] And as Moltmann expresses it, "the relationship is reversed."[54] Understood in personal terms, allowance of this great reversal in roles was a selfless act on the part of the Spirit. We see kenosis here.

Thus we see two apparent stages in the relationship between the Son and the Spirit when viewed in terms of mutual status. For the Son, kenosis (placing himself, as a human, under the guidance and enabling of the Spirit) was followed by an exaltation (to the Father's right hand from where he could grant the Spirit as the Spirit's "Lord"). For the Spirit, in contrast, we see an exaltation (over the Son, whose human life the Spirit enabled and directed) *followed* by a kenosis (when the Spirit now only acted at the behest of the exalted Son). If understood as occurring through time, this looks

51. It is not entirely clear whether Gen 1:2 is best understood as presenting the Spirit hovering like a bird or as presenting a wind sweeping over the water's surface.

52. Warrington's implied counter-argument, that Jesus could perform miracles, for instance, prior to his baptism, fails to convince (*Pentecostal Theology*, 53). So too does Burge's claim that for Luke the earthly Jesus was "Lord of the Spirit" (*Anointed Community*, 62).

53. Turner, "Spirit of Christ," 414, 418–19, 424, 434, 436.

54. Moltmann, *Trinity and Kingdom*, 89.

like a mutual oscillation, in which one partner goes up as another comes down. Viewed as an eternal matter, but as dynamic rather than static, this relationship exhibits what we might characterize as eternal reciprocation. Each eternally and actively exalts the other at the expense of self's kenosis.

The Spirit's kenosis was not to no avail. In emptying and humbling self, the Spirit achieved yet further exaltation of the Son.[55] To this matter I now turn.

THE SPIRIT IN THE LIFE OF THE SON

As I observed at the start of the previous section, the Pentecostal outpouring is usually seen in terms of what the Spirit's arrival did for God's people. This naturally follows Peter's interpretation of the event as recorded by Luke, which built upon Joel's prophecy. This was about what the Spirit would do in and for people and more broadly the cosmos.[56] However, I intend to consider now what the Spirit did in this event for Jesus. I will show that at and after Pentecost the Spirit exalted Jesus. Thereafter, however, I will indicate that even before Pentecost the Spirit, though "in charge" of Jesus in the ways discussed in the previous section, actually exalted the Son in the process. I will then employ imaginative analogy to trace this idea back into the relations of the immanent Trinity. Furthermore, I will suggest that the Spirit upholds both the eternal life of the Son and the Son's eternal relationships with the Father.

The Spirit Exalted the Ascended Jesus

It is easy to demonstrate that Luke regarded the Spirit's descent at Pentecost as the cause of the exaltation of the Son in the eyes of those who responded positively to the gospel, even if this influence was mediated through those who preached the gospel under the Spirit's influence. From start to finish the Spirit's activity was achieving not only a spread of the gospel that brought good to people. It was achieving a spread of the gospel that *brought honor to Christ.* Wherever people who heard the message acknowledged that Christ is Lord, as a result of the Spirit-enabled mission of the fledgling church (Acts 1:8, etc.), the Spirit was thereby bringing further honor to

55. For the Son's exaltation of the Spirit, see below, chapter 3.

56. See my *Baptism in the Spirit.*

Jesus—the Spirit was exalting the Son. A few excerpts will suffice. We read in Acts 19:10 that "all those living in Asia heard the word of the Lord, both Jews and Greeks." While the "all" may be a rhetorical flourish, Luke's claim is impressive: a whole region heard that Jesus is Lord. Admittedly, Jesus of Nazareth's reputation had spread prior to the mission of the young church (e.g., Acts 10:37–38, with its "you know"). But this was not yet the reputation that Jesus is *Lord*. This message (e.g., Acts 10:36, 42–43) came only through those who had seen the risen Jesus and received the Spirit—and through those who in turn believed the message and carried it further. Furthermore, and referring to the Spirit's work in those who were already believers, Stephen is an example of someone to whom the Spirit affirmed Jesus' new place after Jesus' post-resurrection exaltation (Acts 7:55).

Turning now from Acts to Paul's letters, here too we can find a demonstration that the outpoured Spirit exalted the risen Jesus. I consider first Romans 1:3–4 (". . . concerning his Son, born from the seed of David according to flesh, appointed Son of God in power according to [the] Spirit of holiness from resurrection from the dead, Jesus Christ our Lord.") That this text refers to the Holy Spirit, rather than to an aspect of human being or to Christ's divine nature, is assured.[57] Commentators are less confident about the role of the Spirit and the realm of the Spirit's operations here, as is in part attested by the uncertainties about how to translate *kata* (usually "according to"). Fee, Moo, and Dunn, despite their areas of disagreement, all see the Spirit here as operating on or in direct relation to Christ. It is "in the realm of the Spirit" that Christ is appointed (or possibly "declared") Son of God from the resurrection. This encourages Dunn to translate *kata* as "in terms of"[58] and Fee to suggest "with respect to."[59] However, nowhere else in this letter does Paul refer to the operation of the Spirit in the life of Christ, either during Christ's earthly life or during Christ's post-resurrection life. Admittedly, Paul refers in Romans 8:9 to "the Spirit of Christ," but this has to do with the Spirit's operation in believers, not in Christ, and so the term employed is not "Christ of the Spirit." Again in Romans 8:11, Paul speaks of the "Spirit of him who raised Jesus from the dead," but despite the assumptions of many commentators, Fee is rightly insistent that nowhere in this

---

57. Fee, *God's Empowering Presence*, 482–83; Moo, *Epistle to the Romans*, 49–50; Dunn, *Romans 1–8*, 15.

58. Dunn, *Romans 1–8*, 4.

59. Fee, *God's Empowering Presence*, 481. Moo prefers to retain the translation, "according to" (*Epistle to the Romans*, 39, 49).

letter did Paul explicitly assert that the Spirit raised Christ from the dead:[60] the reference here is to the Father who raised Jesus from death.

Paul's habitual concern in this letter was to do with the operation of the Spirit in the lives *of believers*. Why should this be different in Romans 1:4? Paul would later refer to the outpouring of the gift of the Spirit—albeit indirectly (Rom 5:5). While Romans 8:15's cry of Abba Father may suggest a memory of Christ's use of the term, and suggest that he was enabled to see God as Father by the Spirit, this is not asserted. Paul's attention was firmly and consistently on the work of the Spirit in, for, and through believers. Taking these observations back to Romans 1:4, and taking *kata* to carry its usual sense ("according to"), I suggest the following. The flesh, understood neutrally, attested to the fact that Jesus was of human seed—admittedly royal messianic seed. Christ's genealogical origins were in David. The Spirit, *poured out on believers*, attested *in and through their Christian experience* to the fact that Jesus was appointed Son of God with power. The origin of this appointment was the resurrection. This suggestion overcomes concerns about Paul's use of "Spirit of holiness."[61] As Fee points out, it is not satisfactory at this point merely to appeal to Paul's use of traditional creedal language.[62] But if the term means in effect "the Spirit who engenders holiness," as commentators agree,[63] then various strands of thinking come together: the Spirit, poured out on believers to bring holiness to them, is the same Spirit whose outpouring in the lives of believers attests directly to them that Jesus truly is Son of God, to which powerful position the resurrection "appointed" him.[64] Admittedly, it is rare to find such a conclusion expressed by modern commentators, though Fee admits in a footnote that, "some would take the Spirit phrase to refer to the subsequent outpouring of the Spirit by the exalted Son of God as evidence of his present exaltation."[65] Fee

---

60. Fee, *God's Empowering Presence*, 553. However, see further discussion on this point below, pages 68–69.

61. Moo, for example, observes that Paul, like other New Testament authors, never elsewhere used "spirit of holiness" of God's Spirit. "Holiness," used by Paul at 2 Cor 7:1 and 1 Thess 3:13, referred to human sanctification (*Epistle to the Romans*, 50 and n. 54).

62. Fee, *God's Empowering Presence*, 483, n. 34.

63. Ibid., 483; Moo, *Epistle to the Romans*, 50, n. 55.

64. I avoid discussion at this point of Christ's pre-existence, and whether this text alludes to it. Similarly, I eschew discussion of adoptionist christologies.

65. Fee, *God's Empowering Presence*, 482, n. 26.

neither tells us who these "some" are, nor what is wrong, if anything, with their view. I suggest that it is correct.

We find a similar attitude, I believe, in 1 Corinthians 12:3. It is clear that Paul's concerns expressed in this part of his letter were ecclesial. He sought to persuade his readers to behave in certain ways, based on certain beliefs and attitudes, when together as a worshipping community. The most natural questions to ask are therefore about Corinthian misbehavior, as Paul saw it, and about his reproofs. However, there are also theological questions that this text answers. It provides evidence about Paul's own underlying theology, which in turn provides building blocks for a Pentecostal trinitarianism today.

First Corinthians 12:3 declares, "Therefore, I inform you that nobody speaking in the Spirit of God says, 'Jesus is cursed';[66] and nobody can say, 'Jesus is Lord,' if not in the Holy Spirit." Fee quite naturally has his gaze focused on the ecclesial issues when he writes: "The ultimate criterion of the Spirit's activity is the exaltation of Jesus as Lord."[67] In other words, to Corinthians who were perhaps so impressed by unusual phenomena that they took the bizarre or dramatic as a mark of the Spirit's inspiration, Paul wrote: "Careful! See if Christ is being exalted as Lord before you judge that a phenomenon has its origin in God!" All this is no doubt true. But on what theological platform does Paul's assertion rest? As Soards recognizes, it is the "Holy Spirit [who] moves the one under the power of the Spirit to declare, 'Jesus is Lord'!"[68] Put more simply, it is the Spirit who says that Jesus is Lord. It is the Spirit who testifies to the lordship of Christ—the Spirit exalts the Son. In view of this theology, one might in fact be justified in suggesting in response to Fee's comment just quoted, "and vice versa." In other words, "the ultimate criterion of the exaltation of Jesus as Lord is the Spirit's genuine activity." No one and nothing can exalt the Son as well as the Spirit can.

These examples suggest that in Paul's understanding, it was the outpoured—and thus I would say kenotic—Spirit which exalted the Son in the estimation and worship of Christian believers.

---

66. "Jesus is cursed" may have been the verdict of non-Christian Jews at the time of writing. It may even reflect Paul's own early attitude and words. See Garland, 1 Corinthians, 570–71.

67. Fee, God's Empowering Presence, 157–58.

68. Soards, 1 Corinthians, 254. Emphases removed.

I stress again that the exaltation of the Son that thus emerges in the New Testament occurred necessarily by way of the Spirit's kenosis. If the Spirit had not descended, with all that this entailed, the Son would not have been exalted. This much is clear. However, more can be said on the subject of the Spirit exalting the Son, by going further back in time and to some extent by going behind the scenes. I now consider in turn the exaltations of the Son: from earth to heaven; from death to life; during his human history; and, eternally, from non-being to being.

The Spirit Exalted the Resurrected Jesus to the Father's Side

This brief section is about the ascension. It is necessarily speculative: biblical data concerning the ascension are few and far between. Only Luke offered any detail at all. There is, nonetheless, perhaps a hint that Luke regarded the ascension as a work of the Spirit. Admittedly, it is no more than a hint, resting as it does on a somewhat unlikely translation of Acts 2:33. This text indicates that the Jesus mentioned by name in Acts 2:32 was raised—more than that, exalted—by and to God the Father. It is debatable whether the Greek text is intended to indicate that Jesus was exalted by God, implied in what is called a "divine passive," to God's right-hand side, or that Jesus was lifted by the exercise of God's right hand to an unstated position. In favor of the former possibility is the quotation from Psalm 110 in the following verse. This psalm declares in the Septuagint and its quotation in Acts 2:34, "sit on my right." Therefore, this close association of Psalm 110, where the reference is clearly to a position alongside God, suggests that Acts 2:33 can best be translated as "exalted to God's right-hand side," rather than "exalted by [the exercise of] God's right hand." However, in favor of the latter option, as Bruce observes,[69] is the wording of Psalm 118:16 in the Septuagint (where this Psalm is numbered 117): "the right [hand] of the Lord exalted me." As this latter psalm is not quoted or alluded to in Peter's speech, one must conclude that "to God's right-hand side" seems a more likely translation than "by [the exercise of] God's right hand." Nevertheless, the latter is possible, and if it happens to be correct, it raises the question of what Luke would have understood God's right hand to be in this context.

In considering this matter, it can first be noted that biblical authors commonly used anatomical anthropomorphisms to refer to the instrument of God's actions on earth and that Luke was no exception. He included

69. Bruce, *Acts*, 66.

arm, hand, and finger: examples include Luke 1:51 (arm); Luke 1:66; Acts 4:30 (hand); Luke 11:20 (finger). In each of these cases, Luke or his sources might equally have used the word "Spirit." This is clearest in the case of Luke 11:20, where "finger" actually replaces the term "Spirit" found in Matthew 12:28.[70] In the other instances listed here where Luke or his sources used "hand," the context of Luke's thinking would also easily allow "Spirit." Thus, John the Baptist was filled with the Spirit from his mother's womb (Luke 1:15)—and the hand of the Lord was with him from childhood (Luke 1:66); the Spirit enabled the apostles, like Jesus before them, to heal (e.g., Acts 10:38[71])—and they prayed for the stretching forth of God's hand to heal (Acts 4:30).[72] Indeed, God answered this prayer by sending the Spirit (Acts 4:31)! So Luke might well regard "God's Spirit did such-and-such" and "God's hand did such-and-such" as synonymous. We are presented with the slim possibility that Acts 2:33 refers to the Spirit in more ways than are immediately apparent, and that God exalted Jesus to heaven *by means of the Spirit.*

The Spirit "Exalted" the Dead Jesus to Life

When Jesus was dead, the "exaltation" required was from death to life. In chapter 4, I will discuss the obvious idea that the Father raised Jesus the Son from death to life. Christians locate this resurrection in space and time, and rightly so. I will, however, also <u>extrapolate</u> this idea, by means of the pneumatological imagination introduced in chapter 1, "back" into the dynamics of the eternal life of the immanent Trinity and suggest that the Father eternally upholds the Son's life. At this point, however, I tackle the rather less obvious idea that perhaps the Spirit raised Jesus the Son from death to life. My aim is not to suggest, of course, that the Spirit "also" raised Jesus, alongside the Father. On the contrary, a satisfactory full trinitarian statement would surely be that the Father raised the Son *by means of* the

70. For discussion of the most likely wording in "Q," the postulated common source behind Luke and Matt at this point, see Turner, *Power from on High,* 257.

71. For references to discussion of the relation between "Spirit" and "power" in Luke-Acts, see n. 13 above; for discussion of the extent to which Jesus' healing ministry was a paradigm for later apostolic and Christian healing ministries, see Menzies, "Sending of the Seventy," e.g., 108; Williams, "Following Christ's Example," 175–96; and, in contrast, Warrington, *Pentecostal Theology,* 52–53.

72. Admittedly, the word "hand" could also be used in quite different ways in these contexts: e.g., Acts 4:28.

Spirit. I therefore discuss here the Spirit's possible instrumentality in the process of resurrection.

The discussion on this occasion turns quickly to Paul, for neither Luke nor any other canonical Gospel writer offered any evidence that they thought of Jesus being raised from the dead by the Spirit's operation. Whether Paul considered the Spirit to have raised Jesus from death is widely discussed. As noted earlier in this chapter, Fee firmly denies that Paul ever explicitly stated this. However, he has to acknowledge that a host of scholars disagree with him, including Turner.[73] Turner himself not only sees Romans 8:11 and Philippians 3:21 as coming "close to stating this explicitly," but sees such an idea according with intertestamental ideas, themes in Ezekiel on which Paul clearly built, and Paul's other expressions concerning links between the Spirit and resurrection, such as "first fruit."[74] Turner's view is stronger than Fee's at this point, for Paul most clearly linked the Spirit with the life and resurrection of believers (e.g., Rom 8:2,[75] 13; Gal 6:8). Thus, for him to distance the Spirit from the resurrection of Christ seems unlikely, for Paul consistently offered Christ's resurrection as an archetype of subsequent believers' resurrections (e.g., 1 Cor 15:20, 22–23; Rom 8:29; Phil 3:21). One does have to admit that when Paul explicitly related Christ's resurrection to an aspect of God's activity, he chose not to refer to God's Spirit but to God's power (1 Cor 6:14; 2 Cor 13:4; Phil 3:21). Why this is so is not clear. The extent to which New Testament authors separated God's Spirit from God's power conceptually has been much discussed, especially with respect to Luke.[76] Paul linked the themes of power and Spirit at: 1 Thessalonians 1:5; 1 Corinthians 2:4; Romans 15:19 (cf. Eph 3:16; 2 Tim 1:7). Furthermore, he could comfortably ascribe the new life of believers to the power of God in one letter (2 Cor 13:4) and to the Spirit of God in another (Gal 6:8). Therefore, one is hard pressed not to agree with Levison when he writes, "it is difficult to shake off the sense of how integrally related the resurrection and the holy spirit are for someone such as Paul."[77]

73. Fee, *God's Empowering Presence*, 553, and n. 233; cf. 808–11.

74. Turner, *Holy Spirit and Spiritual Gifts*, 125–26, quotation from 125.

75. Probably also Rom 8:11. See Fee, *God's Empowering Presence*, 543, n. 205 for discussion of the textual variants at this point.

76. The strongest argument that Luke largely separated these concepts is perhaps that offered by Menzies, *Empowered for Witness*. For references to discussion of the issues, see n. 13 above.

77. Levison, *Filled with the Spirit*, 311.

If it is the case that the Spirit played a part in establishing the new resurrection life of the Son after death, what might this have to do with trinitarian thought? My claim is that any role of the Spirit in giving life to the Son, as that was expressed in the resurrection, must be a particular instance of an eternal role of the Spirit in establishing the life of the Son. I will develop this idea more when I come to discuss the role of the Spirit in establishing, in the womb of Mary, the incarnate life of the Son. However, just before coming to that material, we must pause to consider the role of the kenotic Spirit in exalting Jesus during his earthly ministry.

The Spirit Exalted the Earthly Jesus

I will give first consideration at this point to the Lukan picture, for Luke more than the other Gospel writers focused on the work of the Spirit in the earthly human Jesus. There is no doubt that during his human history, Jesus was exalted in people's eyes by the Spirit—put another way, God exalted Jesus by means of the Spirit. This is clear from the outset. In Luke 1:35, Gabriel declared that the Spirit's action on Mary would lead to the child's being the holy Son of God. This was not simply an annunciation by the angel to Mary. In Luke's narrative intentions, it was an "annunciation" by Luke to those reading or hearing the text. In turn, it signals an announcement by God to all who listen with faith. These latter considerations are true, as well, of the words from heaven that accompanied the descent of the Spirit on the recently baptized Jesus by the Jordan (Luke 3:21–22).

That Luke regarded the Spirit's work in Jesus as leading to the latter's exaltation in people's eyes also emerges throughout the record of Jesus' public ministry. When Jesus first publicly referred to his anointing with the Spirit (Luke 4:18), all were "astonished by the words" that he spoke (Luke 4:22). When the dramatic visible results of this anointing began to be seen by onlookers, the verdict was that "a great prophet has been raised up among us" (Luke 7:16).

We move now from Luke's witness to consider that of other New Testament authors. There are various references to the Spirit exalting Jesus. Commencing with memories and explanations of Jesus' earthly human history, all the other Gospels in their own ways testify to the idea that the arrival of the Spirit in Jesus' life beside the Jordan River at least coincided with the heavenly voice that affirmed Jesus' identity and importance (Matt 3:16–17 = Mark 1:10–11; John 1:32–34). In the Johannine material it is especially the case that the arrival of the Spirit like a dove served as the direct sign to John the Baptist that the recipient was both the baptizer in the Spirit and the Son of God. Thus the Spirit, by arriving, exalted Jesus in John the Baptist's eyes, and the whole Gospel was expected by its author to exalt Jesus in readers' and hearers' eyes and ears (John 20:31). In this Johannine depiction, the Spirit's later arrival to Jesus' followers (John 7:39) would continue to exalt the earthly Jesus, for instance by reminding these followers of the things—the good things—that Jesus had taught (John 14:26; cf. 15:26). Furthermore, part of this Spirit's work would be to convict people of guilt over their failure to believe in Jesus (John 16:8–9). Even if John 16:14 is understood to refer only to the Spirit's glorification of the risen Jesus, rather than to the glorification of the earthly Jesus, the earlier texts cited indicate that the Spirit exalted Jesus during the latter's lowly ministry. This glorification of the earthly Jesus by the Spirit received further attention in 1 John 4:2 (cf. 1 John 2:20–22).

It needs to be remembered throughout this whole section that the Spirit exalted the Son by means of the Spirit's own kenosis. The dove *descended* to Jesus. As the Son expressed kenosis in becoming human (Phil 2:6–8), so too the Spirit expressed kenosis in joining him in this "descent" from heaven to earth. We can regard this as true of the immanent Trinity: the Son's dynamic eternal exaltation occurs at the "expense" of the Spirit's kenosis. But does the Spirit do more than exalt the eternally existent Son? Does the Son's pre-existence even pre-exist, so to speak, the Spirit's work? Would there be a Son to exalt if it were not for the Spirit's activity? This is the next matter to explore: the "exaltation" of the Son by the Spirit from non-being to eternal being.

The Spirit Establishes the Son's Eternal Life

This section considers the Spirit as the Spirit of sonship, or as the Spirit of adoption. There is plenty of New Testament evidence for the Spirit's role in the sonship of the human Jesus. The action of the Spirit in Jesus' conception, in both the Lukan and Matthean accounts (Luke 1:35; Matt 1:18–20) is relevant. The Spirit played a generative part in the human sonship of the Son. The Spirit's role in Christ's conception ensured his divine sonship as a human (Luke 1:35). That the action of the Spirit in the life of Jesus, in terms of sonship, served as a promise to Jesus' followers for their own experience of "sonship" (if the gendered term be forgiven) can be seen in two ways.

First, the more general promise that Christ's followers would receive the Spirit was articulated not only in words, from those of John the Baptist (e.g., Mark 1:8), to those of Jesus (e.g., Luke 12:11–12; Acts 1:5, 8). The promise of the Spirit for all was also expressed eloquently in Jesus' own "reception" of the Spirit. Some authors have sought to highlight the unique aspects of Jesus' experience of the Spirit at his baptism.[78] Clearly there were unique aspects and these must not be ignored. However, those authors who have sought to highlight ways in which Jesus' reception of the Spirit at this point in his life was at least partly paradigmatic for later receptions of the Spirit by Jesus' followers are surely correct.[79]

Secondly, Paul's writing on the topic (e.g., Rom 8:14–17; Gal 4:6–7) indicates a rare point of contact between Paul's explicit focus and the life of Jesus that we read of in the Gospels. Admittedly, Paul's focus was firmly on God's adoption of believers as children, not on the human history of Jesus of Nazareth. However, Paul's idea of being a child of God was implicitly dependent on Jesus' own experience of God's fatherhood. The likely link here is evidenced by Paul's use of the word "Abba" (Rom 8:15; Gal 4:6). According to Mark, Jesus used this word in prayer to the Father (Mark 14:36). It is even conceivable, though by no means demonstrable, that Paul connected being a child of God who could call God "Abba" to the Spirit because he was aware of the Spirit's role in Jesus' earthly life and relationship to his Father God. Whatever the possible merit of this speculation, we are entitled to see a likely New Testament link between Jesus' experience of sonship by the Spirit and believers' experience of "sonship" by that same Spirit: Paul perhaps worked "forward" from the sonship of Christ to the "sonship" of Christians. With this in mind, we can also work "backward" from the "sonship" of Christians to the sonship of Christ: it is possible to exercise the pneumatological imagination when reading Pauline texts about believers to posit ideas about the role of the Spirit in the sonship of the Son.

What is implied in the term "Spirit of adoption"? It is clear from the Pauline texts mentioned earlier that in the case of the Spirit's role in the lives of Christian disciples, the Spirit *both* achieves believers' adoption as God's children, *and* assures them of this reality. So a twofold work is visible, the first aspect of which is immediately relevant to this subsection, and the second relevant to the next. At this stage, my point is that, just as

---

78. Turner, "Luke and the Spirit," 185; Warrington, *Pentecostal Theology*, 52–53.

79. E.g., Dunn, *Baptism in the Holy Spirit*; Stronstad, *Charismatic Theology*; Menzies, *Empowered for Witness*, throughout.

the Spirit is the Spirit of sonship for believers, so is the Spirit the Spirit of sonship for the Son. I am suggesting that Romans 8:15 could be stated of, and indeed to, Jesus. The Father can be heard saying to Jesus, "You did not receive a spirit of slavery . . . you received the Spirit that makes you my Son, so you can cry, 'Abba, Father.'" By extension, and relying on the relationship between the economic Trinity and the immanent Trinity discussed in chapter 1, the Son's eternal existence and relation to God as Father is achieved by the Spirit: in all eternity, the Spirit is the means by which the Father holds the Son in existence.

We can also consider this matter in Johannine terms. When we think of John's Word-made-flesh, the one who was filled with the Spirit (John 3:34; cf. Matt 12:18; Luke 4:1) was not only the human. The one who was filled with the Spirit was the Word-made-flesh, the divine-human Son. The Spirit filled Christ's *divinity* as well as his humanity. It is a mistake to compartmentalize the divine and human in the earthly Christ. This is well recognized with respect, for instance, to the miracles or to Jesus' hunger and tiredness. Tempting as it may be to suggest that Jesus performed great feats of power in his divinity but hungered and thirsted in his humanity, the Gospels, quite apart from the church's later deliberations, give us no room to think in such a way. So too with the filling of the Spirit: the divine Son, as much as the human, knows what it is to be filled with the Spirit. If this was true on earth, then I suggest it is true in heaven. If it was true in time, then I suggest it is true in eternity. It is true to the eternal state of the Trinity that the Spirit fills the Son. The Spirit empowers the Son to act: in heaven as much as on earth; in eternity as much as in time. The Spirit grants to the Son life, including divine as well as human life. It would be inappropriate, having recognized the combination of divine and human in the earthly Jesus, to separate this facet of the Spirit's work and claim that the Spirit only gives the Son human life but that the Son's divine life is his apart from the work of the Spirit.[80]

The Spirit Establishes the Son's Relations with the Father

For Mark and Luke, the heavenly voice that accompanied the Spirit's descent at Jesus' baptism assured *Jesus*, let alone any onlookers, that he was indeed God's son (Mark 1:11; Luke 3:22). Following Jesus' baptism, Luke

---

80. I return briefly to this theme in chapter 4, where I note that the Father eternally generates the Son *through* the Spirit.

chapter 4 records Jesus' indication both that Old Testament prophecy was being fulfilled in his life, and that the authority he had was mediated to him by the Holy Spirit's anointing. Jesus' words in Luke 4:18–21 are evidence enough that he knew that the dove he had seen descend had been the Holy Spirit. It is a reasonable inference that in Luke's view Jesus linked the *assurance* of his sonship with the arrival of the Spirit.

At the commencement of Jesus' ministry, then, the assurance that he was God's Son was associated with the Spirit. This continued in later events. Admittedly, there is no reference to the Spirit's involvement with the events we call the transfiguration. But it is seen in Luke 10:21, which unlike Matthew 11:27 associates Jesus' awareness of sonship with rejoicing "in the Spirit." Jesus knew of his sonship by a means that was in some way linked to the action of the Spirit. By imaginative analogy, Jesus' divine sonship is assured in the same way: in all eternity, the Father speaks to the Son by means of the Spirit, assuring the Son of this relationship. By the Spirit, the breath of his mouth, the Father speaks to the Son words of eternal and intimate love.

Returning to the Pauline idea of the Spirit of adoption and to Romans 8:15–16, not only could Romans 8:15 be stated of Jesus, I suggest, but also Romans 8:16. One can imagine the Father saying to Jesus that, because the Spirit is the Spirit of sonship, "My Spirit witnesses along with your spirit that you are the Son of God." The Father speaks to the Son, assuring that sonship, by means of *the Spirit*. Furthermore, the Spirit does not only convey the voice of the Father to others. The Spirit also stands on "our side of the line" between divinity and humanity. The Spirit, as the Spirit of adoption, aids believers' prayers (Rom 8:26). While it is not recorded that Jesus' prayers were enabled by the Spirit, the thesis that at least in some respects Jesus' experience of the Spirit was paradigmatic of the disciples' later experiences would suggest that as they prayed with the help of the Spirit so too did the Spirit aid Jesus in his praying, indwelling him and his prayers actively. By the process of extension I am employing in this book, it seems reasonable to suggest that in all eternity, as well, the Son speaks to the Father with the help of—by means of—the Spirit. One may take this further, guided by Paul's logic in Romans: just as the Spirit actually prays in believers, according to Romans 8:26–27, and thereby in effect speaks to the Father through believers, so too I suggest does the Spirit speak to the Father through the Son.

Turning now from actions and words to vision, the Johannine presentation is of a Jesus who trusted his relationship with his Father such that he could know his Father's responses (e.g., John 11:41–42) and perceive his Father's deeds (e.g., John 5:19). While it is suggested by Hurtado with reference to the work of Sproston[81] that the Johannine Jesus expressed pre-incarnate memories at the points referred to in John 8:14, 58; 17:5, it seems more likely that what we have here are statements of Jesus' faith in the nature of his relationship with his Father God. There is little indication in the Johannine portrayal of how such a visionary faith might have been granted to Jesus. However, there is reference to God giving the Spirit "without limit" (John 3:34), which is usually understood to refer to the Father's gift of the Spirit to Jesus himself.[82] Thus, there is at least a hint that the Father granted Jesus' faith-filled capacity to see his Father by this Spirit. So, if the human Jesus saw the Father and the Father's deeds by the Spirit, once again by the same extension the eternal Son sees the Father and the Father's deeds by the Spirit. The Spirit eternally enables the Son's perceptions of the Father and thereby aids the Son's eternal relationship with the Father.

We can also see that the eternal relationship between God and the *Logos* ("Word"), as expressed in John 1:1, was and is *pneumatologically* enabled—upheld by the Spirit—and that thereby we come to see that *Logos* christology and Spirit christology are firmly wedded in eternity. Some commentators have suggested that John's Gospel, in comparison to the Synoptic Gospels, downplays the part the Spirit plays in enabling the Son's ministry, reasoning thus: why would the eternal *Logos*-become-flesh *need* the Spirit?[83] However, whatever John's reasoning may have been, we can *build on* John's foundations and suggest that the notion suggested by these scholars rests on a false dichotomy. *Logos* christology and Spirit christology go hand in hand.

In conclusion to this section, I have considered the place of the Spirit in the life of the Son and seen how the Spirit eternally exalts the Son. This can be traced, historically, throughout the church life presented in Acts, and hints of the same idea are found in Paul's letters. Working back, it can perhaps also be traced in the resurrection, and can certainly be seen in

---

81. Hurtado, *Lord Jesus Christ*, 365 n. 29.

82. For earlier consideration of this verse, see above, page 43. Note also Burge's consideration of the reference in John 6:27 to Jesus' being "sealed" (*Anointed Community*, 85).

83. See the discussion in Burge, *Anointed Community*, 71–73.

the earthly life of Jesus. By analogy, it can be traced in eternity: the Spirit upholds the eternal existence of the Son and his relations with the Father. Thus the Spirit is intimately and utterly involved in every aspect of the Son's divine life. I have also noted that none of this would be possible unless the Spirit acted kenotically. The Spirit's kenosis with respect to creation is visible in a variety of ways but with respect to the Son was seen most obviously at Pentecost. This is also important for identifying a causal link between the Spirit's kenosis and the Spirit's contribution to the life and glory of the Son. The latter could not occur without the former being true.

CHAPTER CONCLUSIONS

This chapter has considered the Spirit's place in the Trinity. The Spirit is not a created heavenly intermediary but can be viewed either as God's own being or as an extension of God the Father's own self towards all else. This combination of commonality with and distinction from the Father lends itself to an appreciation of instrumental, relational, and substantial models of the Trinity. I will explore these models in chapter 5. Seen instrumentally, the Spirit is the *means by which* the Father establishes the Son in eternity and the two relate to each other. This position is similar to that espoused by Augustine, in which the Spirit is the love between the Father and the Son but is subtly different: in my rendition, the Spirit is *the means of* the communication of love between the Father and the Son.

The Spirit can also be viewed substantially—ontologically—in both impersonal and personal ways. The former caused me to pause and note various strands of trinitarian thought that will need to be woven into later discussion. These include, for example, the Father's possible kenosis with respect to the Spirit and the nature of the Trinity's perichoresis as pervasive. The latter—viewing the Spirit as personal—arises because the Spirit's actions in relation to the Father and the Son demonstrate the Spirit's kenosis. Most vividly at Pentecost, the Spirit was ready to step down from being "Lord" of the incarnate Jesus so that Jesus became "Lord" of the poured out Spirit. What in time looks like oscillation reflects the eternal *dynamic*, not static, and reciprocal relations in the Trinity. So the main finding of this chapter has been the impact of the Spirit's kenosis on the life of the Son. Beyond Pentecost, I explored various stages in the economy when the kenotic Spirit exalted the Son and drew the analogical conclusion that the Spirit so acts in eternity. By means of the kenosis of self, the Spirit eternally exalts the Son ensuring the Son's utter glory.

3

Pentecost and the Son

INTRODUCTION

I BEGIN THIS CHAPTER, as I began the last, with a word about their order. That the Son should occupy our attention in the *central* chapter of my triad (chapters 2, 3, and 4: Spirit, Son, Father) is entirely in accord with Pentecostal testimony. Pentecostals *center on Jesus*. This can be seen in their famous slogan, "Jesus: Savior; Healer; Baptizer in the Spirit; and Soon-coming King." I have put this in the terms of my own "foursquare" denomination. Pentecostal holiness groups include a fifth element and speak of Jesus as "Savior; Healer; Sanctifier; Baptizer in the Spirit; and Soon-coming King." Whether we concern ourselves with a foursquare or a "fivesquare" gospel, the centrality of Jesus is undiminished. Pentecostal worship is highly centered on Jesus.[1] Pentecostal prayer is often offered to Jesus. Sensing that we are aided by the Spirit in this insight, we have no doubt of Jesus' centrality and lordship.

As a trinitarian Pentecostal, I find that this entirely accords, too, with my own Christian experience. I rarely pray to the Spirit. I suspect that I generally only sing to the Spirit in worship when the words of a song composed and published by someone else lead me to do so. I confess that I probably pray more to Jesus than to the Father. I say "confess," aware of Matthew 11:9, Luke 11:2, and John 16:23. Jesus looms large in my Christian horizon. The Father seems to stand further back, in rather hazier territory.

---

1. See brief discussions in Parry, *Worshipping Trinity*, 2; Cartledge, *Testimony in the Spirit*, 46–47.

Jesus is sharp and clear, visible as a human. The nature of God, other than in the face of Christ, is relatively undefined.

I will tackle this matter later in this chapter, so turning now to the chapter's content, my aim in it is to show how, by beginning with the dynamics of Pentecost, the Son's trinitarian identity, roles, and relationships can be explicated. First, concerning the identity of the Son, I discuss whether or not he is a created intermediary. Thereafter, just as in chapter 2 it was necessary to clarify both the distinctions between and the commonality between the Spirit and the Father, so now I consider the Son's distinctions from and commonality with the Spirit. In the subsequent section, a way of viewing the Son as personal is derived from the prayer life of Jesus. Thereafter, I explore a way of seeing the Son impersonally through the twin metaphors of the *Logos* ("Word") of God and one of the hands of God.

I will then consider the Son's trinitarian roles. First, I will explore the sending of the Spirit as evidence of the Son's role in the eternal procession of the Spirit (that such a role can be distinguished will inform later discussion, in chapter 4, about the famous *filioque* controversy). Then, I will study how the Son reveals, defines, and exalts the Father and the Spirit. Finally, this chapter will consider both the kenosis and the exaltation of the Son. I will link these ideas to each other and discuss their link to the relations the Son has with the other persons of the Trinity.

THE SON'S DISTINCTIONS

In keeping with the focus of this book, I commence, of course, with Pentecost. According to Luke, public reflection on the interactions between the Father, the exalted Jesus, and the Spirit only began on the day of Pentecost, whatever private reflections there may have been. I do not discount the evidence of some manuscripts of Luke 24:52 that Luke may have countenanced some form of worship of Jesus prior to Pentecost. That Luke would have regarded such words as those recorded in for example Luke 9:20 as an act of worship is more dubious. Of course in Luke's eyes there would have been public reflection on the possible relationship between the earthly Jesus and the Spirit, as evidenced for example by Luke 4:18–29; 7:16; 9:19: Jesus claimed to be anointed and people sensed that he was a prophet. By natural extension, this would entail reflection upon Jesus' relationship with the God whom he called "Father." Nonetheless, consideration of the overall relations was a post-Pentecost phenomenon. What spurred this public discussion was the experience Jesus' followers had at this time of the Holy Spirit coming into their lives overwhelmingly.[2] By Luke's account, the Spirit's arrival both gave the boldness to speak of the risen Jesus in public in exalted terms, and supplied evidence concerning the destiny of the ascended and thus invisible Jesus. He had gone into the clouds, but whither? Some spoke of an angelic visitation, indicating that Jesus was in heaven (Acts 1:11). What did that mean?[3] Had Jesus been enthroned in the same way that, according to various Jewish writings, Moses had?[4] Was this merely a sign of God's approval and promotion? Or was something more involved? I will claim the latter.

The Son and Created Intermediaries

It is not my purpose in this section to compare the Son with created intermediaries such as Moses or angels. Instead, by way of contrast with such intermediaries, I study the Son's relationship with the Spirit as evidence of his divinity.

It was the arrival of the Spirit that indicated just how exalted Jesus' enthroned position was. Or, more accurately, it was the recipients' *experience* of the Spirit's arrival that gave this indication. Several of Christ's followers had seen the empty grave and seen the risen Jesus, by all accounts in the Gospels, Acts, and 1 Corinthians.[5] So these followers perceived that Jesus was alive: risen from the dead. By Luke's account they had seen Jesus ascend. So where was Jesus, and what was he doing? Acts 2:33 states that Jesus, after his resurrection by God, of which this first group of his followers in Jerusalem were witnesses, had been exalted to (or "by") the right hand of God. The longer ending of Mark contains a similar claim (Mark 16:19).

2. See chapter 1 for discussion of Hurtado's presentation of factors leading to the veneration of Jesus. I suggest there that he does not adequately distinguish between the resurrection and Pentecost: between the presence of Christ experienced through resurrection appearances and the presence of Christ experienced through the Spirit's new arrival. Testimony to these two types of experience is historically distinguishable. It is my claim that it was only as a result of the experience of the Spirit as the Spirit of Christ that true Christ-worship began and trinitarianism eventually followed.

3. For more general discussion of what the ascension meant in Luke-Acts, see Walton, "'The Heavens Opened.'"

4. See Hurtado, *One God, One Lord*, 56–63.

5. No mention of the Spirit was made in reference to these sightings except in John 20:22.

What really indicated the status of the ascended Jesus was the experience of the arrival of the Spirit. Of course, God's Spirit had impacted the human world on many occasions in the past, according to Old Testament testimony. But now the Spirit was in some intimate way connected to the Jesus who had just ascended. As presented by Luke through Peter's speech, this realization was immediate. It is harder to tell from, say, Paul's letters how long it may have been for the Spirit to have become this intimately associated with Christ, but there is no doubt that within the early decades of Christianity this connection was firm: Paul's letters present this element of his message as entirely uncontroversial to his readers and uncontroverted, presumably, among his opponents. Luke's position is entirely clear. 1 Peter also offers the same connection (1 Pet 1:11).

We will consider Luke's testimony in detail. Peter's Pentecost speech is key (Acts 2:14–40). It is fascinating to consider how it is set out. There is nothing in the early parts of the speech to suggest anything other than the humanity of Jesus. Admittedly, it was a particularly blessed humanity but it was humanity nonetheless. Thus, Jesus was "a man commended by God" (2:22). He was a man *through whom* God worked (2:22)—this in itself hardly suggests the divinity of Jesus! Neither does his mortality, even if his death was according to a divine purpose (2:23). It took God to raise Jesus from this death (2:24). The only hint at something more than humanity, so far, is the statement that "it was not possible" for death to hold Jesus (2:24). Moving on in the speech, even the resurrection does not alter the presentation of Jesus' humanity and need for total reliance on God. It was *God* who raised Jesus from death (2:32). Thus far in the speech, the only specific status of Jesus that the resurrection indicated was that Jesus was David's messianic enthroned descendant (2:30–31). This prophecy alone would, within the logic of the narrative, have convinced Peter that the risen and ascended Jesus was now enthroned. But there was much more to come. It was the experienced arrival of the Spirit in Peter's and the others' lives that enabled Peter to declare Acts 2:33.

And what a declaration! To put it briefly and simply, Peter claimed that this exalted Jesus was now the granter of God's Spirit. Insofar as only God can grant God's Spirit, this is a *declaration of Christ's divinity*. We owe much to Max Turner for explicating this "divine christology" of Luke. In developing his convincing position, he has to overcome the counter-arguments of others, and in particular he discusses the claims in this respect of

James Dunn.[6] Dunn, like others such as Maurice Casey,[7] is not willing to read a great deal of christological significance into Acts 2:33. Dunn has two arguments. First, it is conceivable that the Judaism of the time would have been comfortable with the idea that a non-divine intermediary could be granted the privilege of dispensing God's Spirit. Secondly, it was, according to Dunn, understood by the earliest Christians that *they* could dispense God's Spirit (or certainly so understood by Luke: Acts 8:19) and so there was nothing unique as such in Jesus granting the Spirit.[8]

Turner successfully overturns these and similar suggestions. With respect to the first of Dunn's arguments, the Spirit of God was understood by the Judaism of the day to be God's self in activity among God's people and beyond: "the claim made in Acts 2:33 is made in the context of a Judaism for which the Spirit is not a second heavenly being, but a way of speaking of *God's own* 'vitality,' 'life,' or 'self-expression,' of God *himself* in action."[9] Nobody but God could grant this. I happen to disagree with Turner and agree with Dunn about the understanding John the Baptist may have had of his own prediction that a coming one would baptize with the Spirit. Turner denies that this is a promise that the coming one would grant the Spirit, while I take the phrase more at face value. As I have written elsewhere, "whether or not other pre-Christian Judaism conceived of a coming Messiah who would himself grant the Spirit of God, Luke portrayed John the Baptist as an extraordinary prophet (Luke 1:15–17, 76; 3:2; 7:26). One must allow that God might have revealed this theological novelty to John—and that Luke would have understood the course of events thus."[10] However, this is not to claim that such an idea would have been common currency in wider Judaism. Turner is right: it was not. Thus a claim that Jesus now granted the Spirit would be seen in typical Judaism as a claim of his divinity (and a strange one, given the nature of Judaism's monotheism). Turning, secondly, to the matter of Christians allegedly dispensing the Spirit, in Luke's understanding, this "seems an unhelpful comparison. . . . It is simply a matter of prayerful human incorporative invocation of the

---

6. See especially Turner, "Spirit of Christ."

7. Ibid., 416.

8. E.g., Dunn, *Partings of the Ways*, 187.

9. Turner, "Spirit of Christ," 414.

10. Atkinson, *Baptism in the Spirit*, 57.

Spirit." Most importantly, it "involved no ongoing relationship between the apostles and the Spirit imparted."[11]

This last point is key for, as Turner observes, the relationship that Luke describes between the exalted Jesus and the Spirit is not "merely" that Jesus grants the Spirit but, perhaps more importantly, that the Spirit thereafter mediates the awareness and impact of Jesus, for instance through visions (e.g., Acts 7:55).[12] So while a text like Acts 18:9–10 does not explicitly mention the Spirit, the programmatic linking of visions with the Spirit's activity (Acts 2:17) is sufficient for us to realize that Luke saw Jesus' presence and words on this occasion as conveyed by the Spirit. Such is the implication of the phrase, admittedly used only once in Luke-Acts, the "Spirit of Jesus" (Acts 16:7—there is very little manuscript doubt, despite KJV; NKJV). So Luke's christology was not an "absentee christology" of a Christ now remote in heaven but "Luke's christology . . . is one of soteriological omnipresence."[13]

Turner's contribution here is immense. First, as he points out, the contribution to early christology that the experience of the Spirit made has been overlooked in scholarly discussion.[14] Secondly, his conclusion, expressed provocatively in the accurate claim that Jesus after the ascension became for Luke the "Lord of the Spirit" has, as he notes, significant trinitarian implications. The divinity of the exalted Jesus is implied.

But is this insight only Lukan? No: of course we find Jesus sending the Spirit in John as well. So Turner points out that it is surprising how scholars so frequently relate John's "high" christology to his understanding of the *Logos* without recognizing the place of Jesus' promised relationship with the Spirit that builds throughout the course of the Gospel until finally we find Jesus' breathing of the Spirit on the disciples (John 20:22) "preparing for Thomas's confession, 'My Lord and my God' (20:28)."[15]

---

11. Turner, "Spirit of Christ," 420.

12. Walton makes much the same point by noting the similarity between Luke 12:11–12 and Luke 21:14–15 ("Whose Spirit?" 48).

13. Turner, "Spirit of Christ," 421.

14. Ibid., 413. Similar observations are made by Hultgren (quoted in Turner, "Spirit of Christ," 415 n. 7), Macchia (*Baptized in the Spirit*, 107), and Fee (*God's Empowering Presence*, 836, n. 29). In my first chapter I have already made reference to Johnson's lament that experience *per se* has been largely overlooked by New Testament scholars (Johnson, *Religious Experience in Earliest Christianity*). See also Rabens, "Power from In Between," 138–50.

15. Turner, "Spirit of Christ," 415.

So too with Paul. Here Turner tackles Dunn's position at length. For Dunn, while there is some sense that, for Paul, Christ is the Lord of the Spirit, the more important aspect of the relationship that is summed up in such phrases as "Spirit of Christ" (Rom 8:9) is that the Spirit has somehow become defined—given personal shape—by Christ through the resurrection. The "Spirit of Christ" means the "Spirit stamped by Christ's personality." Turner is again convincing in showing that this is not a sufficient understanding.[16] Such phrases as "Spirit of Elijah" (cf. Luke 1:17) cannot suggest, within the context of Jewish thinking, that Elijah had somehow stamped his personality on the Spirit he had received from God. Rather, the same Spirit God had given to Elijah was now, in the case of Luke's portrayal of John, going to be given to the Baptist. More apposite to discussion of the meaning of "Spirit of Christ" is its direct comparability to "Spirit of God," which means God's own being actively expressed in recipients. "Spirit of Christ" suggests that the now glorified Christ acted by means of this Spirit. This was *the* expression of Christ's continuing activity among recipients.[17]

This Pauline use was somewhat similar to Luke's use of "Spirit of Jesus." However, there are subtle differences from Luke's picture. As I have already noted, Luke used the phrase "Spirit of Jesus" (Acts 16:7) but Luke's emphasis was on the fact that it was Jesus who *sent* the Spirit (Acts 2:33—though ultimately from the Father). Only indirectly did the Spirit convey Jesus' *presence*. Directly, the Spirit granted a vision of Jesus *in heaven* (Acts 7:55). Only implicitly (on the basis of Acts 2:17) did the Spirit grant a vision in which Christ expressed his presence to a disciple (Acts 18:9–10). Notably, Luke never wrote of "Christ in" believers. On the other hand, never did Paul write of *Christ* sending the Spirit: it was always God who did this (see 1 Thess 4:8; Gal 3:5; 4:6; 2 Cor 1:22; 5:5; Rom 5:5). But these subtle differences must not be allowed to overshadow the common ground in Luke and Paul's assessments of Jesus in relation to the Spirit. Jesus acted in this respect as God would act, according to Jewish expectations. Jesus' divinity was thereby announced and assured.

If the exalted Jesus is divine, has Jesus always been so? Of course, this is where the mature theological reflection expressed in John's Gospel comes in. By the time John wrote, the divine pre-existence of Christ was appreciated (e.g., John 1:1). It is more debatable whether we find it in Paul's letters but those scholars who see it in Philippians 2:6–11 are able to present a

---

16. I will, nevertheless, discuss how the Son defines the Spirit later in this chapter.

17. Turner, "Spirit of Christ," 424–34.

cogent case that this is so. Given that this is likely to be a pre-Pauline hymn, by the way, we are probably tracing the development of this view to a pre-Pauline Christianity. The pre-existence alluded to in Philippians 2 was an *exalted* pre-existence. Thus movement in the Son's status is visible: the pre-existent glorious Son humbled and emptied himself in an act of kenosis before being exalted again by the Father. I will return to the idea of this kenosis later and in far more detail. It is sufficient at this point to note that Paul, perhaps through no choice of his own if he was quoting an existing hymn, used the word, as a verb, of Jesus in his self-humbling (Phil 2:7).

Hurtado is confident that, once the import of Philippians 2:6–8 is recognized, more allusive references to Christ's pre-existence can be seen in others of Paul's works: 2 Corinthians 8:9; 1 Corinthians 8:6 (and cf. Col 1:16–17).[18] The latter passages trace Christ's existence back to creation, in which Christ appears as an active agent. But pre-existence is not eternal pre-existence, even if it is traceable back to creation. Even the "in the beginning" of John 1:1 does not explicitly state as much. It raises the question, "the beginning of what?" Did the *Logos* ("Word") only exist from, for example, the beginning of time? Was the Word the first created being, with all other beings then created through the word? The church in the early centuries struggled with this issue, through such episodes as the turmoil of the Arian controversies, but by 325 the doctrine was firmly and justifiably established: the Son was not the first creation of the Father in time but is eternally begotten. This was famously expressed in the Nicene Creed of that year: "We believe . . . in one Lord Jesus Christ, the Son of God, begotten from the Father . . . begotten not made, of one substance with the Father."[19] This disallowed Arianism by stating that Christ is un-created and is of the same divine "substance" as God the Father. Later creedal developments became more emphatic, so that by 451, when the Chalcedonian Settlement was drawn up, the relevant wording was: "We all unanimously teach that we should confess that our Lord Jesus Christ is . . . consubstantial with the Father in Godhead . . .[and] begotten from the Father before the ages."[20]

It is not my purpose in this book to discuss Nicene and post-Nicene developments in christology in any detail. However, I will offer one relevant observation: it is that the Nicene formulation helps to enhance appreciation

18. Hurtado, *Lord Jesus Christ*, 123–24.

19. Quoted in Kelly, *Early Christian Doctrines*, 232.

20. Quoted in ibid., 339. See also Lane, "Cyril of Alexandria," 286–88.

not only of God's being but also of God's grace. This can be seen in the logic of divine love as expressed on the cross. In bringing salvation to this world, Jesus paid an incalculable price on the cross. Whatever way one considers the cross, other perhaps than that of mere "moral example," if Jesus was a creature rather than being divine then this suffering was of another being than God. One does not need to commit to penal substitutionary atonement as a metaphor for the saving work of the cross, let alone appeal to it as the central defining metaphor, to see that a god who allows a creature—a third party—to suffer as Jesus did on the cross in order to bring salvation to humanity is not the same god as the trinitarian God I am seeking to describe. This trinitarian God took upon God's own self the suffering of the cross, for this Jesus who suffered was and is God.

If the Son is eternally divine, is the Son a second God? Are there (at least) two Gods? To be honest, certain New Testament texts sound ditheistic when heard in isolation. Thus, for one example among many, 1 Corinthians 8:5–6 suggests in isolation that there are two deities—God the Father and the Lord Jesus—as opposed to the many deities of certain pagan religions. If this text had been written by a pagan, one might be justified in guessing that "apotheosis" lay in the background: the process whereby some great hero such as a Roman emperor, upon death, supposedly became a god and was assumed into the pantheon. By analogy, the claim might be that Jesus had been rewarded by the supreme god for his exemplary life by now being promoted to be another god. But it is certain that Paul did *not* mean this: a monotheistic Jew would not conceive of a created human becoming a god.[21] This is but one example. New Testament texts have to be heard within the context of the strict Jewish monotheism in which Christianity first took root.

Hurtado's work here is key. He challenges the claims of some scholars that by the time Christianity began, Jewish monotheism had weakened under the sense of God's remoteness and had loosened to include the worship of divine intermediaries. At the time Christianity emerged, Hurtado indicates, Jewish monotheism was undiminished and unthreatened. In particular, there was no incipient "bifurcation of divinity."[22] This was despite the widespread evidence that intermediaries and agents were valued by Jews. These fell into three groups, according to Hurtado's classification. First, certain divine attributes such as wisdom were personified. Secondly,

21. Hurtado, *One God, One Lord*, 98.
22. Ibid., 87.

human heroes such as Moses were seen as exalted after death to a new heavenly status in which they ruled alongside God. Third, angels acted as God's agents. In particular, a chief angel, variously named, appeared to act as God's main heavenly agent.

Hurtado suggests that this interest in angels could be the root from which other interest in heavenly agency grew. Furthermore, Hurtado postulates with some plausibility that this interest in and valuing of heavenly intermediaries and agents gave Jews a conceptual framework that helped them to think through the idea of the exalted Christ as God's ultimate divine agent. However, and most importantly for both Hurtado's thesis and my own, neither this interest in personified attributes, nor the valuing of exalted heroes, nor fascination with angels, represented a threat to Jewish monotheism. Hurtado offers plentiful evidence that such references were placed within contexts where, for instance by the explicit refusal of angels to be worshiped, Jewish monotheism was clearly upheld and demonstrated.[23]

Of course all I have demonstrated so far is that Christianity emerged in a Jewish context that was (still) firmly monotheistic. I have yet to indicate that early Christianity did not in effect explode this monotheism into a ditheism or tritheism. It might be argued, indeed, that trinitarianism is an attempt to rescue the situation from a di- or tri-theism that is present at the New Testament stage of Christian thought, if one looked for it hard enough. In the middle of the twentieth century, when some New Testament scholars thought that they could discern broad strands of Gnostic thought in the New Testament, then this counter-argument might have been strong. However, more recent New Testament scholarship has dismissed these ideas. Paul and John were countering proto-Gnostic ideas, insofar as these yet existed, not espousing them.

Examination of slightly later stages of the early church's struggle against Gnosticism well shows the firm denial of any suggestion that the Son or the Spirit were di- or tri-theistic emanations from a highest god. The Nag Hammadi texts confirm what the anti-Gnostic teachers in the early church had said: that Gnostics' conceptions of "god" involved multiple complex emanations from the ultimate Depth of Being.[24] Given their efforts to dis-

---

23. Hurtado, *One God, One Lord*, 41 (divine attributes), 67 (human heroes), 90 (angels). Examples cited by Hurtado of the worship of the one God in the midst of interest in these figures include: *2 Enoch* 9; 20–21; 33:4–10; *Apocalypse of Abraham* 10:4–17; 11:1–3; *Apocalypse of Zephaniah* 6:11–15 (Hurtado, *One God, One Lord*, 83–84). See also, from a somewhat different perspective, Bauckham, "Moses as 'God.'"

24. See, e.g., Rudolph, *Gnosis*, 53, 61–66.

tance their own teachings from those of the Gnostics, it is unsurprising that proto-trinitarians such as Irenaeus emphasized the unity of God somewhat at the expense of the threeness. While Irenaeus' theology was, according to Kelly, "the most complete, and also most explicitly trinitarian, to be met before Tertullian,"[25] Irenaeus famously introduced to Christian thought the image of the Son and the Spirit as God's two hands. He also wrote of the Son and the Spirit as the Word and the Wisdom of God. Thus there is no reason to doubt Irenaeus' commitment to the unity of God. In the development of genuinely trinitarian thought, the Son has never been, and should never be, conceived of as a second God.

To state, in the context of monotheism, that the Son is not a created intermediary but is eternally divine equates with claiming that the Son is God. This is true however reluctant either the New Testament or later Christian creeds were to posit the claim in quite such bald language. So two questions must be asked. The first is whether the Son is in effect the Father, while the second is: if the Son is God's own self and the Spirit is God's own self, is the Son in effect the Spirit? I will tackle the first of these questions in chapter 4 but I will turn my attention to the latter question now.

The Son and the Spirit

This is an important topic that needs to be explored: are "Son" and "Spirit" perhaps two names for the same divine person? Might it be that the terms refer to different phases in the life of this one person, or that they refer to this person operating in different spheres? As I seek to tackle these questions, I briefly consider, first, the pre-incarnate life of the Son—if there was one. What I mean by introducing this element of doubt is that it might conceivably be argued that prior to the Christ-event, there was either a unitarian God, who adopted the human Jesus by means of the Spirit, understood functionally as a mode of God's action, or there was a binitarian God—Father and Spirit. This God "took over" the life of the human Jesus, and adopted him into what then became trinitarian life.

Such pneumatological adoptionism might be construed from Luke's writings if they were all we had. It would be a moot point when the adoption happened. Contenders would be: Jesus' conception, which would be understood as an action of God's Spirit transforming an otherwise human embryo into a divine being; Jesus' baptism, in which the descent of the dove

25. Kelly, *Early Christian Doctrines*, 107.

would be interpreted as the union of the divine with the previously merely human; or the resurrection/ascension, which enthronement would be seen as Jesus' "promotion" as reward for carrying out successfully—as a mere human to that point—his earthly career and ministry.[26]

However, we do not only have Luke's writings, and even if we did, the possibilities I have just set out would be considered by many to be mis-readings of Lukan texts.[27] When we turn from Luke to Paul or John, we find expressions of the pre-existence of the Son that are offered without any recourse to references to the Spirit. That this Son is then the one who, incarnate, was called Jesus indicates clearly that there is no room in their christologies for the idea that the pre-existent one was the Spirit, who then became the Son at or around the time when Jesus was conceived or born. Key relevant texts include John 1:1 and Philippians 2:6.

Turning now to the incarnate life of the Son and tracing the relation-ship between the Spirit and Jesus the Son in Luke's Gospel, the distinction is consistent: the Spirit came down on Jesus (Luke 3:22); the Spirit led Jesus (Luke 4:1); the Spirit was "upon" Jesus (Luke 4:18, 21); the Spirit probably granted Jesus joy (Luke 10:21). It is not surprising, then, that Smail opines: in "the writings of Luke the distinction between Son and Spirit is empha-sized more strongly than anywhere else in the New Testament."[28]

I now move on to discuss the post-incarnate life of the Son. Some authors have argued a "binitarian" reading of several key New Testament texts, with the argument that New Testament writers used "Christ" or the like to refer to Jesus in post-resurrection exaltation and "the Spirit" to re-fer to Jesus in his immanence within the church. Thus it is necessary to peruse the New Testament with a view to tracing distinctions between the Son and the Spirit. Starting once more with Luke's account of Pentecost, Acts 2:33 distinguishes between the Son and the Spirit as clearly as it does between the Son and the Father. Jesus, God the Father's exalted Son,[29] has both received and poured out the Spirit. It is difficult to imagine how the Son could possibly be understood to *be* the Spirit here. In line with this,

---

26. For a brief presentation of adoptionism in the early church, see Kelly, *Early Christian Doctrines*, 115–16.

27. See, e.g., Menzies, *Empowered for Witness*, 137–38; Witherington, *Acts*, 149.

28. Smail, *Giving Gift*, 49.

29. That Jesus is God's Son is both implied by the unusual use of the term "Father" (see above, chapter 2, n. 6) and by the reference in Acts 2:30 to the enthroned descendant of David. This carries allusions to 2 Sam 7:12–14, where the enthroned son of David is to be a son of God as well.

although in less clear-cut terms, is the distinction between the Spirit filling the dying Stephen and thereby enabling him to have a vision, and the exalted Christ who is standing at God's right hand in that vision (Acts 7:55). Only in writing both Luke 12:12 and 21:15 did Luke conceivably identify the Son with the Spirit. However, given the distinctions of identity offered elsewhere by Luke, Walton's understanding is more likely, that this pair of verses further confirms that the Spirit in Luke-Acts conveyed the presence of Jesus from Pentecost on.[30]

It is certainly the case that in the writings of Paul and John a stronger case can be made for a conflation of the Son and the Spirit. Paul's letters contain statements that might be read as explicitly identifying the two (1 Cor 15:45; 2 Cor 3:17); and in John's presentation, Jesus identified himself, it seems, with the coming Paraclete (John 14:17–19). I will explore these in turn.

Paul's identification of the Son with the Spirit is clearest at the level of believers' experience. Thus for instance in Romans 8:9–10 to have the Spirit within (here called both the Spirit of God and the Spirit of Christ) seems simply to be the same experience as having Christ within. As Fee rightly observes, it is unlikely "that Paul somehow envisioned both Christ and the Spirit indwelling the believer, 'side by side' as it were." Thus "'Christ in you' is simply Pauline shorthand for 'the Spirit of Christ in you,' or perhaps better in this case, 'Christ in you by his Spirit.'"[31] This might suggest that the Spirit, in Paul's thinking, was no more than an immanent mode of action of the exalted Christ. Furthermore, Paul wrote elsewhere in more clearly substantive terms of the Spirit, on some of these occasions implying that Christ and the Spirit were to be entirely identified.

In 2 Corinthians 3:17 he famously wrote that "the Lord is the Spirit" (cf. 3:18; although 3:17 also contains reference to "the Spirit of the Lord"). As the Lord in 3:16 is apparently the Christ to whom believers turn (cf. 3:14), the natural conclusion is that Paul indicated, "Christ *is* the Spirit." This, however, is not firmly the case, plausible as it may seem. Paul's argument here rests on his understanding of Exodus 34:34—Moses, whenever he "turned to" the LORD's presence and glory by entering the tent or climbing the mountain, removed his veil. Reference here to the LORD/Lord actually refers, Paul perhaps indicated, to the Spirit. If this is so, "the Lord is the Spirit" is a condensed way of expressing the idea that the Lord whom Moses

---

30. Walton, "Whose Spirit?" 48.

31. Fee, *God's Empowering Presence*, 548. So also Dunn, *Romans 1–8*, 430.

met, unveiled, was actually, or represented, the Spirit. This Pauline passage does not clearly equate the Son with the Spirit. If anything, in trinitarian terms, it might further identify the Spirit with the Father.

First Corinthians 15:45 offers no such ambiguity. The "last Adam" is undoubtedly Christ. This man *became* (the) life-giving Spirit. Here most clearly Paul identified the Son and the Spirit. Now, it would not be true to Paul's depiction to suggest that the Son after the resurrection became the Spirit and no more—as if all that could be said about the exalted Christ could be expressed in terms of the Spirit. Thus the Spirit within believers could inspire objective declarations about Christ in his lordship (e.g., 1 Cor 12:3); and the exalted Christ could be described without any reference to the Spirit (e.g., 1 Cor 15:20–28). Equally, it is not the case that all that could be said about the Spirit could be expressed in terms of the exalted Christ. Fee is quick to point out that for every time Paul called the Spirit "Christ's Spirit," he called the Spirit "God's Spirit" many times over.[32] Nevertheless, Paul's identification of Christ with the Spirit has led some commentators to conclude that when Paul was describing the post-resurrection situation, "Christ" referred to the Son's exaltation and "Spirit" to the Son's immanence among believers: there is only one person. Such a view could cohere with such apparently "trinitarian" texts as, for instance, Romans 8:26, 34 and Galatians 4:4–6. Romans 8 could be read such that the Son intercedes *in believers* as the Spirit (8:26) and intercedes *before the Father* as the exalted Christ (8:34). In Galatians, one might understand that God sent the Son as a man "born of a woman" (Gal 4:4); thereafter God sent the Son as Spirit (Gal 4:6)—after all, does not *the Spirit* cry out "Abba, Father"?!

If texts such as those examined above were all the evidence that lay to hand, one might have to conclude that Paul, if anything, was a "proto-binitarian," rather than a "proto-trinitarian." However, they are not. Among the undisputed Pauline letters, perhaps the clearest—though not indisputable—evidence for a distinction between the Son and the Spirit (see also Eph 4:4–6) is to be found in 1 Corinthians 12:4–6. Here Paul listed in carefully parallel wording three divine sources of gifted service in the church: the Spirit, the Lord (Jesus), and God (12:3). Admittedly, priority is given to the last, who alone "works all things in all." Nevertheless, the parallels speak against any suggestion that here one can simply read of God or Christ working by the Spirit. The Spirit seems to be one of three sources. A plausible counter-argument would be that 1 Corinthians 12:4–6 is simply a rhetorical

---

32. Fee, *God's Empowering Presence*, 835.

"piling up" of terms, and Paul happened to stop after three of them. After all, we do not argue from Paul's use in these verses of the terms "gifts," "services," and "works" for a "trinity" of charismata. This counter-argument would thus suggest that even here Paul did not distinguish between the exalted Christ and the granted Spirit. It would carry considerable weight if it were not that it would demand, in turn, that 1 Corinthians 12:3 be read as an "auto-testimony" by and to the one Spirit-Jesus. This is unlikely.

The following verses tend if anything to confirm this distinct hypostatization of the Spirit: Paul could write that these gifted services were given (no doubt a "divine passive"—given by God) *through* the Spirit (1 Cor 12:8—suggesting that the Spirit might still simply be seen as a mode of divine operation); but a few words later could write that the Spirit energizes, distributes, and determines these gifts (1 Cor 12:11).[33] If these distinctions between the Son and the Spirit in Paul are acknowledged then of course texts such as Romans 8:26, 34 can be read in this light: as references to two conceptually distinguishable intercessors interceding in two quite different ways in different "places."

Turning now from Paul to John, we find the same mix of identification and distinction between the Son and the Spirit. Perhaps the clearest note of identification is in John 14:17–18. Here, Jesus had just mentioned the Spirit of truth that the world was unable to receive but the disciples would have within them (John 14:17).[34] Then he immediately promised, "I will not leave you as orphans; I am coming to you" (John 14:18). This, among other evidence, leads Burge to declare:

> The Spirit appears to be the life of the Messiah himself after and before the resurrection. This is most clear in Johannine eschatology . . . , where the presence of the Spirit is the presence of Jesus. It is most pronounced in the Johannine Paraclete, who compensates for Jesus' absence, or better, who extends and communicates the presence of Jesus while Jesus is away. . . . Jesus is the visible

---

33. See also Fee, *God's Empowering Presence*, 840. However, Fee, in his determination to demonstrate that "Paul's understanding of God was functionally trinitarian" (ibid., 839), overstates his argument, claiming to find trinitarianism in at least fledgling forms not only in Rom 8:26, 34 (ibid., 838) but in a host of other texts in which there is no need to see clear distinctions between the Son and the Spirit at all (ibid., 841–42).

34. There is manuscript uncertainty here as to whether the original text stated that the Spirit "will be" or "is" in the disciples.

presence of the Father, and the life and being of Jesus waiting to be poured forth into the world is the Spirit.[35]

However, this is not the whole story. In the same discourse, Jesus firmly distinguished between himself and the Spirit in saying, "if I do not leave, the Paraclete will not come to you; but if I go, I will send him to you" (John 16:7). Furthermore, Turner, who criticizes Burge for overstating the identity of the Son and the Spirit in John, points out that the Spirit-Paraclete conveys not simply the presence of the Son but in fact the joint presence of the Son and the Father, thereby distancing somewhat further the identity of the Spirit from that of the Son (John 14:23).[36] Thus in conclusion, John exhibits the same duality of perspective as both Luke and Paul: the Son is intimately linked with the identity of the Spirit but not so closely that no conceptual distinction can be offered.[37] If anything, the distinctions are clearest in Luke and most obscure in Paul, but all these authors provide evidence of distinction as well as identity. The Spirit is a mode of the action of the Son; however, the Son and the Spirit can also be conceived as different entities from one another.

THE SON AND PERSONHOOD

The Son Seen Personally

Of all the persons of the Trinity, it is in my opinion easiest to argue for the personhood of the Son. If one thinks of the Son's life in three dynamic stages—pre-incarnate, incarnate, and post-incarnate—then the Son's personhood is most obvious in the latter two stages. In the central, incarnate stage his personhood shines through his humanity. In his post-incarnate stage, in which he does not cease to be human, his personhood is assured not only

---

35. Burge, *Anointed Community*, 99–100.

36. Turner, *Holy Spirit and Spiritual Gifts*, 58 n. 4; 80–81.

37. Arguably, a similar position is evident in the book of Revelation. If the "seven spirits" in front of the throne in Rev 1:4 are a reference to the Holy Spirit rather than to the seven angels of Rev 2:1—3:14, then this Spirit is to be distinguished from the glorified Jesus of Rev 1:5. On the other hand, the Spirit speaking to the churches in Rev 2:7, etc. is closely identified with the voice of the glorified Jesus who tells John to write the seven letters at this point (Rev 1:17–19; 2:1, etc.). See discussion in Waddell, *Spirit of the Book of Revelation*, 9–26. By the time the *Vision of Isaiah* was written in the second century, the Spirit was firmly distinguished from the Son both as an object of heavenly worship and as a worshiper of the Father (*Martyrdom and Ascension of Isaiah* 9:33–42).

by his continuing humanity but also by his lordly reign and his reception of worship in personal terms. The Pauline (1 Thess 4:15–17; 1 Cor 15:25–27; Phil 2:9–11), Lukan (Acts 2:33; 3:20–21; 7:55–56), and apocalyptic (Rev 5:6–14) heavenly and eschatological visions all make this perfectly clear. However, it is in his pre-incarnate stage that the Son's personhood is least easy to demonstrate. I will consider the incarnate and pre-incarnate stages in turn.

Turning first, then, to the incarnation, the personhood of Jesus seems to me so self-evident as hardly to need demonstrating. Insofar as Jesus was a human who related to other humans through relationships, exhibiting with total consistency all the usual awareness of self and others, his personhood cannot be doubted. This personal sense of self in relation to others included without doubt his relation to God. Jesus believed in a God who was personal. I mean this in a straightforward way, according to the norms of human interpersonal relationships. Jesus regarded his God as a being who could be spoken to, and who would speak to others. In this, Jesus demonstrated his own personhood. Furthermore, as I will explore in the next chapter, it is clear that Jesus did not regard this God as being the same person as he was. Jesus addressed this God as "you." He gave no impression whatever that he thought he was speaking to himself. Jesus, in ways that were unusual to the religion of his day, addressed God as "Father." While it is true that he invited others into this filial relationship, encouraging them for instance to pray to "our Father in heaven," and describing God as "your Father" (e.g., Matt 7:11), it is nevertheless the case that Jesus clearly regarded God as in some special way his own Father.

So there is no doubt concerning the personhood of the human Jesus; but does this demonstrate the personhood of the incarnate Son? It could be counter-argued that personhood might only have been actual in Christ's humanity, and that this was perfused with the entirely non-personal divine *Logos* ("Word"). However, this cannot stand. Whatever nuances of incarnational christology one holds to, it remains the case that the incarnate Christ was *one* person. The ideas bound up in concepts such as the hypostatic union and the communication of attributes forbid the position that Christ's personhood was to be found *only* in his humanity.

Rahner's version of trinitarianism falls into this trap. Rahner is to be congratulated for his challenge to a false distinction between the economic and the immanent Trinity, and for achieving this by reasoning from the incarnation and salvation history.[38] However, in a commendable attempt to avoid the dangers of tritheism, he postulates an unduly modalistic trinitarianism. His reasoning exhibits weaknesses. Of particular relevance to my present discussion, Rahner virtually ignores the prayer life of Jesus. His one reference to it forces it solely into Jesus' humanity,[39] thereby "protecting" the Trinity from genuine interpersonal relationships, for "there is properly no *mutual* love between Father and Son"![40] This artificial "slicing up" of Jesus' earthly life into human and divine features, not to mention this etiolating of the love between Father and Son, does not faithfully reflect the Gospel witness. In John's Gospel, the one that most explicitly stated the divinity of the Word (John 1:1), it was precisely this divine Word that became flesh (John 1:14). The flesh cannot be excised from the Word and then accorded merely human features. Neither is it an accurate reading of the Gospels to see Jesus as sometimes acting as divine and sometimes as human.[41] As Reed observes, some Oneness Pentecostals have offered this explanation of Jesus' prayer life.[42] Thus at this point, both Rahner and some versions of Oneness Pentecostalism are to be criticized for failing to take with due seriousness the prayer life of Jesus as evidence of bi-personality (at least) in God.

So it was Jesus' prayer life that indicated most particularly the personhood of the Son and that warns us away from a trinitarianism that is unduly modalistic. It might, however, be counter-argued that I am naively extrapolating from human personhood (albeit the human personhood of Jesus) to divine personhood and thereby committing the error of anthropomorphism in which I view God as if God were a human. My working definition of personhood, presented in chapter 1, obviates this difficulty, for it enables me to speak equally in this context of human and divine personhood. Furthermore, the very fact that it is Jesus' personhood that I am considering draws human and divine personhood together in the one divine-human person of Jesus, who is God the Son.

---

38. Rahner, *The Trinity*, 15–22. See the similar stances in Torrance, *Trinitarian Perspectives*, 142–43; Alan Torrance, *Persons in Communion*, 222.

39. Rahner, *The Trinity*, 76, n. 30.

40. Ibid., 106; italics his. Alan Torrance criticizes Rahner for not allowing "mutuality and reciprocity between" the divine persons (*Persons in Communion*, 273).

41. See also Lane's reference to Nestorius ("Cyril of Alexandria," 289).

42. Reed, "In Jesus' Name," 296–97.

Thus, the personhood of the incarnate Son is assured. But this does not in itself demonstrate the personhood of the *pre*-incarnate Son. Could it be that when, to use Johannine terms, the Word *became* flesh (John 1:14), the Son concomitantly *became* a person? In other words, the eternal divine Word was impersonal, and the event of becoming in which the humanity began was by the same process the event of becoming personal. In seeking to respond to this thought, it will not do to appeal to the declaration in John 1:1 that the divine Word was "with" God. There are many entities that could be with or alongside God without thereby being persons. And even if a personal hint is detected here, it could simply be that of personification, along the lines of the personification of wisdom in Proverbs 8:27–30, where we read that she too was with God at the beginning.

Other arguments must be mounted before one can conclude that the eternal divine Son is eternally personal. First, one can presume that the historical personhood of Jesus indicates the eternal personhood of the Son unless and until a counter-demonstration is offered. This arises from the recognition, developed in chapter 1, that the economic Trinity is a genuine revelation of the immanent Trinity. While the immanent Trinity may be *more than* the economic Trinity, the immanent Trinity is not *other than* the economic Trinity. There is no contradiction between the two. God is honest. The self-revelation of God will be a genuine revelation of God as God is, however many the complexities and paradoxes that arise when this revelation occurs in and through the particularities of a historical human. On this logic, the eternal Son may be *more* than personal, but will not be *less* than personal.

This presupposition is given ample confirmation by appeal to kenosis, drawing on the evidence of Philippians 2:6–8, matched and supported by 2 Corinthians 8:9. The kenosis that the Son underwent did not arise as the result of a set of *human* choices. It is clear from Philippians 2:7 that the choice to empty self in order to honor another (God—Phil 2:6) "predated" Christ's humanity. One gains the same impression from Hebrews 10:7, for while verse 5 is placed chronologically *within* the incarnation ("entering the world"), the relative timeframe of verse 7 predates verse 5 ("I *have* arrived ... to do your will"), placing the kenotic attitude *prior* to the incarnation. This kenosis, as I argued in chapter 1, is of the very essence of personhood. This choice to lay aside all potential status and self-aggrandizement for the sake of another is at the heart of a loving personal relationship. The eternal Son was and is a person. This recognition of a personal pre-incarnate Son kenotically relating to the Father (I presume the personhood of the Father at this stage) lends itself to a relational model of the Trinity. As I also found the personhood of the Spirit in the Spirit's kenosis, we have the potential, if the Father's personhood can be established, for a tri-personal relational or social trinitarianism.

The Son Seen Impersonally

I have made much of the evidence that in all eternity there is a person—the Son—who relates interpersonally to the Father. But is there any value in thinking of the Son in impersonal terms? Is this a model that also has explanatory power—and a model that the Bible invites us to keep in our minds beside that of personhood? I believe so. It is first noteworthy that the New Testament offers impersonal metaphors in discussing the Son. The post-incarnate Son is clothing believers put on (Gal 3:27). The pre-incarnate Son was a rock from which Israelites drank (1 Cor 10:4). These analogies must not in themselves be pressed too hard. We may call someone a "rock," referring perhaps to her reliability, without suggesting at all that the woman in question should be defined in impersonal terms as well as personal ones. However, in the case of the Son, two metaphors show their defining value in the frequency with which they are used and the conceptual weight that is placed upon them.

For all that the personhood of the pre-incarnate Son can be demonstrated, there is no doubt that the term *Logos* ("Word") connotes most directly an impersonal concept. That it was used of the Son invites us to think here in impersonal terms. The matter can be overstated, as it was by Rahner when he wrote that the "Son is the Father's self-utterance which should not in its turn be conceived as 'uttering,'" and that the "Logos is not the one who utters, but the one who is uttered."[43] Rahner's affirmations are correct—the Son-*Logos is* the Father's self-utterance and *is* the one who is uttered—but his denials are inaccurate, for the Son *should* also be conceived as uttering: the *Logos* utters. A paradoxical "both-and" is nearer the mark at this point than an "either-or."

While drawing back, then, from overstatement, one can still see that the idea of the *Logos* as God's Word uttered has value. This impersonal model has two significant uses in trinitarian thinking. First, it offers, in the realm of *impersonal* relations, a link between the Son and the Spirit,

43. Rahner, *Trinity*, 76 (n. 30), 106.

for as the Spirit can be conceived not only as, metaphorically, oil or water, but as the breath that carries the word forth (e.g., Ps 33:6), so the Son can be conceived as the Word that proceeds from the Father's mouth on that breath. The Son and the Spirit work cooperatively in achieving the Father's purpose. Each needs the other and is nothing without the other. Together, in eternal balance and synthesis, they speak God's mind. This way of seeing the Son and the Spirit as impersonal modes of action of the Father has also been expressed historically, from Irenaeus onwards, with reference to the "right and left hands" of God. I indicated in the previous chapter that "the hand of God" is paralleled in biblical thought and language with "the Spirit of God." It is a simple extension of thought to include the Son as "the other hand." While the model has its weaknesses, its use is evident in the frequency with which it is referred to in the literature.[44]

There is a second trinitarian use to which this impersonal model of the Son can be put. Combined with the impersonal ways of looking at the Spirit introduced in the previous chapter, this idea allows for a modal or instrumental trinitarianism to be expressed. But it is not a modal trinitarianism in which each of the three "persons" is a mode of an ontologically prior divine essence. And it is far from the ancient modalism of Sabellius and his predecessors, in which God could act at different times towards the world in different modes, now as Father, now as Son, and now as Spirit.[45] On the reading of modal or instrumental trinitarianism that I am espousing, there is a person—the Father—who has and expresses modes of action. All the Father's actions are achieved *by means of* the Son and Spirit. This instrumental model of the Trinity, which would never suffice *alone* as an explanation for the inner-trinitarian relations that the Bible attests to, is a useful balance to a social or relational model.[46] Apart from anything else, this model is far less "awkward" than the social when it comes to articulating the *unity* of God. There is one God—the Father—who has two

---

44. E.g., Gunton, *Promise of Trinitarian Theology*, xxvi–xxx, 197; Parry, *Worshipping Trinity*, 19, 34; Smail, *Giving Gift*, 125; Yong, *Spirit-Word-Community*, 50–59; similarly, Volf refers to the two arms of God (*Exclusion and Embrace*, 128).

45. See Kelly, *Early Christian Doctrines*, 119–22. I acknowledge, however, that it does bear some resemblance, when taken in isolation, to that aspect of Sabellius' thought that Kelly expresses thus: "the Father was, as it were, the form or essence, and the Son and the Spirit His modes of self-expression" (ibid., 122).

46. I will explore these models and the relationships between them in more detail in chapter 5.

hands with which actions are performed, and who utters words by means of breath.

ROLES OF THE SON

So far in this chapter, my concern has been to establish the identity of the Son: the Son is fundamentally distinct from, though closely identified with, the Spirit; is divine; and is to be understood primarily as personal, though an impersonal understanding also has merit. In this section I explore the Son's role in the trinitarian relations of God, considering both the procession of the Spirit and the Son's part in revealing, defining, and exalting the Father and the Spirit.

The Son Sends the Spirit

Acts 2:33 is perfectly clear about the origin of the Pentecostal outpouring of the Spirit, in two respects: its ultimate source is the Father; its immediate source is the Son, Jesus. This is in perfect accord with the blend of statements offered in John 14:26; 16:7; and especially 15:26. Insofar as Jesus sends the Spirit, he does not do so autonomously, but does so on behalf of and in fulfillment of the promise of the Father. This takes place—took place—in time, and the inception of the church. But the congruent relationship between the economic and the immanent Trinity that I have been utilizing in this book allows us, by way of imaginative analogy, to understand the same dynamic at work in the eternal relations of the Trinity: the Spirit's eternal existence "arises" ultimately from the being and will of the Father; the Spirit's eternal existence "arises" through the obedient cooperation of the Son.

More can be said. The Spirit, in time, does not merely proceed from the Father through the Son: the Spirit proceeds from the Father through the *exalted* Son. As experience of the Spirit's "descent" was *evidence* of the Son's exaltation—precisely the evidence that sparked off the early Christian reflections that would lead in due course to fully fledged trinitarianism—so too the Spirit's arrival was a *result* of the Son's exaltation. If the Son were not exalted to the right hand of the Father, the Son would be in no position to send the Spirit. Furthermore, the Son's exaltation was a direct result of the Son's prior kenosis. This is stated clearly and concisely in the hymn reflected in Philippians 2:6–11. Without the kenosis, there would be no subsequent exaltation. I will not explore why this might be the case. One could conjecture that if the Son had not chosen the path of kenosis, he would not, so to speak, have *deserved* to be exalted. One might, in close relation to this idea, regard the exaltation as some sort of *reward* for the Son's kenosis (as is perhaps evidenced by the "therefore" of Phil 2:9). One might on the other hand simply argue that if there were no kenosis there would be no need of exaltation, for a low point from which he needed to be raised would not have been reached. I will not seek to argue for or against either of these positions or any other. I will simply leave it that the Son's kenosis, we are told, *was* a necessary prerequisite to his exaltation by the Father. Thus it was also a necessary prerequisite to the sending of the Spirit. If the Son had not chosen to empty himself, the Spirit of Christ would not have been sent. In time, so in eternity: without a kenosis of the Son, I infer, there would be no eternal procession of the Spirit. But this raises a question that must be faced: clearly, trinitarianism understands the generation of the Son and the procession of the Spirit to be eternal. However, the kenosis of the Son that we have traced was expressed in time: the Son became a human and submitted to the humiliation of death hanging from a cross. Could it be, then, that the Son's kenosis was also eternal—a primal prerequisite of the eternal procession of the immanent Spirit? I discuss this question in detail and in the affirmative later in this chapter. At this stage, I simply claim that the trinitarian relations expressed in time and in the economy truly express the trinitarian relations in eternity. Furthermore, I submit that this eternal kenosis of the Son is the dynamic behind the eternal procession of the Spirit.

What is the connection? I am not sure that we can know. I simply offer here a speculation. We must remember that the first and foremost recipient of the Spirit is the Son. He was not, of course, the first human in history to receive God's Spirit. But he is the archetypal recipient of the Spirit. Thus, in the immanent Trinity, I suggest that the procession of the Spirit is not only *through* the Son—and through the Son's kenosis—but also *to* the Son. Thus the Spirit is, in all eternity, the Father's *reward* to the Son for the Son's loving kenosis. The very Spirit that is and expresses the life and vitality of God is granted by the Father to the Son. If there were no kenosis, there would be no reward (again, I do not explore why this might be, for I do not believe I can); if there were no kenosis, there would be no Spirit.

I cannot leave the subject of the Son and the sending of the Spirit without exploring the so-called *filioque* question but I will do this in chapter 4, in relation to the procession of the Spirit from the Father.

The Son Reveals and Defines the Father and the Spirit

I turn first in this section to my own experience. At this point my mind goes not to my Christian experience of God but to my pre-Christian experience (or non-experience) of God. In my earlier teens, I sensed at times that the whole question concerning Christianity was one I had to face at some point. My usual attitude to this challenge was the sense that it would be better to wait until after I had my school exams out of the way before I put concerted effort into the question. I suspect that, if this policy had been followed through rigorously, I would still be deferring the question today. I am most grateful that God had other plans. However, on those occasions when I did try to think about God at that stage, all that would come to my mind was the picture of an old man with a gray beard sitting on a cloud. This did not help me to draw any closer to God at the time. However, what interests me from my present vantage point about those early musings is that I was, I suggest, seeking to conceptualize the *Father*. As I recall, I took no interest at that stage in Jesus. I doubt whether I had given serious thought to whether Jesus was a historical character or a product of fiction. It was, later, to be the palpable, unavoidable historicity of Jesus that first began to draw me to him. But at that stage I seem to have tried vaguely to imagine the Father—and without any real success. Without the Son, the Father was obscure, to say the least.

Of course, the New Testament also declares that without the Son, the Father is obscure. One need only think of the words: "nobody knows the Father except the Son—and anyone to whom the Son wishes to reveal him" (Matt 11:27; Luke 10:22)—the "Synoptic bolt from the Johannine blue."[47] One might suggest that the Old Testament gives a rather different picture, and that God was perfectly capable of a self-revelation to Moses that did not need to be mediated by Jesus. This raises awkward questions about how God was active and self-revealing prior to the incarnation. Which person of the Trinity was revealing God to Moses? Who or what was the angel of the LORD? From a trinitarian point of view these questions are probably best avoided, for they are unanswerable except by reading back anachronistically rather than working with data emerging from the pre-Christian era.

What can be stated with some confidence is that before the incarnation, God had not been revealed as Trinity. Thus, the Father had not been

---

47. Karl von Hase wrote that the text "gives the impression of a thunderbolt fallen from the Johannine sky" (quoted in Smail, *Forgotten Father*, 52–53).

revealed as the Father of the Son. Although some relationship between God and the Spirit was to be gleaned from the various Hebrew Scriptures, this relationship, too, remained mysterious to a degree that the incarnation began to overcome. But my thesis, consistently, has been that even the incarnation did not "tell the whole story." It was at Pentecost—or people's own "personal Pentecosts"—that more pieces fell into place. In human experience, it was at Pentecost that the Spirit of God "became" the Spirit of Christ. In other words, the Spirit as experienced by old covenant believers conveyed the action, influence, or presence of God, and this God was the God of Abraham, Isaac, and Jacob. After Pentecost, this experience of God, and of God's relation to the patriarchs, was undiminished. But a new dimension was added. Now the Spirit touching the lives of new covenant believers brought the influence, presence, and action of Jesus Christ, and so the God sending this Spirit was confirmed as the Father of Jesus. In other words, the Christ-event, culminating in the granting of the Spirit to Jesus' first followers, had the effect of bringing into sharp revelatory focus the being of both the Spirit and the Father. The Spirit was both experienced and known as the Spirit of Christ. God came to be seen and known as "the God and Father of our Lord Jesus Christ," for as the Son brought and brings definition to the Spirit so too the Son brought and brings definition to the Father. Smail wrote of the Spirit as "the person without a face."[48] But without the Son, the Father too is a "person without a face." The only face the Father has is Jesus ("The one who has seen me has seen the Father," John 14:9). In more strictly trinitarian terms, then, the only face the Father has is that of the Son. Without the Son, the Father is, so to speak, expressionless: as John 1:18 notes, nobody has ever seen God; however, as Hebrews 1:3 puts it, the Son is the very "stamp" of the Father's being.

As soon as these greater degrees of definition were perceived, of course, they begged the question of hindsight: had God and God's Spirit been always thus? 1 Peter 1:11 answers in the affirmative with respect to the Spirit: with hindsight, the Spirit had always been the Spirit of Christ. As the exalted Christ is Lord and sender of the Spirit after Pentecost, so too the pre-existent Christ spoke by the Spirit prior to "the sending of the Son." Similarly, with respect to the Father, the context in which Old Testament Scriptures were quoted in Hebrews 1:5 to indicate God's fatherhood of the Son is one in which pre-existence is assumed: it was through the Son that God created the universe (Heb 1:2). Thus God the Father always

---

48. Title of chapter 2, Smail, *Giving Gift*.

has been and always can be "defined" in terms of the Son. It is difficult to delineate what this defining role might be within the immanent eternal relations of the Trinity. To *whom*, for example, is the Father or the Spirit identified by the Son? Perhaps all that can be stated is that the Son shapes—"embodies"—the Father and the Spirit.

Before leaving this topic, it is worth noting that this definition may be regarded as at least somewhat mutual. By eternally generating the Son (for details of this, see chapter 4), the Father gives definition, by means of granting eternal divine existence, to the Son. So too the Spirit, through whom the Son is generated in eternity (for details of this, also see chapter 4), thereby plays a part in defining this Son's everlasting identity.

The Son Exalts the Father and the Spirit

It is clear that in his earthly ministry, Jesus exalted God his Father, in word and deed. One might go so far as to say that, especially as presented in John's Gospel, Jesus had no greater joy or purpose than this (e.g., John 17:4). It is important to appreciate, however, that this earthly glorifying of the Father could not have occurred unless the Son had made his kenotic pre-incarnate choice to dwell on earth and serve his God as a human being. For the Father to be glorified on earth, the Son had to undergo kenosis. This is an expression, imaginative analogy suggests, of the eternal relations of the Trinity. The Son eternally glorifies the Father, and does so by means of personally chosen kenosis. The Son empties self to raise up the Other.

Clearly, too, the incarnate Son exalted the Spirit in his teaching and promises, as presented in the Gospel record. The Spirit was the power needed for future living and mission (Luke 24:49). The Spirit was to come as "another Paraclete" who would do great works in Jesus' absence (e.g., John 14:26). While Jesus' promises on this subject could be expressed elsewhere in the Gospels without reference to the Spirit, but simply to his own future presence (Matt 28:20; Luke 21:15), there is no doubt that mention of the Spirit was always presented in ways that honored the Spirit as on some par with Jesus' own influence and presence. Again, however, it is vital to note that this honoring of the Spirit among people could only occur because the Son first kenotically accepted the humbling of the incarnation. Thus by analogy the Son's eternal exalting of the Spirit requires the Son's eternal kenosis. To fuller consideration of this matter of the Son's kenosis, therefore, I now turn my attention.

THE KENOSIS OF THE SON

I have introduced the idea of kenosis in earlier sections but will discuss the matter more fully in this one. This section will first consider the Son's kenosis in general terms as a concept, before tracing it in the crucifixion, the Son's eternal generation, and the final eschaton.

It is with respect to the Son that kenosis has most often been the subject of scholarly attention. This is hardly surprising. One has to look rather hard to find the kenosis of the Spirit (see chapter 2—and I may not have convinced all my readers!) and of the Father (see chapter 4). The kenosis of the Son shines out in his human history and is articulated in the New Testament using this term. Admittedly, the word is used only once, in verb form (Phil 2:7). However, it has been the subject of much scholarly discussion and has formed the basis of a whole doctrine, such that the term "kenoticism" has been coined.

Kenoticism flourished in the nineteenth and early twentieth centuries. It took various forms, in which the Son, in becoming human, divested himself of either some or all of his divine attributes. For instance, by some accounts, the Son retained such qualities as truth and holiness but forsook omnipotence, omnipresence, and omniscience.[49] As a vehicle for trying to understand the incarnation from the point of view of the divine and human attributes of Christ, it was of extremely limited value. So to suggest that the divine attributes can be categorized, and those in one category can be regarded as having been laid aside by the Son in his incarnation, while those in another category were not, smacks of artificiality. If this were the case, furthermore, the incarnate Son would be "somewhat" divine, retaining some divine attributes but losing others. So this form of kenoticism has, not surprisingly, fallen from favor.

However, kenosis understood as a relational dynamic between the trinitarian persons is undoubtedly valuable and it is this type of kenosis that I am seeking to develop. Given that kenosis means emptying, it is important to tread with caution in delineating the concept. If one were to decide, on the basis of Philippians 2:7, that the Son emptied himself in the incarnation in such a total and unbalanced sense that there was no self left, this would be remarkably unhelpful. First, it would not be true to the passage in Philippians, for a further self-emptying is described immediately

---

49. For discussions of kenoticism, see Baillie, *God Was in Christ*, 94–98; Balthasar, *Mysterium Paschale*, 23–36; Lewis, *Between Cross and Resurrection*, 169–75.

afterwards in Philippians 2:8. Not only did the Son undergo the self-humbling of incarnation but he then went further still—to the cross. There was still a "self of the Son" to do that. Secondly, as Volf shows when critiquing the views of Ratzinger, the "no-self-left" view is logically meaningless. Ratzinger proposes, according to Volf, that divine persons are no more than the relationships in which they are involved (an idea that can be traced back through Aquinas to Augustine) and that the Son empties himself entirely of self *to the Father*. However, the logical outcome of this move is that there is then no Son left to relate to the Father: the Son's being and identity has been entirely subsumed within that of the Father. As Volf puts it, Ratzinger "is unable to guard the distinct identity of the Son. If the self of the Son consists in *complete* self-giving who would then be doing the giving? How are the Son's 'coinciding' with the Father, and the Father's and the Son's 'coalescing' into unity, different from the dissolution of the Son in the Father?"[50] There is then no Son for the Father to relate to: the Son's "'I' is that of the Father." The Son is in effect "colonized" by the Father, such that the Father is all and the Son is nothing. The "Son is not a participant but a ventriloquist."[51]

I believe that the way to overcome this difficulty is twofold. First, with Volf and Gunton,[52] I believe that persons, divine or human, are more than the clusters of relationships they enjoy. Such a functional definition is reductionist. There is an ontology to person. A person is a some*one with* a potential sense of self and capacity to relate to others as non-self. The kenosis I am exploring is *relational*. Secondly, the answer to the difficulty does not lie in softening or sidestepping kenosis but in ensuring that it is not seen in isolation. In the dynamics of the trinitarian relations, kenosis goes hand-in-hand with exaltation. Insofar as the Son's self-emptying for the sake of the Father is total, the Father gives back to the Son life and identity—and much more—through resurrection, exaltation, and all that these processes involve.

The Son's Primal Kenosis

We are now in a position to consider the biblical record concerning the kenosis of the Son. I will start, somewhat paradoxically, with the Son's

---

50. Volf, *Exclusion and Embrace*, 178–79; italics original. See also Volf, *After Our Likeness*, 67–69.

51. Volf, *Exclusion and Embrace*, 178–79.

52. Ibid., 179–80 (following Moltmann); Gunton, *Promise of Trinitarian Theology*, 92, 200.

exaltation and work back. Several texts attest to his exalted state as being above every other name. This eschatological reality is only partially realized in time: a case of "now but not yet." Thus in one sense the Son is already exalted over all names. In another important sense, the kingdom of the Son is invisible during the church age (Heb 2:8). Not every name yet submits to the Son. The Son's reign is progressive: he rules, but not all submit. Gradually, however, this rule is extended through the church's mission. Finally, all will bow; every enemy will be destroyed (1 Cor 15:25–26).

By extension, this idea of progressive exaltation also implies exaltation *from* some humbled or humiliated state. In the human history of Jesus of Nazareth, this humility and humbling are obvious, most particularly on the cross. However, the cross is part of a wider picture. In terms of incarnational christology, it is possible to conceive of this humbling in terms of the Son "stepping down" from a previously exalted state into the humility of incarnation, and this theme is not absent from the biblical witness: New Testament writers had already begun to conceive of the matter in these terms. The best known passage is Philippians 2:5–11 but John 1:14 and Hebrews 10:5–7, where the Son is portrayed as indicating to the Father at the point of incarnation an already existing desire to do the Father's will, carry the same connotation. Combining the messages of these texts, the picture is of the eternally pre-existent word freely choosing to walk the path of humility in this world as a servant, and taking the ultimately kenotic path to the cross.

So the Son's incarnational kenosis was taken to the extreme on the cross, which was the ultimate kenosis of the human Son. This is where kenosis "hits one between the eyes." It has been widely explored by theologians and by some has been used extensively in helping to fashion their trinitarianism. Perhaps most famously, Moltmann begins his trinitarianism with the cross.[53] This has much merit. It has the historical merit of commencing with the most firmly attested event affecting Jesus of Nazareth. It potentially offers a theodicy expressed in both God's acts and God's being, by commencing with the event that evidently cost God the most.

However, this starting point has the decided disadvantage of lending itself to a binitarian rather than a more obviously trinitarian view of God. Moltmann struggles to include the Holy Spirit in his account of the cross,[54]

---

53. See especially Moltmann, *Crucified God*; Moltmann, *Trinity and Kingdom*.

54. E.g., *Crucified God*, 247: Golgotha is "the event of love of the Son and the grief of the Father from which the Spirit who opens up the future and creates life in fact derives."

despite the fact that Lewis gives Moltmann praise for doing just this.[55] Moltmann's description is for the main part binitarian and his theology at this point is insufficiently pneumatological. Of all points in Jesus' human career, the Spirit is absent from the cross. If the Spirit conveyed to Jesus a sense of the Father's presence, then the fact that he could cry out to his God, "Why have you abandoned me?"[56] implies if anything the *absence* of the Spirit at that point. Suggestions that the reference to Jesus' giving up the spirit (John 19:30) was intended by John to refer to *the Holy Spirit* are less than convincing.[57] Even if they were, however, they would not negate my point, for by these accounts John 19:30 refers to a *departing* of the Spirit.

Nonetheless, this recognition of the Spirit's relative absence at the crucifixion, so to speak, does open up another line of trinitarian thinking. I suggested earlier in this chapter that the Father eternally gives the Spirit to the Son. Of all the gifts from the Father to the Son, this has to be the most important. It is the one upon which the Son's very existence and divinity rely. For the Son on the cross to experience the absence of, so to speak, not only the Father but also the Spirit or the Father's absence *through* the Spirit's felt absence is surely the emptiest that the Son could be and the lowest to which the Son could go.

Rather than follow Moltmann in exploring what the cross itself means for the Trinity, I am choosing to focus simply on the kenosis this represents, and the results of this kenosis. We need to see the Son's kenosis as the necessary prerequisite to his exaltation that allowed for the procession of the Spirit. The kenosis was so deep that it involved "absence" of the Spirit. The resultant exaltation was so high that it involved not only reception of the Spirit but "becoming" the source of the Spirit. Understood in terms of eternity, this is the bedrock of the Trinity. Without the eternal kenosis of the Son that "lets go" of the Spirit in love to the Father, there could be no eternal procession of the Spirit from non-being to eternal being.

But in what sense can we say that the Son's kenosis is eternal? In answering this question we need to recognize that the incarnational and cruciate kenosis of the Son is not an isolated expression of divine love that emerges in the life of the Trinity by, so to speak, economic necessity. Rather,

55. Lewis, *Between Cross and Resurrection*, 226.

56. See Atkinson, *The "Spiritual Death" of Jesus*, 160–68, for discussion of possible meanings of this cry.

57. Against Burge, *Anointed Community*, 134–35; Bennema, "Giving of the Spirit," 91–93. For arguments against their view, see Beasley-Murray, *John*, 353.

it is an expression in our human world of the Son's *eternal*, or *primal*, kenosis, by which through all eternity the Son humbly submits to the will of the Father, not through the Father's coercion but by the Son's free love for the Father. As Balthasar put it, "in this primary Kenosis the second is already contained."[58] Certainly Philippians 2:5–8 does not stand against such a conclusion. If one can dissect the poetry with such precision, it places the choice that Christ made prior to the kenotic act of being born in human likeness that followed. And, we might well ask, how could it be otherwise? So, and again I acknowledge that I am placing quite a lot of semantic weight on a piece of poetry, I understand that Christ's choice was an eternal one: the lamb was, so to speak, slain from the foundation of the world (Rev 13:8; one possible translation).[59] I posit therefore that the Son is eternally kenotic: the Son's relationship to the Father is one in which the Son empties himself for the sake of the honor of the Father and the fulfillment of the Father's purpose and promise. In this sense the Son did not have to "change his mind" to undergo historical kenosis as a human. The Son did not merely *become humble and humbled* at the incarnation, being converted as it were from an attitude of pride. Philippians 2:6, hard as it is to translate, denies this. The incarnation revealed the humble and humbled nature of the Son. The Son ever is humble. In "eternity before time," devoid of created beings, the One in comparison to whom the Son "was" humble and humbled is best understood to be the Father. This can perhaps be understood as the Son's eternal choice to submit to the Father, for the Scriptures allow no suggestion that the Father imposed this humility on the Son (indeed, would an imposed humility be a true humility at all?).

The church has traditionally taught that the three persons of the one God are equal. There is indeed a very real sense in which this is true, for we speak of all three persons as truly divine, in a monotheistic sense. However, the Bible's consistent focus is not on the equality of the Son with the Father but on the submission of the Son to the Father, evident of course in the incarnation, but deduced from this in every other aspect of their relationship. The claim by Giles that the Son was submissive in his incarnate form but not prior to or following this makes the mistake of suggesting that the incarnation was an *inaccurate* revelation of the trinitarian relations.[60] So the kenosis of the Son is far more than simply an incarnational dynamic. It is, I suggest, an eternal truth.

58. Balthasar, *Mysterium Paschale*, 24.

59. See ibid., 34–36.

60. Giles, *The Trinity and Subordinationism*, 17–18, 81, 116.

The Son's Eschatological Kenosis

If the kenosis of the Son is an eternal reality, then in the economy one will expect to find it expressed at least in the final state of things. According to Paul's writing, this is the case. Ultimately, when the dynamics of God's intervention in this world are complete, and the "end" has come (1 Cor 15:24), the Son freely allows himself to be subject in humility to the Father (1 Cor 15:24, 28). We may call this the Son's *eschatological kenosis*.

The wording of 1 Corinthians 15:28 is surprising. One might expect the Son's active choice to be evident, so that we would read, "the Son will subject himself." But we do not. We read that "the Son will be subjected . . ." by the Father. What then are we to make of Paul's surprising wording? Is it the case that, finally, the Son loses all choice and is coerced by the Father into submission? While such a reading of verse 28 is possible in isolation, this does not fit with the immediate context of the passage, or the wider context of Paul's christology. With respect to the immediate passage, the passive voice, and sense, of this verse is balanced by the active in verse 24: the Son will "hand over the kingdom to [his] God and Father." So the Son's active choice is in view; we recognize that at the end, as elsewhere in the economy, the Son is freely emptying himself. As for Paul's wider christology, Philippians 2:7, while referring to the Son's kenosis in incarnation rather than in eschatology, nevertheless indicates that for Paul free choice could be located in the Son. Why then might Paul have expressed verse 28 as he did? Perhaps we see here the very deepest depths of kenosis, when the Son accepts from the Father this final act of subjection.[61]

It is important to observe what 1 Corinthians 15:24–28 does not state, as well as what it does. While it indicates that finally the Father, not the Son, has ultimate kingship (the kingdom is handed over), and that finally the Son is subject in obedience to the Father, it does not state that the Son plays no further part in exercising this kingship.[62] Neither does it state that the Son's humanity, being, or person is subsumed into the Father in this final "transaction." The last clause of verse 28 must be read with care. The common

---

61. Whether, in turn, we must accept that the Father is here being presented as a tyrant will depend on Paul's, and wider Christianity's, presentation of the Father. Only a deep eternal kenosis of the Father will save the Trinity from such "imbalance." See chapter 4 for discussion of the Father's kenosis.

62. See Lewis, *Between Cross and Resurrection*, 221, n. 62, for discussion of Moltmann's "highly controversial" handling of this passage, according to which the "Son's reign . . . is not eternal, for at the end he surrenders his lordship to the Father."

English translation of the final phrase, "all in all," is potentially misleading. It might suggest that the Father, here in view, is the finally existing person of God. The Son, and thus by extension the Spirit, has been absorbed into the eternal being of the Father. This would be an unfortunate reading. The Greek plural is noteworthy: "that God might be *all things* among all things." Because there is not a plurality of Gods in view here, the meaning is clearly functional. Ultimately, all credit goes to the Father. The Father's centrality is recognized in every possible context.

I now broaden discussion from this one text, seeking all the while to utilize its message. In the view of the Trinity I am suggesting, this final state of the Son at the eschaton is an expression of the eternal state of the Son in dynamic relationship with the Father. The Son is utterly kenotic in relation to the Father. To express eternal ideas in temporal terms, we might declare that the Son is *always* abased before the Father. However, this abasement is before a Father who himself is utterly full of self-emptying love. If it were not so, we might need to accept the reality of the picture of the Trinity for which Volf criticizes Ratzinger. As I mentioned in the previous section, Volf's concern is that if a person is only a set of relations, then relational kenosis represents loss of personhood—of self.

This picture of the Trinity will not do. Volf accesses Moltmann's ideas in countering Ratzinger's picture. Volf is rightly concerned to indicate that a person is more than a web of relations.[63] This fits with my own working definition of "person" for the purposes of this book. In a person, there is a capacity to relate, but there is too a sense of self. There is a self that relates. Divine kenosis, I am suggesting, does not involve loss of self, but emptying of self *relationally.* The Son eternally exists, but eternally lays that existence down in humility before the Father. The Son, then, is eternally *kenotic*, or self-humbling, while the Father eternally exalts the Son. To this exaltation, discussion now turns.

THE EXALTATION OF THE SON

As this and the previous chapter have developed, much that needs to be said on this topic has already come to the fore. Therefore at this stage I can afford to offer relatively brief summaries of arguments that have been discussed in detail earlier. I will consider the Son's pentecostal exaltation and then his eschatological exaltation.

63. Volf, *Exclusion and Embrace*, 179–80.

In chapter 2, I discussed at some length ways that the Spirit exalts the Son. I linked this to the kenosis of the Spirit, which I saw expressed most vividly at Pentecost. Turning our attention more now to the Son himself, and questioning the dynamics of Pentecost, how far was the Son exalted, and who was the Son who was exalted? The former question may be answered in three ways, the third of which takes us to the latter question. These three ways of answering the question relate to the Son in relation to others. First, in relation to the Father, and accepting the more likely translation of Acts 2:33, the Son was exalted to the Father's right hand. One may not directly infer from this aspect of Acts 2:33 alone that this exaltation was absolute rather than relative. However, the aspect in question does lead in this direction. Secondly, in relation to every other name, this exaltation was therefore to a higher position than those names, for the Father is higher than all: to be at his right hand is to be above all. Even this, however, does not offer an account of a complete exaltation. It is still, conceivably, relative to others, even if it happens to be higher. Thirdly, in relation to the Spirit, the Son was exalted to such a position that the Spirit could now be given to him for him to grant to others. This is the highest place: the place of divine activity within the trinitarian relations. Here, the Father gives the Spirit to the Son not as to a creature. He gives the Spirit to the Son that the Son may "handle" the Spirit (I express myself loosely) as the Father himself would "handle" the Spirit. The Son is given the privilege of "acting upon" the Spirit precisely in the way that the Father does, though always at the initiative and behest of the Father. And so we can answer the second question. As only God can thus grant God's Spirit, so the Son is revealed in this exaltation as God. I have related this paragraph very specifically to Acts 2:33 and only demonstrated thereby that *Luke* offered a divine christology. However, as I have shown in earlier sections, there is broad New Testament agreement that the Spirit was "now" the Spirit of Christ. This reflects a broad New Testament agreement about Christ: a divine view of the Son is implied.

I come, finally, to the eschatological exaltation of the Son and return momentarily to the passage so recently discussed, 1 Corinthians 15:24–28. Despite my lengthy discussion in the previous section about what this passage states regarding the eschatological kenosis of the Son, there is here a magnificent exaltation of the Son expressed as well, and this is all the gracious gift of the Father. It is ultimately by the Father's power and authority that the Son "destroys all rule and all authority and power" (1 Cor 15:24). It is by the Father that the Son "must reign" (1 Cor 15:25). It is by the Father that the Son will destroy death (1 Cor 15:26). All this is explicitly declared to be the gracious gift of the Father in verse 27, where the "he" in "he has put all things under his feet" is best understood as the Father. This is clear from the quotation's source, Psalm 8:6.

At the risk of undue repetition, I am suggesting that what we see so clearly indicated in the economy, be it at one point in time or at the end of time, is also true of the immanent relations in the Trinity. The eternally kenotic Son is the eternally exalted one. It is by the gracious working of the Father that the Son is so exalted. The exaltation is, in all regards external to God, absolute. There is none higher save the Father himself.

CHAPTER CONCLUSIONS

This chapter has considered various matters pertaining to the place of the Son in the Trinity. First, it sought to demonstrate that the Son is not a created intermediary or a second God. Neither is the Son simply identifiable with the Spirit, though the two are very closely linked in New Testament thought. The Son is divine and is a distinguishable being in the life of the Trinity. That the Son is personal is considerably easier to demonstrate from the New Testament than that the Spirit is personal. One might say that the overriding characterizations of the Son are of a person. In turn, this personal view of the Son provides conceptual apparatus, along with the personhood of the Spirit discussed in chapter 2 and the personhood of the Father to be considered in chapter 4, for a model of the Trinity that is tri-personally relational or social. On the other hand, while ascribing impersonhood to the Spirit comes as a natural conclusion from the New Testament witnesses, doing so with respect to the Son seems to rely on a "minority report" in the New Testament. This impersonal view of the Son is useful, however. It coheres with an instrumental approach to the Spirit and in turn offers ideas for an instrumental model of the Trinity. I will give further consideration to these models in chapter 5.

The Son's roles within the life of the Trinity include a part in the procession of the Spirit, as seen in the exalted Christ's part in the pouring forth of the pentecostal Spirit. I will address the *filioque* question directly in the next chapter but at this point it is more central to my focus to stress that the Son only operates in this role because of his kenosis. Only by way of emptying himself in utter humility was the Son exalted to the position of granting the Spirit in time. Only by eternal kenosis does the eternally exalted Son have a role in the procession of the Spirit. Similarly, the Son brings defini-tion to the Spirit and to the Father. The Son reveals and exalts the Father and the Spirit. In all this, the kenosis of the Son is a prerequisite.

This kenosis can be traced "backwards" from the cross, through the incarnation, to a primal kenosis—an eternal truth that expresses itself in time throughout the economy. It can also be seen as an eschatological re-ality. Undoubtedly, this filial kenosis raises questions about the Father. If no kenosis of the Father can be identified, then there is great risk that the trinitarianism I am espousing will be unbalanced, with an autocratic Father to whom the other persons of the Trinity are subjugated. Even before that question is tackled, however, it is noteworthy that the Son's kenosis is itself "balanced" by his exaltation. In particular, though not solely, the Son's exal-tation shines out at Pentecost as the Son grants the Spirit and at the escha-ton as every enemy is placed beneath his feet. The Son is divine Lord of all.

4

Pentecost and the Father

INTRODUCTION

To HAVE A CHAPTER on the Father *following*, rather than preceding, chapters on the Spirit and the Son might strike readers as strange. I have sought, in introducing earlier chapters, to explain my choice of chapter order. At this point, I simply want to state that turning now to the Father must not in any sense be seen as a relegation of the Father to "last place" in the Trinity. I would like to suggest that if one looks at the Trinity from a suitably eschatological viewpoint, then to study the Father last is potentially to consider him as the peak and pinnacle of all that the Trinity is and is becoming.[1]

First, who is the Father? My previous chapters have had early sections titled, "The Spirit and the Father" (chapter 2) or "The Son and the Spirit" (chapter 3). Now in this chapter I come to the final example in this triad: the Father and the Son. In this section, I return to discussion I commenced in the previous chapter: the Son's role in defining the identity of the Father. I also consider the degree of differentiation that can be drawn between the Father and the Son. Then, in the subsequent section, I discuss the personhood and impersonhood of the Father.

The purpose of later sections of this chapter will be to discuss the Father's trinitarian roles and relationships. I will consider the Father's eternal generation of the Son and the Father's eternal spirating of the Spirit. Thereafter, I will discuss the kenosis of the Father, identifying this in the events of Pentecost before exploring the possibility of an eternal, or as Balthasar put

1. For discussion of the possibility of change in God, see chapter 1.

it, a "Super-Kenosis," of the Father.[2] I will find this kenosis of the Father in the eternal generation of the Son. Finally, I will consider the Father's exaltation. In so doing, I will begin a discussion concerning the unity of God that I will continue in the next chapter.

THE FATHER AND THE SON

I start as usual by referring to Pentecost, in order to note the distinctions it draws between the Father and the Son. There is no suggestion in Acts 2:32–33 that God the Father is Jesus. On the contrary, the Father raised Jesus, and was the one to whom Jesus was drawn close from some other, here unspecified, position. I am aware that the phrase, "the Father is not Jesus," is one with which Oneness Pentecostals are entirely comfortable. However, the sense in which I mean the phrase leads in a clearly trinitarian direction, for I mean that the Father is not the same person as Jesus. The interactions between God the Father and Jesus in these verses, in which the Father raised Jesus, drew him into proximity, and gave a promised gift to him, speak of personal relationships between the two. And if that text were not enough evidence on which to base this point, the Gospels are replete with evidence that Jesus related to God his Father as to another person.[3] One person of God could, at least under the circumstances of the incarnation, talk to another. Each loved the other. We are here viewing two persons in relationship.

There is less New Testament evidence, unsurprisingly, for any interpersonal relations between the Father and the Son in the Son's pre-incarnate life. As I mentioned in the previous chapter in a slightly different context, one must not place too much weight, for example, on the word "with" in John 1:1, as tempted as one may be to do so. One might assume that the pre-incarnate decisions of the Son implied in Philippians 2:6 and Hebrews 10:7 suggest some interactions between the Father and the Son that led to those decisions, but that would be an assumption. Nevertheless, one does not need to for the purposes of trinitarian discussion. It suffices to see Jesus and the Father relating in prayer as two persons in the incarnation. The pneumatological imagination employed in this book suggests that this is a true representation in the economy of the immanent eternal Trinity. The Father is not the Son.

2. Balthasar, *Mysterium Paschale*, viii.
3. See chapter 3 for further discussion.

If, however, the Father and the Son are distinguishable as two persons, how could I have been so confident in the previous chapter that the Son reveals and defines the Father? If the degree of revelation and definition were only analogical to a map indicating the contours of a terrain, then this might be possible: the Son is sufficiently similar to the Father to indicate something true about the latter. But on this level, any human reveals something of the Father, if we believe that humans are in the God's image, however marred that image might be. The degree to which the Jesus revealed the Father would only be directly analogous to the extent to which any other human did the same, albeit that perhaps Jesus did so to a particularly accurate degree. This is an acute problem with all functional christologies, in which Jesus was merely an exemplary human, most uniquely in contact with and filled by God.

Incarnational christology claims far more. While the Father and the Son are not the same person, there is an identity between them such that it can truly be stated of both: "he is God." The New Testament points us in that direction. Hurtado's *Lord Jesus Christ* is a masterly study of the early historical developments that led to the worship of the Son "alongside" the worship of the Father. However, studied on a superficial level, the New Testament does not give us as much cause to identify the Father with the Son ontologically as it does to identify the Spirit with the Father or the Son with the Spirit. It took the next few centuries of careful theological reflection, as affected as it was by cultural and philosophical factors and political constraints (what theological reflection is not?), to come to the conclusion that the Son is "one-in-being" with the Father. I do not intend to consider the process of that development in detail, for my focus is on Pentecost, but suffice it to say that there is in my view no Pentecostal trinitarianism without incarnational christology, and incarnational christology identifies the Father with the Son in this way. Therefore, though my sources for reaching the conclusion are different, I come to the same conclusion about the Father and the Son as I came to in previous chapters about, in turn, the Spirit and the Father, and the Son and the Spirit: the Father and the Son can be distinguished from one another ontologically in important ways that can be well expressed by saying that they are different persons. They are not, however, so distinguishable from one another that their identity can be torn apart. There is an identity of being.

THE FATHER AND PERSONHOOD

To some, it may seem strange that I am even raising the personhood of the Father as a question. However, as I noted in chapter 2, McFague writes of the Old Testament depiction of God: "nonhuman images are frequent and especially powerful for intimating feelings of the sublime and mysterious as well as for balancing [personal, relational] images which domesticate."[4] For non-human, one might read "impersonal." I referred to McFague's observation in discussion about the Spirit. However, this observation also has relevance to the Father. This is because the God of the Old Testament is the one the New Testament identifies as Father. Thus these non-human, impersonal images can be seen to refer to the Father. Just as the New Testament may call the Son "clothing" or a "rock," so too God (the Father) is light (1 John 1:5) and a consuming fire (Heb 12:29). I do not claim that such non-personal images are common, but they are important. Repeating McFague's point quoted above, they help us to avoid the danger of domesticating God. The two images just referred to, especially, point to the overpowering brightness of the glory of the Father and to the dangers incumbent in taking this Father for granted, as if the Father were merely a "buddy" or indeed merely a "daddy." Viewing God the Father in impersonal terms helps us to stand in awe.

Turning now from impersonhood to personhood, it may seem self-evident that the Father is as personal as the Son is. However, the personhood of the Son is so clear precisely because it is evident in and through the person of Jesus, whose human personality we see displayed in the Gospels, and whose divine personhood we surmise "behind" the human, precisely because Jesus was and is one person, not two.

In the case of the Father the situation is different. As I sought to demonstrate in the previous chapter, the Father is defined by the Son. Whatever we are to make of the personal interactions of Old Testament characters with God, it is only in and through Jesus that the Father's personhood really emerges. Quite clearly, as I stated in the previous chapter, Jesus enjoyed a relationship, not least through prayer, with his Father that we can only characterize as personal. We see a mutual relationship between two persons who communicate with each other as two human people would. If nothing else, the personhood of the Father is revealed in his relationship with his own eternal Son in incarnate form. Therefore, pneumatological

4. McFague, *Metaphorical Theology*, 43.

imagination permits one to see the eternal relatedness of the personal Father to the personal Son. While this is undoubtedly the case, more can be said. The personal relationship that the Father shares with the Son expresses kenosis on the part of the Father as well as the Son. At the risk of laboring an oft-repeated point, voluntary relational kenosis is a feature of personhood *par excellence*. The Son's kenosis towards the Father has been discussed in chapter 3. Later in this chapter, I consider the Father's kenosis in relationship to both the Son and the Spirit. As this book has constantly sought to indicate, the relationships between the three persons of God, however else they might validly be presented, can be characterized by kenosis of the self and exaltation of the others.

ROLES OF THE FATHER

The Father Raises the Son

I start with the resurrection because of its centrality to the Christian gospel, the breadth of its attestation in the New Testament, and the consistency with which the New Testament refers to this achievement of the Father. In chapter 2, I considered the slim New Testament evidence for the idea that the Spirit raised the Son from death. This idea should not be seen as contradicting the idea that the Father did so: one might understand the dynamic to be that the Father raised the Son by means of the Spirit. I also need to acknowledge another strand of New Testament evidence that ascribes the resurrection to Jesus himself. The authors of the three Synoptic Gospels tended to do this at times, seen in the active voice used for instance in Mark 9:9–10. This idea is combined with God raising Jesus in John's Gospel: if the discussion of death and life in John 5 can be applied to Jesus' own resurrection, then the Father raises the dead (5:21). But because what the Father does the Son also does (5:19), the Son thereby has the power of life, implying power over death (5:26), including his own (cf. John 10:18).

The most consistent New Testament testimony concerning who raised Jesus from death, however, is that God did so. In trinitarian terms, we may express this as: the Father raised the Son. We see it in the Gospels in the employment of a "divine passive" (e.g., in Luke 24:6, obscured in common English translations). The testimony in Acts is clear (e.g., Acts 2:24, 32; 3:15; 4:10; 5:30; etc.). In the letters, many references can also be found to this (e.g., 1 Thess 1:10; Gal 1:1; 1 Cor 6:14; Col 2:12; 1 Pet 1:21). Presumably, we might add, the God who raised Jesus from death also thereafter maintained his resurrection life. The relevance of this for understanding the Trinity is that if the Father has raised the Son to life—and presumably keeps the Son in life—in time, then one is already prompted with the idea that the Father sustains the life of the Son in eternity. That is why I gave this brief section a title that employs the present tense: "The Father Raises the Son." I do not mean to deny that the Son, any less than the Spirit, plays a part in the sustenance of his own life. I have just indicated how in John's Gospel we see a combination of the thought that life comes from the Father with the thought that the Son thereby has the power of life. We are justified in carrying that combination into our thinking about the immanent Trinity. Nor do I wish to imply that the resurrection of Jesus from death to life happens continuously. It happened in our past. However, I do wish to imply that the dynamic that enabled the resurrection is eternally present between the Father and the Son: the Father is eternally the source of the Son's life and the power behind the Son's life. The Father stands between the Son and death. Christianity has traditionally taught that this granting of life to the Son by the Father has a logical, if not a temporal, "beginning." This traditional doctrine is expressed as "the eternal generation of the Son." To this dynamic my discussion now turns.

The Father Generates the Son

It is worth considering why the terms "Father" and "Son" are used by trinitarians for these two divine persons. After all, Christianity emerged out of a Judaism that rarely called its God "Father." The term was used relatively infrequently of God in the Old Testament (e.g., 2 Sam 7:14; Ps 89:26; Isa 63:16; 64:8; Mal 2:10; cf. Ps 68:5), and Israel only occasionally heard itself referred to in its Scriptures as God's "son" or "children" (e.g., Exod 4:22–23; Deut 14:1; Jer 3:19; 31:20; Hos 11:1–4). In later Jewish writings, we continue to see fairly infrequent use of either designation: God as Father of the nation;[5] or Israel as God's sons or children.[6] (Sometimes, these ideas were

---

5. See, e.g., Sirach 23:1; 51:10; *Jubilees* 1:28; Tobit 13:4; 3 Maccabees 2:21; 5:7; 6:8; Wisdom of Solomon 11:10; 14:3; *Joseph and Asenath* 12:14–15. For discussion about addressing God as Father in Jewish prayers somewhat postdating Jesus, see McKnight, *New Vision for Israel*, 51.

6. See, e.g., Wisdom of Solomon 18:13.

combined in a single text.[7]) We also find the terms "son of God" or "child of God" used of any righteous person.[8] A famously righteous person such as Moses could be referred to as God's "heir."[9] An outstanding priest would be able to address God as "Father."[10] Nevertheless, McKnight, who is keen to highlight the number of occasions when such language was used, is still able to conclude: "'Father' occurs only occasionally in the evidence that survives from Second Temple Judaism."[11]

Returning to the OT, we do not find "father" and "son" language used frequently, either, with respect to heavenly intermediaries. The Spirit in the Old Testament was never called God's child. Divine wisdom in Proverbs 8 was personified as a woman and as God's companion (Prov 8:30) but not necessarily as God's daughter, despite a possible translation of Proverbs 8:30 that suggests wisdom here was a child at creation. In the Old Testament some heavenly beings were sometimes called "sons of God" (e.g., Job 1:6; Gen 6:2[12]). However, this was always in the plural, and did not suggest anything beyond a heavenly relationship with God, as expressed in Job 1:6 and later reflected in Luke 1:19. It is not surprising, given this background, that in Judaism closer to the time of Christ angels should continue to be designated as God's children.[13]

There was, however, a particular development in the Judaism of this era: a conceptual link gradually strengthened between the idea of sonship and that of an awaited Messiah. Jews began to see this Messiah relating to God as son. Clearly, 2 Samuel 7:14 supplied plentiful conceptual apparatus for such a link. To offer but one example, the Qumran community expressed this idea, combining the messianic theme of anointing by the Spirit with the idea of sonship: "[The spirit of God] dwelt on him, he fell down before the throne[;] . . . he will be great on earth. . . . The son of God he will be proclaimed (or: proclaim himself) and the son of the Most High

---

7. See, e.g., *Jubilees* 1:24–25; 19:29; *Joseph and Asenath* 12:8.

8. E.g., Wisdom of Solomon 2:18 (cf. 2:16); 5:1–5; 12:19.

9. Philo, *Life of Moses*, 1:155, quoted by Hurtado, *One God, One Lord*, 60.

10. *Testament of Levi* 17:2. The priest in this case would be involved in bringing salvation. Messianic connotations are thus identifiable.

11. McKnight, *New Vision for Israel*, 54.

12. The import of Gen 6:2 is widely disputed.

13. E.g., *1 Enoch* 6:2, heavily dependent on Gen 6:2.

they will call him. Like the sparks of the vision, so will be their kingdom. They will reign for years on the earth . . ."[14]

While acknowledging all this background, there seems no reason to doubt that the fundamental reason that early Christians began to adopt Father and Son language when discussing God lies in Jesus' own use of these terms, as expressed in the Gospels and reflected in the letters. Jesus called his God "Father" and called himself God's "son." As I stated earlier, McKnight is keen not to minimize unduly the use of "father" language by Judaism. Yet he notes, accurately, "Even though God is addressed in prayer as Father in the Hebrew Bible and in early Jewish literature, there is a singular difference in the case of Jesus. . . . The centrality he gave [use of the term "Abba"] . . . reserved for it a special significance . . . that shows this distinctive emphasis of Jesus."[15]

While Jesus clearly invited his followers also to call God "Father," notably in the prayer he taught, Jesus still retained a distinction about his own relationship with God as Father, such as in Luke 10:22, paralleled in Matthew 11:27, and most notably in the Johannine portrayal. God was for Jesus *my* Father (e.g., John 5:17; 8:54; 15:23–24; 20:17). It seems clear that early Christianity was left with a distinct impression of a unique paternal/filial relationship that, though mirrored in Christian relationships with God, was ultimately a relationship that Jesus alone shared with God.

It is hardly surprising, then, to find Jesus' followers writing of the relationship between Jesus and God as that between a Son and a Father, not only in the Gospels but also in other New Testament documents (e.g., Rom 15:6; Heb 1:5; 1 Pet 1:3; Rev 1:6) and then in Christian discourse down to our own day. Such is, surely, the historical explanation. But what is the conceptual significance? Fathers are fathers to the children they have taken part in conceiving or have adopted. Unsurprisingly, both these ideas expressed themselves in early (and later) christological thinking, whether it be Arian or adoptionist. It is not my purpose to discuss the early evolution of incarnational christology. Needless to say, I support this position, as I am a trinitarian. But the retention of "Father" and "Son" language is useful in that it constantly reminds trinitarians that the eternal being and life of the Son is dependent on that of the Father.[16] The Father has not adopted

---

14. 4Q 246, translation from Vermes, *Complete Dead Sea Scrolls*, 577.

15. McKnight, *New Vision for Israel*, 55.

16. This is despite the objections of, e.g., D'Costa, *Sexing the Trinity*, 21–22, 76–77, 94.

the Son from another family. Nor does the Son have a temporal beginning. But the Father *eternally* generates the Son. As soon as I use this traditional language about the "eternal generation" of the Son, I want to stress how decidedly metaphorical it is. To quote D'Costa, it is "startling to speak of an eternal begetting, which linguistically is like the sound of one hand clapping."[17] Metaphors lose their shock value with use and become "dead metaphors." Perhaps D'Costa's fresh simile helps us to hear anew the remarkable paradox that the Son is dependent for existence on the Father (which, by the way, is not a statement with which D'Costa would agree) *and* that the Son is eternally existent with an existence that is, by the Father's gracious provision, divinely self-existent.

The idea that is presented by the metaphor, then, is that the Father is the eternal source of the Son's eternal existence—is the source of the Son's eternal life. The repeatedly attested idea that the Father was the source of the Son's resurrection life after the cross and the grave is then reflected in this eternal dynamic. I wish to emphasize the imbalance in this relationship, in the face of pressures from various theological voices to "flatten out" or equalize the Trinity. Paul declared to the Corinthians, "the head of Christ is God" (1 Cor 11:3). It matters not for the purposes of my present discussion whether the term "head" is understood as "source" or "authority."[18] This stark statement is not an exception to the New Testament rule. There is an *inequality* between the Father and the Son. Fee writes that "'God is the [head] of Christ' is not a christological statement in the ontological sense; that is, Paul is hardly thinking of the 'eternal generation' of the Son from the Father."[19] I am sure that what Fee writes is accurate as it pertains to Paul's focus. My concern for trinitarian thinking, however, is the distance that Fee implies between a "christological statement in the ontological sense" and what we see of the relationship between the incarnate Christ and his God. If the head of Christ is God, then I suggest the head of the Son is the Father—in an ontological sense. I do not merely lift this from the text of 1 Corinthians 11:3. But I derive it from the whole witness of which 1 Corinthians 11:3 is a part.

As soon as one dares whisper any reference to an inequality between the Father and the Son, one is confronted with the long-held Christian

17. Ibid., 87.

18. For discussion of this question, see, e.g., Fee, *First Epistle to the Corinthians*, 501–3, and the references cited there.

19. Ibid., 505.

declaration, expressed in ancient creedal liturgy,[20] that the Father and the Son are co-equal as well as co-eternal. I firmly believe this to be true, for anyone or anything not equal to God cannot, surely, be God. How can equality and inequality thus co-exist? Broadly, I appeal to the place of paradox in Christian theology. It is hard to think of a central Christian doctrine that does not carry within it some degree of paradox. More precisely, however, there is more to be said.

At the risk of pressing an analogy too far, I wish to use the case of a human parent and child. The analogy offers some degree of explanatory help whether they be father and son or mother and daughter. I will refer to a father and son simply for the sake of the clarity of the parallel I seek to draw. A father and a son are unequal in terms of their relationship with each other. The father will always be in that paternal relation to the son whereby it is the father who is a source of the son's existence and not the other way round. But in respects other than this relationship, no such inequality can be traced other than that of age. So, all other things being equal, the son at the age of, say, thirty is entirely equivalent to the father when he was thirty years old. The son is not rendered inferior to the father in any sense, as a human being, by being that man's son. He is no less a man. The analogical link to the Trinity is, I trust, clear. The inequality that exists between the eternal Father and the eternal Son *only* pertains to their relationship with each other. The Father is the source of the Son's eternal existence and not the other way round. But the Son is no less God than the Father.

We can go further—and the analogy comes some way with us but is limited by the nature of father-son relationships at different stages in life, across different cultures and eras, and in terms of how healthy the relationships are. The Gospels and other New Testament witnesses indicate that the incarnate Son, Jesus, was obedient to the Father's commands, responsive to the Father's initiatives, dependent on the Father's enabling, and so on. Such inequalities of relationship can be detected in *some* aspects of *some* relationships between parents and children in *some* cultures at *some* points in people's lives and so forth. So this analogy, like all analogies, provides some explanatory help but has its limitations. We must observe how, as presented to us in the witnesses, the Son on earth related to the Father in heaven and trust the pneumatological imagination that sees all these aspects—unequal aspects—reflected in the eternal immanent relations between the two co-equal persons of the Trinity.

20. See, e.g., *Quicunque Vult*, in the Anglican Book of Common Prayer.

It is noteworthy that Christians are more used to declaring in creeds that the Son is eternally generated by the Father than that the Father eternally generates the Son. We seem naturally to focus on the Son when considering this dynamic and see the Father in the background to the Son's existence, as the primordial explanation of this eternal fact. It somehow feels more uncomfortable to focus our gaze on the Father and see him, so to speak, eternally generating the Son. This leads me to consider *by what means* the Father eternally generates the Son. Smail, who as we will see in the next section views the procession of the Spirit from the Father as occurring *through* the Son, insists that the eternal generation of the Son must also be seen pneumatologically: the Son is eternally generated by the Father *through the Spirit.*[21] Smail regards this as important in terms of "trinitarian balance": it prevents any relegation of the Spirit "beneath" the Son. Smail's book, *The Giving Gift*, is ostensibly a work of pneumatology, as its title implies. However, Smail's reflections concerning the Holy Spirit are set in a firmly trinitarian framework, and many of his insights are about the Trinity overall as much as the Holy Spirit in particular. Like Rahner and Moltmann, Smail begins his trinitarian reflections with the Christ-event. It is a trinitarianism "from below." However, while Rahner begins his with the incarnation of the *Logos* ("Word") and Moltmann begins with the crucifixion of Jesus,[22] Smail begins with the conception of Jesus.[23] His point here is simple: Jesus was conceived from the Father in the womb of Mary, according especially to Luke, by the action of the Spirit. The Son's human existence was dependent on that of the Father, yes. But that human existence was dependent on the action of the Spirit. The Father operated by the agency of the Spirit in giving human life to the Son. Smail also regards what he perceives of the economic Trinity to be inferable of the immanent Trinity.[24] If this is true in the economy of God's dealings with the world, then it is surely true as well of God's own immanent nature: the Father eternally generates the Son and thereby grants him eternal life by means of the Spirit's action. For reasons that I developed in chapter 2, I can only agree with his conclusions.

So far in this section I have been considering the role of the Father— and the Spirit—in giving the Son eternal life. Now I wish briefly to discuss

21. Smail, *Giving Gift*, 141–42.

22. Rahner, *The Trinity*, 9–33; Moltmann, *Trinity and Kingdom*, 21–31.

23. The title of chapter 1 of Smail's *Giving Gift* is "Beginning with Mary."

24. Smail, *Giving Gift*, 145, 164.

how I see the Father also giving to the Son eternal divinity. Insofar as the history of Jesus of Nazareth sheds light on the dynamic relationships between the persons of the Trinity, we learn from Acts 2:33, supported by Philippians 2:9 and other texts, that the Son was exalted by the Father at a certain point in time. The status to which he was exalted was above every other name—on that point, New Testament witness is unanimous. To be above every other name and to grant God's Spirit is to be the supreme Name—to be God.[25] The Father exalted the Son to divinity. In stating this, I do not wish to suggest that the Son had at some point in time been less than divine. Once more we face paradox. But the exaltation of the Son after his humiliation affirmed and declared, as well as appointed, the Son to his eternal rightful place as the *divine* Son. Furthermore, insofar as these dynamics enlighten our understanding of the eternal relationships between the persons of the Trinity, we learn that the Son is *eternally* exalted by the Father to the latter's right hand. It is by the Father's action that the Son is eternally higher than any other name. The Father establishes and maintains the uttermost exaltation of the Son. We discover in effect that the Father establishes and maintains the divinity of the Son. I am tempted to suggest that, again, the Father does so by means of the Spirit. I have little textual support for such an idea, and would need to rest on a less than likely translation of Acts 2:33, which would read "exalted by God's right hand [i.e., the Spirit]" rather than "exalted to God's right hand" (see chapter 2). However, I think, given all the other aspects of intra-trinitarian relations that one can trace in the economy and thus understand of the immanent Trinity, it seems reasonable to speculate that this too is the case: the Father eternally establishes the divinity of the Son by means of the Spirit.

The Father Grants the Spirit

One need hardly turn to Acts 2:33 as a key source for the idea that the Father grants the Spirit in the economy, for such a dynamic is expressed plentifully throughout the Scriptures. The Father is the source of the Spirit. There is no source of the Spirit "behind" the Father. To argue from the economic to the immanent Trinity, then, the Spirit owes eternal existence to none other than the Father. In and through all eternity, the Father "exhales," "exudes," or "spirates" the Spirit.

---

25. See my earlier discussion of this point in chapter 3.

Placing together the thoughts expressed in the previous section with this thought, the Father emerges as the eternal source of both the Son and the Spirit. The Father, ancient Greek theologians such as the Cappadocian fathers recognized, is the sole cause.[26] This idea has not gone unchallenged in modern theology. Later in this chapter, when I will return to discussion of this topic from a slightly different angle, I will note Moltmann's seeming embarrassment with this matter: an embarrassment that forces him to see the Father as sole cause in some respects but not in others. John Zizioulas, in contrast, is enthusiastic about the Cappadocian doctrine: the "concept of agency or causality in the existence of God is one of the most important and least recognised areas of Christian doctrine."[27] Alan Torrance is critical of Zizioulas' enthusiasm. In Torrance's view, to say that the person of the Father is the first cause in God fails to recognize the notion of trinitarian *communion* as foundationally contributing to the being of God. Furthermore, claims Torrance, causation is a "cosmological category."[28] In other words, we must beware "uploading" worldly categories such as cause and effect into God's being. While these criticisms are important, neither is without counter-argument. To say that the Father is the sole cause is not to suggest that God is *complete* solely as the Father. God is "completed" in the communion of the Father, the Son, and the Spirit. If one were, so to speak, to "take away" the Son and the Spirit, one would not have God left. (One might suggest that one would not even have the Father left, for by analogy a person is not a father without a child.) Thus the relations within the Trinity are still conceptually foundational to the being of God. On the matter of causality being a "cosmological category," granted: we live in a world of causes and effects and must be careful before we project our world into God's being. But it is an assumption that there can be no causality in God's being. T. F. Torrance offers a similar critique of the Cappadocian doctrine. "The Holy Spirit certainly proceeds from the Father, but because of the Unity of the Godhead . . . , he issues . . . from out of the indivisible perichoretic relations within the One Being of the Holy Trinity in which he himself is eternally and fully participant."[29] The reluctance of Torrance's agreement with the thesis that the Spirit pro-

---

26. See the exposition offered by Zizioulas, *Lectures in Christian Dogmatics*, 50–53, 59–61.

27. Ibid., 59.

28. Alan Torrance, *Persons in Communion*, 290–91, quotation from 291.

29. Torrance, *Trinitarian Perspectives*, 142.

ceeds from the Father is indicated by the way Torrance has to nuance it immediately by offering a counter-statement that consists of two ideas: the Spirit proceeds from the trinitarian relations and the Spirit proceeds, in effect, from the persons. Each is problematic. The former suggests that relations are logically antecedent to persons. However, one cannot have relationships without persons. Persons and relations go hand-in-hand. The latter idea is circular: the persons proceed from the persons. The most fundamental difficulty, however, with Torrance's statement is its reluctance to agree wholeheartedly with the testimony of Scripture concerning the economic Trinity. In the latter case, the Spirit is poured out by the Father through the agency of the Son (e.g., Acts 2:33, of course). There is no need to posit an immanent Trinity that acts and relates differently.

Perhaps there is a way in which *biblical* ideas can be utilized to suggest some reciprocation between the divine persons in the matter of procession. John 4:24 states that God is spirit. These words were spoken by the Johannine Jesus and, as I have noted previously (in chapter 2), he was speaking of another, not himself. Thus, I take it that he was referring to the Father. The Father is spirit. This is not a metaphysical statement; nor should it be read as, "The Father is the Spirit."[30] However, one might be justified—in line with my point in chapter 1 that the Father eternally chooses to subsist as spirit: it is the *Word*, not the Father, who became flesh—in suggesting that the Father chooses to allow his existence to be expressed and maintained through the resources that belong to the Spirit. If there is any possible truth in the statement that "the Father proceeds from the Spirit," then it may be along these lines that the truth could be sought. However—and it is a firm "however"—such an idea has only a tiny fraction of the biblical support that the Spirit's procession *from the Father* has. The latter is the one with plentiful and clear support throughout the Scriptures, and then in turn throughout the ancient creeds.

To whom does the Father grant the Spirit? To whom does the Spirit proceed from the Father? Acts 2:33 is a useful place to turn (though again not the only one) as a source for the idea that, first and foremost, the Father grants the Spirit *to the Son*. At an earlier stage in the economy, we saw the Father granting the Spirit to the Son in the sense that the Son became the recipient of the Spirit—the Spirit now acted on the Son, in some ways analogously to how the Spirit acts on any human recipient (e.g., Luke 3:22;

---

30. Burge, *Anointed Community*, 192; Beasley-Murray, *John*, 62.

4:18).[31] However, at the later stage in the economy described in Acts 2:33, we see the Father granting the Spirit to the Son as his to give in turn to others. In the immanent Trinity, two ideas are thus suggested to us. The first is that the Father in all eternity grants the Spirit to the Son so that the Son is the recipient—so that the Son's eternal life and divine capacities are upheld by the infusion of the Spirit into him. The other idea suggested to us is that the Father eternally grants the Spirit to the Son so that the Son can in turn grant the Spirit at will. One is tempted to speculate that in "eternity-before-time," in the absence of any created order and thus of any other potential recipients, the Son then offers the Spirit back to the Father. To put this another way that makes best sense, I suggest, when understood in terms of the impersonhood rather than the personhood of the Spirit,[32] the Father and the Son grant to one another, in eternal reciprocal giving, their very own life.

The *Filioque* Question

The *filioque* controversy arose in response to the creedal statement that the Spirit proceeds from the Father. While this universally accepted statement remained unchanged in the East, in the Latin West an addition came more and more to be included in the statement, so that it became in time standardized as: the Spirit proceeds from the Father "and from the Son." *Filioque* is Latin for "and from the Son." This became the cause of much dissension, and led, among other factors, to the division between the churches of the East and West in around 1054.[33]

The *filioque* clause is commonly regarded as problematic in that it relegates the Spirit in relation to the Son. Indeed, on a practical level this is connected in commentators' minds with the neglect of the Spirit that I described in chapter 1 (The "Binitarian" Challenge).[34] However, this is not its only problem. It also relegates the Father, so that the Father and the Son

---

31. See chapter 2 for references to discussion of the extent to which the Son Jesus' experience of the Spirit at his baptism was archetypal for other human receptions of the Spirit.

32. See chapter 2 for discussion of both personhood and impersonhood with respect to the Spirit.

33. See, e.g., McGrath, *Historical Theology*, 69–72.

34. Gunton, *Promise of Trinitarian Theology*, 199; Moltmann, *Trinity and Kingdom*, 178; Smail, *Giving Gift*, 132–35.

seem to be two equals in the procession of the Spirit, both equally primary as causes of the Spirit's existence and activity. This does not do justice to the biblical testimony, repeated often and in multiple ways, that the *Father alone* is the fount of all. We can perhaps discern that the *filioque* clause is useful in general terms in that it resists isolating the Son from the procession of the Spirit. The Son is involved in some way. To state that the Spirit proceeds from the Father and the Son is thus more helpful than to say, merely, that the Spirit proceeds from the Father, period. However, we can also discern that, given the problems that arise when the Spirit's procession is thus formulated, there might be better ways of presenting the matter.

Moltmann and Smail have suggested different ways to express the relation of the Son to the procession of the Spirit. Moltmann writes about the Spirit proceeding from the Father *of* the Son.[35] Moltmann's starting point is a straight denial of the *filioque*: "The Holy Spirit does not proceed from the Son. Consequently it is a correct interpretation to say that the Holy Spirit proceeds 'solely' from the Father."[36] However, leaning rather heavily on the term "Father" (for we do not say, "The Spirit proceeds from *God*"), he considers whom this Father is the Father of. He does not accept that God's fatherhood is in relation to all creation by being its creator. Rather, for Moltmann, this fatherhood is uniquely the fatherhood of the Son—and then by extension a fatherhood of all those in the Son as sisters and brothers in Christ.[37] So the Son's involvement in the procession of the Spirit from the Father is, one might say, that of defining who this Father is: he is the Father of the Son. Moltmann takes this a step further when he explains later that the Spirit in this eternal process receives from the Son "relational form" and "visage"[38]—in other words, the Son grants definition and identity to the Spirit as well as to the Father. Furthermore, for Moltmann, if the Spirit is to proceed from the *Father*, then God must "already" be a Father—to the Son. Thus the eternal generation of the Son is presupposed in the procession of the Spirit. The two cannot be disentangled. Finally, because "Father" and "Son" indicate two persons in relation, the Spirit proceeds from this relationship.

35. Moltmann, *Trinity and Kingdom*, 182–85.

36. Ibid., 182.

37. Ibid., 183.

38. Ibid., 186. This is comparable to Dunn's understanding of Paul's "Spirit of Christ," as critiqued by Turner ("Spirit of Christ," 429–30).

There is much here that is worthy of careful consideration. Moltmann's first idea, that the Son defines who is the Father from whom the Spirit proceeds and defines who this Spirit is, is particularly useful. The Spirit proceeds from that particular Father who has been specified, defined, and particularized by the Son. So too is the Spirit specified by the Son. This is helpful, and in the previous chapter I briefly discussed how the Son defines the Father and the Spirit. However, one is hard pressed to acknowledge this as a role of the Son *in the Spirit's procession*. Admittedly, it is a role of the Son in defining the Father and the Spirit, but not in that which gives the Spirit eternal existence. Moltmann is at pains to separate these ideas. The Spirit's eternal existence is derived from an action of the Father alone ("Objectively speaking, the procession of existence preceeds [*sic*] the reception of form in the relations we have described"[39]). Only then, so to speak, does the Son step in and "mold" this existing Spirit. The problem is that Moltmann is referring to *another* role of the Son, which happens to have relevance to the Spirit's procession but plays no part in effecting this procession. In the case of Moltmann's second idea, that the Son's generation comes logically "before" the Spirit's procession, the Son has no role: the Son is passive. Only in the third idea, that the Spirit proceeds from the paternal-filial relationship, is there perhaps an implicit role for the Son. Even this seems unlikely in Moltmann's thinking, for he prioritizes the role of the Father in this relationship: the Spirit "does after all issue from the fatherhood of God, which is to say from the Father's relationship to the Son."[40] Thus all of Moltmann's thinking at this point about the immanent Trinity seems to stand in some contrast from the roles of the economic Trinity, in which the Son is clearly active in the procession of the Spirit to the world (Acts 2:33, etc.). Moltmann seems to have failed to maintain his own dictum that the economic Trinity is the immanent Trinity: "there are not two different Trinities."[41] Thus he is not on safe ground. It is not adequate to state merely that the Spirit proceeds from the Father of the Son.

During his discussion of the idea that the Spirit proceeds from the Father of the Son, Moltmann also toys with another suggestion, which is that

---

39. Moltmann, *Trinity and Kingdom*, 187. Moltmann's full formulation is, "The Holy Spirit, who proceeds from the Father of the Son, and who receives his form from the Father and the Son" (ibid., 187, italics removed).

40. Ibid., 184.

41. Ibid., 153; cf. 159–60, in which Moltmann states that he is here following Rahner.

the Spirit proceeds from the Father *through* the Son.[42] This idea is one that is given full consideration by Smail. For Smail, it is clear that the Spirit does indeed proceed eternally from the Father through the Son.[43] This useful characterization seems to cohere with the roles of the Father and the Son in the sending of the Spirit in the Christian economy, as Acts 2:33 so ably attests. However, it can be further defined, in ways that Pentecost illuminates. First, as I have already suggested, the Son does not merely owe existence to the Father, as eternal generation suggests, but owes divinity to the Father: the Father both generates the Son and exalts the Son (in eternity, of course) above every other name, effectively naming the Son as divine. Next, it has been more tentatively suggested that the Son is eternally exalted to this divinity by the Father *through the Spirit* (the right hand of God in Acts 2:33), and in this the Spirit has clearly *proceeded* from the Father to the Son. It has also become clear that the Spirit proceeds from the Father both through the Son's kenosis and through the Son's exaltation. In other words, it is as a *result* of kenosis (Phil 2:9—"therefore") that the exaltation occurs; and it is only as eternally and exaltedly divine that the Son *deserves* to receive the Spirit to grant to others. Thus, putting all these thoughts together, I conclude that: the Spirit eternally proceeds from the Father *through the Son's kenosis and exaltation*. I would then wish to add that: the Son is eternally exalted by the Father *through the Spirit's procession—and kenosis* (see chapter 2).

THE KENOSIS OF THE FATHER

In keeping with the central focus of this book, I want to explore in particular those aspects of the Father's relationship with the Son and the Spirit that can be described as kenotic. While my earlier chapters, in which I discussed the kenosis of the Son, and even of the Spirit, may have occasioned no great surprise in this respect, it may come as more of a shock to find me suggesting a kenosis of the Father (though I am not the first to have done so).[44] Surely, it might be argued, the Father, of all that is God, is the one who exists

---

42. Ibid., 182 ("*per Filium*"), 185 (approvingly quoting the Russian orthodox Boris Bolotov).

43. Smail, *Giving Gift*, 128, 138–39. This idea is not new to Smail (nor does he claim that it is). Moltmann traces it back to Tertullian (*Trinity and Kingdom*, 137), Alan Torrance to Cyril of Alexandria (*Persons in Communion*, 293).

44. I have already noted a hint of the Father's kenosis, with respect to the Spirit, in chapter 2.

eternally in unapproachable light and glory, who does not share his glory with another? However, even in the Old Testament one finds strands that speak of the voluntary self-humiliation of God (e.g., Isa 57:15). One must be cautious: it might be that this Old Testament self-lowering of God is fulfilled not in the actions of the Father but in and through the actions of the Son and the Spirit. To solve that uncertainty, one needs to seek evidence not of the Father's kenosis with respect to creation (for this might indeed have been achieved by means of the Son and Spirit as the "right and left hands" of God, with no stooping of the Father's own person) but of the Father's kenosis with respect to the Son and the Spirit themselves. Can it possibly be stated that the Father lowered or lowers himself in lifting up the Son and the Spirit?

I believe that it can. However, before possible examples are explored, an important caveat must first be offered. In previous chapters, when I sought to consider the mutual, dynamic kenosis of the Son and the Spirit in the economy of God's dealings with creation, I noted that, as long as the language was used loosely, one might helpfully speak of a kenosis of the Son in the incarnation in which the Son placed himself "beneath" the Spirit, such that the Spirit became "Lord" of the Son. For example, the Spirit sent the Son Jesus into the wilderness after his baptism. Conversely, as at least presented in Acts 2:33, after the ascension we can delineate a kenosis of the Spirit with respect to the Son that placed the Spirit "beneath" the Son now, so that at that point, and thereafter consistently, the Son was "Lord" of the Spirit, so that the Son sent the Spirit (ultimately from the Father) into the church.

In the case of the kenosis of the Father, which we do find, the situation is different. The Father's kenosis, real as it is, does not involve his placing himself beneath the Son or the Spirit. The Son never leads the Father. The Spirit never sends the Father.[45] There is no "role-reversal" of any form. There is a dynamic that presents a deep and costly emptying of the self but there is not an emptying of self that leads to an exaltation of the other above the self. The equivalent exaltations that occur, for instance, do not involve the Father's ever taking "second" place. The Father never exalts the Son to a place "higher" than that occupied by the Father—so too with the Spirit. On this matter, if "proof text" be needed, we can press into service

---

45. I state this despite my tentative suggestion earlier in the chapter that there might be some truth in the statement "the Father proceeds from the Spirit."

1 Corinthians 15:27—"when it says that all things have been subjected, clearly the exception is the One subjecting all things to him."

In turn, this means that there is in a real sense an inequality in the Trinity. For all that no person of the Trinity is less than God, no person is less than eternal, and no person is less than perfect, it remains the case that the primal ultimacy belongs to the Father, and to the Father alone. So reciprocity is limited: it never threatens the ultimacy of the Father. This exaltation of the Father will be considered in a subsequent section, after we turn in detail now to different aspects of the Father's kenosis.

The Father's Pentecostal Kenosis

I turn first, as usual, to the Pentecostal outpouring of the Spirit and specifically this time to the exaltation of Jesus that preceded it. Acts 2:33 tells how Jesus was exalted by the Father to his right hand. Perhaps it is in this event that the kenosis of the Father is easiest to detect. It would be bizarre to suggest that in exalting the Son, the Father was demeaned or demoted, even if this demotion was self-imposed (though the analogy of the parent who stoops down to lift the small child may not be entirely inappropriate). Nevertheless, exaltation of another person, even another person of the Trinity, is a loving act, and as such a selfless act. The Father acted selflessly in exalting the Son. Furthermore, the Father had to be ready to share the position named "highest" with the Son. So to speak, the Father had to "shuffle along" and make space on the highest throne for the Son to share. The Father had to let go of any suggestion of keeping the highest glory as his own. He had to empty himself of such a notion (of course, I do not aim to suggest that the Father was even tempted to do otherwise or that the Father ever did occupy that position alone). Thus for the Father to exalt the Son, the Father had to undergo kenosis. The exaltation of the Son was for the Father a kenotic act.

However, the kenosis of the Father evident in Acts 2:33 does not end there. For all that the exaltation of the Son involved the kenosis of the Father, how much more, we might say, did the outpouring of the Spirit. I can put it this way: for all time, so to speak, the Father had poured out the Spirit as *his* Spirit: the Spirit of God. Now, for the first time (I write loosely) the Father could no longer simply pour out the Spirit autonomously. Now the Father chose to delegate the outpouring of the Spirit to the Son. The Father divested himself of his eternal right to pour out the Spirit. He emptied himself of this privilege, granting it to the Son. As I say, I am writing loosely. One in fact can only say that *at the level of believers' experience* did the Spirit of God become at this stage the Spirit of Christ, granted by the Son. With the benefit of hindsight, at least one New Testament author realized that in reality the Spirit of God had *always* been the Spirit of Christ (1 Pet 1:11). And of course he was right. So this kenosis of the Father did not *start* with the event of Pentecost. This is an eternal truth. The Father has eternal prerogative to pour out the Spirit; but the Father eternally and kenotically hands this divine privilege over to the Son. In the eternal relations of the Trinity, the Father has the eternal prerogative to "spirate" the Spirit, but the Father eternally and kenotically grants to the Son a central role in this spiration or procession, such that the Spirit proceeds from the Father *through* the Son.

More can be said. Not only does this "delegation" of spiration represent kenosis. The Father *gives* the Spirit to the Son. I suggest that this giving "away" of the Spirit is kenotic. I would not wish to suggest that the Father, in consequence, lacks the Spirit. That is why I must place the word "away" in inverted commas. But neither would I wish to suggest that the Father gives the Spirit casually, as if this cost the Father nothing. In giving the Spirit, the Father is giving God. In giving the Spirit, the Father is giving the divine fabric of himself to the Son.

Furthermore, this giving is eschatological. Acts 2:17, quoting Joel, tells us: "it shall be in the last days that I will pour out from my Spirit upon all flesh." The reference to the last days points to the eschatological import of Pentecost, referred to elsewhere throughout the New Testament. It is noteworthy that this eschatological outpouring on all flesh requires, first, the eschatological granting of the Spirit to the Son. While it "has always" been true, in "eternity past," that the Father gives the Spirit to the Son, yet it is also an important truth to which we look forward that at the eschaton the Father will most supremely—and therefore most kenotically—give the Spirit to the Son. Admittedly, Pentecost is only eschatological in a proleptic sense, expressed through the metaphor of first-fruit (e.g., Rom 8:23). But precisely insofar as first-fruits point forward *and are themselves part of* the full and final harvest, so too does the pentecostal kenosis of the Father point forward to and participate in a full and final eschatological kenosis of the Father towards the Son: the "final" eternal state of these persons is that the Father eternally and kenotically pours his life-nature out in love to the Son. He puts his own life at the Son's disposal.

The Father's Primal Kenosis

It is relatively easy to see a kenosis of the Father in the events of Pentecost. However, can this kenosis of the Father be identified elsewhere in the history of God's dealing with the world? Moltmann believes it can: he finds the kenosis of the Father in the events of the cross. The Father gives away the Son, but in doing so experiences God-forsakenness—self-emptiedness—in and through the Son. The Father "does not merely enter into the situation; he also accepts and adopts it himself, making it part of his own eternal life."[46] One is encouraged by Moltmann's explorations to seek the kenosis of the Father elsewhere as well. Once the thought is implanted in the mind, it "leaps out" in the incarnation. The Father's sending of the Son surely involved a self-emptying. This is not to suggest the crude conclusion that the Son's arrival on earth left the Father lonely in heaven.[47] Quite apart from challenging the traditional notion of the eternal creative Word's continued upholding of the universe during his incarnate earthly ministry,[48] it fails to do full justice to the biblical testimony to the relationship that the heavenly Father and earthly Son Jesus enjoyed. Nonetheless, for the Father to have sent his Son into the world, knowing what the world would do to him, must surely have cost deeply within the Father's own being.

We can "trace" this kenosis of the Father further still, into eternity: to the generation of the Son. While traditional christology speaks of the eternal generation of the Son, it speaks less often of the "other side of the coin": the eternal *kenosis* of the Father in and through this generation. But more recent theology has gone where classical theism feared to tread. Balthasar is remarkably outspoken: "We shall never know how to express the abyss-like depths of the Father's self-giving, that Father who, in an eternal 'super-Kenosis', makes himself 'destitute' of all that he is and can be so as to bring forth a consubstantial divinity, the Son. Everything that can be thought and imagined where God is concerned is, in advance, included and transcended in this self-destitution which constitutes the person of the Father."[49] This is

---

46. Moltmann, *Trinity and Kingdom*, 119. He also finds the kenosis of God in creation: the omnipresent God has to "create space" for creation to inhabit (*Trinity and Kingdom*, 59).

47. McGrath quotes the hymn by Germanus in the seventh century: "The Word becomes incarnate and yet remains on high!" (*Understanding the Trinity*, 122).

48. On this point, see Lossky, *Mystical Theology*, 144; Lane, "Cyril of Alexandria," 292; and, from a different perspective, Lewis, *Between Cross and Resurrection*, 171, n. 18.

49. Balthasar, *Mysterium Paschale*, viii. Alan Lewis makes a similar point in less

a remarkable piece of writing. It cuts to the heart of what it must have cost the Father to "share" divinity with the Son. If one's immediate reaction is to state that Balthasar is exaggerating (after all, the eternal generation of the Son did not cost the Father his divinity), one must understand that for Balthasar, the generation of the Son is not simply a costly act in and of itself: it cannot be undertaken, in divine foreknowledge, without accepting too the cost of the cross, where the Father's—as well as the Son's—kenosis would come to full expression before the eyes of humanity. Thus Balthasar can continue, in words that explicate the kenosis of both:

> God, then, has no need to "change" when he makes a reality of the wonders of his charity, wonders which include the Incarnation and, more particularly, the Passion of Christ. . . . All the contingent "abasements" of God in the economy of salvation are forever included and outstripped in the eternal event of Love. And so what, in the temporal economy, appears as the (most real) suffering of the Cross is only the manifestation of the (trinitarian) Eucharist of the Son: he will be forever the slain Lamb, on the throne of the Father's glory, and his Eucharist—the Body shared out, the Blood poured forth—will never be abolished, since the Eucharist it is which must gather all creation into his body. *What the Father has given, he will never take back.*[50]

I have so far in this section explored the kenosis of the Father in relation to the Son in the latter's exaltation, death, incarnation, and eternal generation. I have not yet considered whether the Father acts kenotically with respect to the Spirit. I must confess that I can find no evidence for this in the economy. In chapter 2, I did find a hint of the Father's eternal kenosis with respect to the Spirit, in that God the Father is spirit. This suggests that the sustenance of the Father's eternal existence and life is attributable to the Spirit's pervasion of his being. But in the economy I have not traced this dynamic. As the Spirit did not die, was not raised to life, and was not exalted to the Father's right hand, opportunities do not arise to parallel the Father's relationship with the Spirit to his relations with the Son. Only in the case of the Spirit's eternal procession can such parallels be analogically traced. The analogy is simple. As the eternal generation of the Son cost the Father in, to quote Balthasar again, "an eternal 'super-Kenosis', mak[ing]

---

outspoken terms: "Being or essence is exactly what the Father in love and self-giving shares with the Son and does not withhold" (*Between Cross and Resurrection*, 146).

50. Balthasar, *Mysterium Paschale*, ix; italics added.

himself 'destitute' of all that he is and can be so as to bring forth a consubstantial divinity," so we can infer the same kenosis must have played a part in eternally pouring forth the divine being of the Spirit.

THE EXALTATION OF THE FATHER

This section considers two matters: one is the Father's inherent glory—his self-consistent exaltation; the other is the dynamic exaltation that comes to the Father from the Son and the Spirit—they lift him up. In approaching this topic, I will as usual work from the divine history we find in Scripture. Here, the Son clearly glorified the Father, at least in the "external" sense of magnifying the Father's reputation among people. So, too, the Spirit glorified the Father by empowering the mission of the early church that brought people into a reconciled relationship with God. These elements of glorification in history are but small foretastes and preliminaries of the great eschatological glorification of the Father that the Bible promises. However, we can trace the Father's exaltation "back" into eternity as well as forward to the eschaton. First, then, I consider the Father's primal exaltation, before going on to discuss his economic and ultimate exaltation.

The Father's Primal Exaltation

The Bible clearly affirms the utterly and uniquely exalted nature of the monarchy of the Father. This is evident within the Trinity in terms of practical rule—who obeys whom—and in terms of origin. Jesus' life is clearly portrayed as one of obedience to the Father, both in the Gospels and in certain other texts such as Hebrews 5:8. The same is true of the Spirit, which being often portrayed in impersonal terms is even more clearly seen to act at the behest of God the Father. Turning from obedience to origin, the message is again unequivocal, as I indicated earlier in the chapter (and here I take up and extend some of the discussion introduced there). Jesus was "sent" by God into the world, as was the Spirit (e.g., Gal 4:6). The pre-existent origins of the Son, the Word, are not set out so clearly, but while texts such as John 1:1 and Philippians 2:6 might in isolation suggest that the Son is unoriginate, the early church was right, taking all into account, to decide that the Son is eternally generated by the Father.

So the Bible is clear: the Father is the ultimate fount and monarch. But this idea is contested by some theologians today as being unduly "subordinationist." For Moltmann, it carries the problem that this justifies the monarchical oppression of some humans by others.[51] But Moltmann has to recognize the consistent testimony to the Father's uniquely exalted place in the Trinity. This forces him to divide his discussion of the Trinity between God's nature, in which he does allow for the Father's supremacy, and the trinitarian relations, in which he does not.[52] This distinction, which smacks of artificiality,[53] causes him to run into a problem: he veers towards positing some logically pre-existing "divine nature" from which Father, Son, and Spirit derive. He is, for example, forced to write of differentiating "between the relationship of the Holy Spirit to the being of the Godhead, and his relationship to the Father and to the Son."[54] What is this "being of the Godhead" that can be distinguished from the being of the three persons of the Trinity? Moltmann seems to have posited a "quaternity" of: the Divine Substance; the Father; the Son; and the Spirit. I will return to this matter later in this section.

Others go further than Moltmann. They take the "flattening" of the Trinity to a more logical conclusion. The Father must not be allowed any monarchy—any unique exaltation in the Trinity—at all. D'Costa, who is stringently critical of Moltmann in this respect, is one such writer: to speak of the "first"[55] person of the Trinity as exalted over the others by being their cause and origin runs into three problems, he claims. First, an anthropomorphic idolatry occurs. To "upload" the earthly concept of "father" to the divine is "univocally attributing to God what we find in the created world."[56] Second, because the concept is also gendered, when the Father is exalted within the Trinity, "patriarchal subordinationism occurs."[57] Thirdly, to prioritize the Father thus is a "denigration of the Spirit and the denigration of co-equal subsistent relations as constituting the very being of God."[58]

---

51. Moltmann, *Trinity and Kingdom*, 157–58; and compare the comment by LaCugna, in a similar context, about "those whose full personhood has been diminished by patterns of hierarchy and inequality" (*God for Us*, 273).

52. Moltmann, *Trinity and Kingdom*, 165, 177, 183.

53. For other criticisms of Moltmann on this point, see D'Costa, *Sexing the Trinity*, 84–88.

54. Moltmann, *Trinity and Kingdom*, 186.

55. D'Costa generally places the word *first* in inverted commas when referring to the Father (e.g., *Sexing the Trinity*, 77, 82; though contrast 83).

56. Ibid., 42–43; cf. 21, 77.

57. Ibid., 77.

58. Ibid., 22–23, in discussion with Thomas Weinandy (cf. ibid., 89).

D'Costa's alternative is a Trinity in which no one person is "above" the others in any sense. The term "Father," which if used at all should be used with a liberal mix of other biblical metaphors that are non-gendered, refers only to entire relationality and reciprocity.[59]

These "flattened, democratized" presentations of the Trinity have departed markedly from those offered by the New Testament. The God of the Bible is much more hierarchical than Moltmann and D'Costa allow. We might argue from our cultural vantage point that the Bible is culturally determined and that its view of God is simply a product of its cultural and social location. However, we need to exercise some humility at this point and recognize that God's chosen vessel of self-revelation was a male Jew living in the ancient (from our stance) world on the eastern shores of the Mediterranean. We have no other. While we might struggle with questions about how the universal God can choose to be revealed in and through the particulars of this Jewish man, I repeat that we have no other. If this Jewish man of ancient Mediterranean culture is in fact the exact impress of God's being, then we must accept that, for example, his insistence in word and deed that he was *obedient* to the Father displays not only an entirely normal cultural response to an authority figure but also a genuine aspect of the trinitarian relations.

However, how can the exalted monarchy of the Father be maintained in the face of D'Costa's and Moltmann's criticisms that this is grossly anthropomorphic, dangerously patriarchal, derogatory of the Son and the Spirit, and liable to justify the monarchical oppression of some humans by others? To tackle the last first, D'Costa actually supplies a response to Moltmann's criticism. D'Costa observes that Moltmann makes an assumption that how God is seen will necessarily lead to a certain type of government or leadership among people. He offers life in the Old Testament prophetic tradition as a historical combination of a firmly hierarchical view of God with a human society where kingly leadership could be challenged by the prophets.[60] But then D'Costa's claim that granting the Father a uniquely exalted status in the Trinity as origin, for instance, of the other persons, justifies abusive sexist patriarchalism is surely to fall into the same trap. One cannot draw such a clear-cut parallel. To give one example, Pentecostalism, though not uniformly, contains within its history accounts of the remarkable emancipation of women in church groups that maintained a

59. Ibid., 81, 83, 94.
60. Ibid., 40.

highly traditional view of God—groups that would never dream of calling God anything other than "He," and would never dream of referring to the Father as "Parent," for example.[61] The criticism of anthropomorphism is not as strong as it initially sounds. First, God has taken the initiative in developing significant points of contact between the divine and the human: God created humanity in God's own image, and even more to the point the Word became human flesh. Secondly, anthropomorphism is actually useful, as long as one recalls that one is engaging in *metaphor*.

It is the criticism that exalting the Father derogates the Son and the Spirit that I want to attend to in most detail. To acknowledge the exalted monarchy of the Father is to risk the danger of subordinationism: the Son and the Spirit appear to be subordinate to the Father in a way that questions their divinity. Moltmann again is an example of someone who expresses this concern. He says that the Father cannot be an authoritarian, patriarchal kind of Father. His fatherhood must only be understood as the fatherhood of the Son, and certainly cannot be fatherhood over creation, for the latter would be unduly hierarchical and authoritarian.[62] But Moltmann's form of trinitarian belief protects him from subordinationism at a high price. His version of the Trinity is flattened out in a way that skews the biblical picture.

I believe that a better answer to the problem is at least approached by Macchia. With frequent reference to Pannenberg, Macchia indicates that the Father's exalted monarchy is "hemmed in" by the limits of reciprocation. The Father "needs" the Son and the Spirit in order to be, within the Trinity, monarch. Without a Son, the Father is no Father. Without the Spirit, the Father is no sender. Thus, to say that the Father is monarch is not to say that the Father is absolute ruler, with no reference to the existence of the Son and the Spirit. Rather, it is to say, among other things, that the Son and the Spirit, by means of their eternal existence, give to the Father the capacity to be monarch.[63]

This is a start, but I do not think this is the whole answer to Moltmann or D'Costa's concerns. All rulers need the existence of others in order to

---

61. See articles in Alexander and Yong, *Philip's Daughters*. E.g., Powers writes of the "unprecedented number of women being licensed or ordained in Pentecostal churches" in its early years. She continues, "even today, over fifty per cent of all women who have ever been ordained come from the Holiness-Pentecostal tradition" ("Pentecostalism 101," 134).

62. Moltmann, *Trinity and Kingdom*, 162–64.

63. Macchia, *Baptized in the Spirit*, 122–24. D'Costa also makes considerable use of Pannenberg (*Sexing the Trinity*, 89–93).

rule over them. The answer also needs the insights that kenosis can offer. The Father's rule over the Son and the Spirit is eternally kenotic. The rule is a self-giving, self-emptying one. Only by recognizing the extraordinary loving kenosis of the Father in and from all eternity can we support the idea of the monarchy of the Father. Only when the kenosis of the Father is deliberately brought into focus can we dare to gaze at the exaltation of the Father.

In other words, the answer does not lie in Moltmann or D'Costa's theses. It lies in the Father's kenosis. The Father's authority over the Son was and is a *kenotic* authority. It is not the case that the Father and the Son discuss together and come to a mutually agreed decision, as Moltmann effectively implies. No—the Father "calls the shots." The Son obeys. The Father sends. The Son and the Spirit are sent. But the initiator in these dynamics is filled with utterly selfless kenotic love for the other persons of the Trinity. In brief, what recognition of the kenosis of the Father offers is an understanding that the trinitarian relations are deeply reciprocal. While the Father is ever the fount and originator, there is not a "lording it over" of the Son and the Spirit. The Father's role might be described as "servant-leadership." The Father's role is not egalitarian but neither is it totalitarian, egocentric, or megalomaniac.

This exalted monarchy of the Father is also a most important factor in the unity of God. Moltmann is careful to avoid appealing to the monarchy of the Father to defend divine unity, pointing out not only, as I noted above, that this leads to the justification of acts of human monarchy, where one rules over others to their detriment, but also that traditional arguments for God's unity fail to recognize the mutual relations of the persons of God. Keenly sensitive to the ills that have been perpetrated in the name of a monarch-like God, Moltmann cannot conceive that God could in fact be so. God must be a "community" of loving, reciprocally relating persons. It is interesting to note at this point how often Moltmann's form of social trinitarianism has been criticized for its dallying with tritheism.[64] Moltmann's social trinitarianism is so concerned to "level" the Trinity and deny leadership to it that he cannot adequately define the divine unity and his trinitarianism does indeed sit awkwardly close to tritheism. The three

---

64. See Lewis, *Between Cross and Resurrection*, 219; cf. Jowers, "Theology of the Cross as Theology of the Trinity," 26 and n. 87—Jowers offers a noteworthy bibliography of similar critics. In contrast, Bauckham defends Moltmann's social trinitarianism against any charge of tritheism (*Theology of Jürgen Moltmann*, 25).

persons are so distinct in their relations with one another as to appear all too easily to be three Gods.

Moltmann is of course aware of this danger. He appeals to the concept of perichoresis to protect the divine unity. But his argument at this point seems unconvincing. Perichoresis as described by him only seems to be functional—it refers to the mutuality of loving relation in the Trinity. This is evidenced by his repeated use of the phrases, "interpersonal, perichoretic" and "relational, perichoretic."[65] Thus the unity of God, as presented by Moltmann, seems to be no more fundamental to God's being than the unity of a family is to the being of one or all of its members.

I will return to study the nature of perichoresis in chapter 5. For the purposes of this section on the Father's primal exaltation, however, I simply propose that the unity of God is actually protected, according to scriptural testimony, by the exalted monarchy of the Father. He is the head of Christ. He sends the Spirit. It is to the Father that both owe their eternal existence. One must acknowledge the usefulness of such terms as unity of "substance" but also recognize their danger. This example implies that there is some prior substance, known as "God," of which Father, Son, and Spirit are "merely," so to speak, examples. The resulting picture almost seems to be of four "somethings" comprising God: first, divine substance, then, formed "from" this, the three persons: Father, Son and Holy Spirit.[66] It is better, surely, to see the unity of God invested within the monarchy of the Father.

At this point, the picture offered to us by Irenaeus, and often repeated since, of the Son and the Spirit as the two hands of God comes to mind (see chapter 3), as therefore does an instrumental model of the Trinity. In this model the one divine person, God the Father, acts by means of the Son and the Spirit, as his word and breath or his right and left hands. However, the monarchy of the Father is not foreign to a social model of the Trinity either. The perichoretic relations of the persons do not necessarily need to be *equal* relations or relations of equals. I have, for instance, already indicated that their kenosis is not identical—of equal quality, we may guess, but not of equal type. In that it is true to say that the Father generates the Son but the Son does not generate the Father, further inequality of relation can be

---

65. Moltmann, *Trinity and Kingdom*, 186–88.

66. For criticisms of this "quaternity," see, e.g., Lewis, *Between Cross and Resurrection*, 205–6; Lossky, *Mystical Theology*, 56, 62, 64–65; Rahner, *The Trinity*, 68–70; Alan Torrance, *Persons in Communion*, 236. See also above within this subsection.

seen. Perichoresis does not need to be seen as an *alternative* to the Father's monarchy as sole cause."[67]

The Father's Economic and Eschatological Exaltation

Perhaps nothing is more obvious, in terms of the type of trinitarian discussion I am advancing, than to assert that in the economy the Father is exalted by the Son and the Spirit. I have written about this already in the previous chapter and little more needs to be discussed at this stage. I only want to share the insight presented by Yong when he writes, with reference to the work of David Coffey, "the 'incarnation' of the Spirit is detectable in the love that those in the body of Christ show to one another, to the world, and to God, each integral aspects of the movement in and by the Spirit 'inward' back to the Father through recreation in the image of the Son."[68] What is fascinating about this is the sense of direction towards the Father. To exalt the Father is to point to the Father. All eyes should be on the Father. There is no justification for being distracted from him. One of Smail's relevant books is titled, *The Forgotten Father*. We must not forget the Father.

When we turn our attention from the economic exaltation of the Father to his final eschatological exaltation, a key text is 1 Corinthians 15:28. I have studied this topic and this text in detail in chapter 3 and I will not repeat that detail here. Suffice it to mention at this point that here we are left in no doubt by Paul that the final state of all things will see not just the ultimate triumph and glorification of God, but of the Father specifically, as even the Son himself is subjected to him. To quote Smail, "just as the Father is the source of everything both in creation and redemption, so also he is the goal of everything, and the mission of the Son and of the Spirit is to advance his glory and let him be all in all."[69]

CHAPTER CONCLUSIONS

In this chapter I have considered the distinctions and commonality between the Father and the Son. I had to acknowledge that while the distinctions are

---

67. LaCugna suggests that, historically, perichoresis *did* take the place of the Father's person as the basis for defending God's unity in those early accounts of the Trinity that emphasized the relations of the persons (*God for Us*, 270).

68. Yong, *Spirit-Word-Community*, 68–69.

69. Smail, *Forgotten Father*, 21.

clear, the commonality at an ontological level is not as observable in the New Testament as it is between the Spirit and the Father on the one hand, and the Son and the Spirit on the other. It is necessary to consider the logic behind incarnational christology, which lies beyond the scope of this book, to understand the cogency of the view that there is an identity of being between the Father and the Son.

The Father can be considered impersonally, in ways which serve to protect Christians from the error of "domesticating" God, but the primary presentation of the Father is personal, and in keeping with the key aspect of personal relationships that I have sought to explore—kenosis—the Father's kenosis towards the Son can be discovered, when careful consideration is given, in several respects. The Father's kenotic relationship with the Spirit cannot so readily be established through study of the economy, even though it is perhaps detectable in God's simply being spirit. The Father's kenosis towards the Son can be seen at Pentecost, when the Father, so to speak, divests himself of any right to a sole place on the throne and of the sole right to grant the Spirit. This divestment of rights can be understood to be eternal. Furthermore, kenosis can be seen in "eternity past." For the Father to grant eternal existence to the Son is not only to "share" divinity with another but also to accept the destiny of the Son and the cost therein destined for both. No greater expression of the selfless love of the living God could be imagined than to empty oneself of all for the sake of the divine other.

The Father who kenotically empties himself in love is also the Father who is eternally exalted. The Father's primal exaltation is seen in his being the origin of the eternal existence, life, and divine glory of the Son and the Spirit. They owe all to him. The subordinationism this implies does not threaten the persons of the Son or the Spirit, precisely because this Father loves them in an eternal kenosis. He empties himself of sole glory in order to exalt them to the name of "God" and to that of "life-giver." The Father's eschatological exaltation also reflects the eternal dynamic of the trinitarian relations. To state that the Father will finally be "all in all" (1 Cor 15:28) is not to suggest that in the final state of things the persons— the relating selves—of the Son or the Spirit will be subsumed into that of the Father. Rather, it is to recognize that all eyes will be on the Father. His ultimacy and totality will be clear for all to experience in every respect. While Pentecost began, for those who had recently started to follow Jesus, with experience of the Spirit poured out, and while it thereby revealed the extraordinary glory of the Son, yet ultimately it was *for* the Father. The same could be said of creation, of the incarnation, of the cross, of the resurrection, of, indeed, the whole economy. The same can be said of eternity. All is for the Father, as in love the Father is for all.

5

Pentecost and the Trinity

INTRODUCTION

IN THIS BOOK I have been looking at the Trinity from the viewpoint of Pentecost. Certain consequences have transpired. The first is that I have found myself starting with the Spirit. It was the Spirit, after all, that the first disciples most immediately experienced. What link their experiences had with God or with the present status of Jesus were matters of the faith that built on this experience. So I too start with the Spirit and suggest a thoroughly pneumatological trinitarianism. Starting with the Spirit entails a second important consequence, which is that I have found myself invited to think about God in ways that include impersonal aspects as well as personal ones. This breadth of view has its impact on how one "models" the Trinity. In my view, no one model will suffice. A third consequence, which depends upon my viewing the trinitarian persons as *persons*, in a "naive" straightforward way, is that I could not ignore loving selfless kenosis. I will consider all these important aspects in this final chapter. In many ways, too, this chapter will serve to summarize the findings of my previous chapters.

In the next section, I will summarize my thoughts about the twin ideas of kenosis and exaltation that have been so central to this book's thesis. Then, I will go on to consider the matter of reciprocation and the degree of equality and inequality that can be seen in the Trinity, for instance relating to personhood and impersonhood. Thereafter, I will discuss the nature of perichoresis in order to explicate the unity of God in the face of trinitarian distinctions and plurality. In the subsequent section, I will consider the use of models in characterizing the Trinity. I will need both to set out what useful models I think there are and also to indicate how these models might relate to one another. Finally, I want to consider a brief survey of what I may call the "missing chapter" in this book. It was tempting to write a chapter on the Trinity and humanity but I decided not to. I will briefly set out what it might have covered and why I have decided not to include it.

KENOSIS AND EXALTATION

Throughout the book, I have explored the eternal mutual movements in which each divine person empties the self of self in order to elevate the other or the others. This dynamic within the life of God lies, I believe, at the heart of the trinitarian relations. It is the ultimate expression of selfless love for the living God to undergo genuine kenosis for the sake of the divine other. This is visible to the eye of faith through the divine actions expressed in the economy and is "visible" to the pneumatological imagination in the immanent Trinity of eternity. These are not polar opposites. God is eternal and yet God is also acting and becoming. The final eschatological state of the Trinity, expressed in the eternal being of the immanent Trinity but not yet been fully seen in the time-bound activity of the economic Trinity, will nevertheless be expressed at the end of this world's history. Both God's primal and eschatological states are easier to identify with the eternal nature of the Trinity than are the "works in progress" that make up the dynamics of the economy, but the incarnation and Pentecost must not be ignored in this regard. They offer the clearest, sharpest evidence for the divine relations at work in the economic Trinity. Thus, what emerges is an enduring dynamic reciprocal "dance" of the persons of the Trinity, in which each ceaselessly empties self in order to exalt the other, and in return as "reward" is exalted by the other.

Within this world's history and starting from Pentecost, especially as conceived by Luke but also as an umbrella term for the new covenant experience of the Spirit of Christ, I have consistently found the inner dynamic of the relationships within the Trinity to be a loving mutuality of kenosis and exaltation. This pair of loving activities has in many ways been my focus. I have suggested that trinitarian relations, including the eternal generation of the Son and the eternal procession of the Spirit, flow from this. I have suggested that Pentecost, and most particularly Acts 2:33, has offered a window into this trinitarian kenosis and exaltation as an expression of divine love, both as it is expressed in the economy and is it is expressed within the invisible realm of the immanent Trinity.

I have discovered that kenosis is identifiable in the roles and relations of all three persons of the Trinity. The kenosis to which I have perhaps given greatest attention is the Spirit's kenosis in what Moltmann called, as I have noted earlier, a reversal of relationship.[1] I have observed how, as long as the language was used loosely, one might helpfully speak of a kenosis of the Son in the incarnation in which the Son placed himself "beneath" the Spirit, such that the Spirit became "Lord" of the Son. For example, the Spirit sent the Son Jesus into the wilderness after his baptism. Conversely, after the ascension we can delineate a kenosis of the Spirit with respect to the Son that placed the Spirit "beneath" the Son now, so that at and after that point, the Son was "Lord" of the Spirit in the sense that the Son sent the Spirit (though, of course, from the Father). Beyond Pentecost, there are various stages in the economy when the kenotic Spirit's role is visible in exalting the Son and thereby the Father. This is wonderfully demonstrated in the observation that the dove *descended* to Jesus. The analogical conclusion can be drawn that the Spirit acts thus in eternity: by means of the kenosis of self, the Spirit eternally exalts the Son ensuring the Son's utter glory. The dynamic includes the Spirit's role in the eternal generation of the Son. I also suggested that one can see the Spirit's kenosis in the Spirit's willingness, as a person, to be understood in impersonal terms: the person of the Spirit is, so to speak, even prepared to go without personhood.

The kenosis of the Son is the one that I have had to introduce least, as it has been written about at length by others and is most obviously attested within the New Testament. Interestingly, I did not detect a kenosis of the Son in the events of Pentecost—far from it. However, I considered the Son's incarnational and cruciate kenosis and extended discussion, as some others have before me, beyond these to the Son's primal kenosis—an eternal truth that expresses itself through the economy—and to his eschatological kenosis. Only by eternal kenosis does the eternally exalted Son have a role in the procession of the Spirit. Similarly, the kenotic Son brings definition to and exalts the Spirit and the Father. Undoubtedly, the Son's kenosis is "counter-balanced" by his exaltation. The Son's exaltation is highlighted at Pentecost, as the Son even grants the Spirit, and at the eschaton, as every enemy is placed beneath his feet.

---

1. Moltmann, *Trinity and Kingdom*, 89.

I suspected the Father's kenosis in relation to the Spirit in that the Father perhaps allows himself to exist only in and by the Spirit. The Father's kenosis towards the Son can be seen at Pentecost, which expresses the Father's eternal willingness to divest himself of any right to a sole place on the throne, and of the sole right to grant the Spirit. Equally, for the Father to grant eternal existence to the Son is not only to "share" divinity with him but also to accept the destiny of the Son and the cost therein destined for both. This kenotic Father is the Father who is eternally exalted. The Father's primal exaltation is seen in his being the origin of the eternal existence, life, and divine glory of the Son and the Spirit. The subordinationism this implies does not threaten the persons of the Son or the Spirit, because this Father loves them in an eternal kenosis. He empties himself of sole glory so as to exalt them, with the result that each is "God" and each is "life-giver." The Father's eschatological exaltation also reflects the eternal dynamic of the trinitarian relations. The Father will finally be "all in all" because the Son and the Spirit, in their eternally kenotic relations with the Father, are lovingly willing to give him all the ultimate glory. While Pentecost began with experience of the Spirit poured out, and while it thereby revealed the glory of the Son, yet it pointed forward to an eschaton that is *for* the Father. The whole of the economy is directed towards the eschaton. The same can be said of the dynamics of eternity. As the Trinity fashioned on Pentecostal thinking is dynamic rather than static, the Trinity is eschatological: God is active and is "going somewhere." Eternity has broken into time in the economies of the Son and the Spirit but the ultimate "economy of the Father" is yet to come.[2] The Son will hand everything over to the Father, so that ultimately it is the Father who is the first and the last. The Son and the Spirit kenotically lay down their glory before him.

RECIPROCATION IN THE TRINITY

Reciprocation in this context refers to a dynamic within relationships and so between persons. It presupposes distinctions of being and therefore the capacity for the personal self to relate to non-self. Thus, an early requirement in this section is to summarize the findings of previous chapters on both the distinctions of the Father, the Son, and the Spirit in the Trinity, and on the degree of personhood and impersonhood that can be found in

2. I echo the titles of chapters 7 and 8 ("The Economy of the Son"; "The Economy of the Holy Spirit") in Lossky, *Mystical Theology*.

God. With this task in mind, the next two paragraphs merely condense the findings of previous chapters.

Of the three persons of the Trinity, the Spirit's being is the hardest to identify. The Spirit is not a created heavenly intermediary but is best understood as God's own being or as an extension of God the Father's own self towards all else. Regarded instrumentally, the Spirit is the means of the Father's establishment the Son in eternity. Equally, the Spirit is the means of the communication of love between the Father and the Son. By way of the incarnation, the being of the Son is more clearly on display than that of the Spirit. The Son is not a created intermediary or a second God. Neither is the Son merely identifiable with the Spirit, though the two are very closely linked in New Testament thought. The Son is divine and is distinguishable in the life of the Trinity. The Son's roles within the Trinity include a part in the procession of the Spirit: the Spirit proceeds from the Father through the Son. When I considered the distinctions and commonality between the Father and the Son, I had to acknowledge that though the distinctions are clear, the commonality is not as observable in the New Testament as it is between the Spirit and the Father or the Son and the Spirit. The Father is the ultimate fount and cause: the Father is Father in that he eternally generates the Son through the Spirit. So too is the Father the ultimate cause of the Spirit's eternal existence and life, pouring out the Spirit into this existence through the Son.

The Spirit can be viewed in both impersonal and personal ways, but ways of viewing the Spirit impersonally rise more easily to the surface in both the New Testament and typical Pentecostal experience. Viewing the Spirit as personal is not impossible, however. It arises from recognition that the Spirit's actions in relation to the Father and the Son are kenotic. That the Son is personal is considerably easier to demonstrate from the New Testament than that the Spirit is personal. Indeed, the overriding New Testament characterizations of the Son are of a person. This is reinforced in normal Pentecostal religious experience. In contrast, though the New Testament witnesses provide ample reason for ascribing impersonhood to the Spirit, only a slim sample provide a basis for ascribing such impersonhood to the Son. However, this impersonal view of the Son is not without its uses. Taken together with an instrumental approach to the Spirit it provides a foundation for an instrumental model of the Trinity. The Father can be considered impersonally in ways that serve to protect us from domesticating God. However, the primary New Testament presentation of the Father is personal. This is true in terms of the Father's relations with Christian believers but seems especially true of his relationship with the Son. In keeping with this, the Father's kenosis towards the Son can be discovered in several respects. In keeping, too, with the possibility of seeing personhood in all—Spirit, Son, and Father—is the possibility of tracing reciprocation.

Turning, then, specifically to reciprocation, I commence once more with Acts 2:33. All I am concerned to note at this stage, having considered various aspects of this text in previous chapters, is that it can be seen as a fulcrum, in time, between the Spirit being "Lord of the Son," and the Son being "Lord of the Spirit." This seems to me to be highly revelatory for the way in which the persons of the Trinity reciprocate with one another in eternity. None is selfishly motivated to hold on to glory. Each is ready, in deference to the others, to stoop low in kenotic love, thereby exalting the other. The whole dynamic of kenosis followed by exaltation, and of kenosis leading to the exaltation of the other, is exquisitely expressed in the kenosis and exaltation that I have sought to demonstrate from Acts 2:33. This reciprocal vertical movement is well expressed in the perichoretic metaphor of the dance.

However, it has also become clear that the nature of the reciprocation evident between the persons of the Trinity is limited. There are points at which no reciprocation is seen to occur. For example, while an economic kenosis of the Spirit is discernible, no eschatological exaltation of the Spirit is evident as such. The degree to which speculation about the immanent Trinity may move beyond the perspectives offered by the economic Trinity is moot. One might be tempted to assume that, as there is a pentecostal kenosis of the Spirit, so there must be an eschatological exaltation of the Spirit, so as to "balance" the matter and thereby reward the Spirit for the prior kenosis. However, I am not convinced that this degree of assumption is warranted. There is an eternally kenotic aspect to the Spirit—the person without a face—that I do not see reciprocated in the other persons of the Trinity. Limitations to reciprocation are also evident in the relations of the Father to the Son and to the Spirit. The Father's kenosis, real though it is, does not involve his letting go of being the source and fount of the eternal existence and divinity of the Son and the Spirit. One cannot find the type of self-abasement that ever places him "beneath" the Son or the Spirit. The Father is always and ever first. While it is vital to see reciprocity in the trinitarian relations, there is no need to imagine the trinitarian persons as three dancers who have an equal say in the moves. The Father is the leader of the dance. In other words, there is, so to speak, an inequality among the persons of the Trinity—there is a limit to the reciprocation that one can detect.

As soon as I write this I must recognize the "danger" of suggesting a Trinity ruled by an autocratic Father. However, the answer to this danger is not to "democratize" the Trinity. Some modern theology has so "flattened" or "democratized" the Trinity that what has been lost has been a truth that must be held in paradoxical tension with the very real equality within the Trinity. I have sought to demonstrate in earlier parts of the book that an important corollary to the idea of kenosis that I have explored at such length is that there is no need to "flatten out" the relationships in the Trinity to guard them, so to speak, from the autocracy of the Father. The Father's kenosis—or in other words, the Father's utterly selfless self-giving love for the Son and the Spirit expressed in the most sublime and unimaginable self-emptying—is what actually guards the Trinity against a paternal "corruption of power." This is true even if reciprocation cannot be detected in every aspect of these relationships.

Another way in which one can detect a sense of inequality within the Trinity is with respect to the degree of personhood that each person exhibits. I disagree with Baillie, who wrote, "God is always and wholly and in every respect *personal*. Nothing in God is impersonal. His Word is personal. His Spirit is personal. . . . God is the only perfectly personal Being."[3] In contrast, I believe there is value in considering both personhood and impersonhood with respect to all three persons of the Trinity, as I have explored in previous chapters. Each has both personal and impersonal characteristics. This combination of personhood and impersonhood within the Trinity does not threaten the use of the word "person" when referring to the Father, the Son, and the Spirit. However, there is, so to speak, an imbalance in the Trinity with respect to personhood and impersonhood. The majority of biblical pictures of the Spirit are impersonal while in the main the picture painted of both the Father and the Son is personal. I do not thereby wish to imply that the Spirit as portrayed in the Bible is inferior to the Father or the Son. I simply note that there are differences that must be acknowledged and thereby note that in this further respect the genuine reciprocation that we detect in the Trinity has its limits.

---

3. Baillie, *God was in Christ*, 143. Baillie offered no reasoning behind these assertions.

GOD'S PERICHORETIC UNITY

The observation that the Spirit can usefully be viewed in impersonal terms as well as personal ones leads to diverse ways of defending and expressing the unity of God. These ways appear on the surface to be incompatible with each other but only in the same way that trinitarian doctrine itself, in terms of one God in three persons, expresses paradox—as does the incarnation. Trinitarians cannot be afraid of paradox. Viewing the Spirit functionally and then extending that perspective to the Son allows for a model of the Trinity that sees God as the Father who operates by means of right and left hands and speaks the Word by means of breath (an instrumental model of the Trinity). God speaks, with the Word carried on divine breath. God acts, with right and left hands in perfect coordination. It is pointless to try to separate the one who speaks from the speaker's out-breathed word. It is meaningless to say, "God's hand performed this deed, but God did not." In this case, the unity of God need hardly be discussed, for it is plain.

At the other end of the spectrum, so to speak, lies a view of the Spirit in fully personal terms. Viewing the Father and the Son in the same terms arises naturally both from New Testament material and from typical Christian experience. This tri-personal view leads to a relational, social model of the Trinity. It is this that has a much greater danger than does a functional model of slipping into ditheism or tritheism, for it accentuates the persons in relation to one another and therefore it is this social model of trinitarianism that has the greatest difficulty in suggesting how the unity of God is maintained. Moltmann offers a prime example of this. He has often been criticized for straying perilously close to tritheism in his presentation of the Trinity, and yet has actually gone to some lengths to demonstrate how this social Trinity is but one God.

There are two solutions to this problem that he rejects forthrightly and repeatedly. The first of these is the idea, false in his mind, that there is some "divine essence" behind the persons but in which all three persons participate.[4] I agree that this is an unnecessary and unhelpful idea. The Bible is clear—and so, in *some* respects, is Moltmann—that the Father is the source of the being of the persons. They do not originate from some eternally "pre-existing" essence. To posit as much would be to turn the Trinity into a Quaternity of Essence, Father, Son, and Spirit. The second

---

4. Moltmann, *Trinity and Kingdom*, 10–12, 17. However, I suggested in chapter 4 that Moltmann seems to fall into this very trap at times.

solution, also rejected by Moltmann, is that there is some unitary subject to which the threeness of the Trinity is secondary.[5] Here I must be more cautious in my degree of agreement with Moltmann. In effect, he is rejecting modal models of the Trinity—anything that smacks of unipersonhood. But my position is that, while the social model is primary, it needs to be partnered by an instrumental model. The Father can, as I have mentioned earlier in this section, be regarded as a single person with two hands. The extent of my agreement with Moltmann at this point is therefore limited but real: insofar as the social model is primary, I accept that the existence of a single subject cannot be regarded as the key explanation for the unity of the trinitarian God.

Having rejected these two explanations for God's unity, Moltmann offers his own: he sees the answer lying in the doctrine of *perichoresis*.[6] Traditional doctrines of the Trinity explain the unity of the three persons in terms of perichoresis, by which term is meant the mutual interpenetration of each divine person with the others. They belong to one another and share each other's "personal space." They are not divisible into individuals.[7] Moltmann refers at some length to the thinking on the subject of John of Damascus and, building on that discussion, offers a characterization of perichoresis that is entirely relational or interpersonal. As I showed in chapter 4, his linkage of perichoresis to the ideas of relationality and interpersonality is consistent and clear. Thus his implication is that the unity of God is found in the quality of relationships between the different persons of the Trinity. While this may be an enlightening way of viewing these relationships, it hardly represents an adequate way of framing the unity of God. God seems on Moltmann's account to be no more "one" than a human family is. Each person of the Trinity seems no more united to the others than each member of the family is to the others. In Moltmann's conception, then, the unity of God is fragile.[8]

5. Ibid., 13–16, 18.

6. Ibid., 175 and, more generally, 148–200.

7. The statement of the Council of Florence, in 1441, contained the words, "because of this unity the Father is wholly in the Son and wholly in the Holy Ghost; the Son is wholly in the Father and wholly in the Holy Ghost; the Holy Ghost is wholly in the Father and wholly in the Son" (quoted in Crisp, "Problems with Perichoresis," 137).

8. Moltmann appeals to the Father's being as sole cause and source but can only identify this in the divine essence, not in the trinitarian relations. As I set out in chapter 4, this is an unsatisfactory division of God's essence from the very relations that are essential to God's trinitarian being.

I want to agree with what Moltmann affirms but disagree with what he implicitly denies. I agree that perichoresis can be understood relationally. One graphic way in which this relational aspect is sometimes portrayed is, as I mentioned earlier in the chapter, through the metaphor of dance.[9] The origin of this comparison lies, it seems, in one understanding—probably a misunderstanding—of the etymology of the word "perichoresis" itself. It is viewed by some as rooted in the idea of dancing around each other. LaCugna admits that, "the philological warrant for this is scant."[10] Whatever the merits of the etymological link, James Barr showed long ago that etymology is no sure guide to a word's meaning.[11] Nevertheless, the idea of the eternal dance of the trinitarian persons has much to commend it, with or without an ancient verbal rootedness. Considered as a social entity, the Trinity is an *utterly* tight-knit unit of persons who relate to each other in *utter* intimacy. They dance together in beautifully and intimately coordinated moves. The moves are "vertical." Each stoops down to lift the other up. Each lovingly bows in order to exalt the other to a place of honor. Never does one promote the self at the expense of the other. The dance of relational perichoresis, then, speaks volubly of interpersonality, of intimacy, of empathy, and of course of movement. Furthermore, it highlights plurality in God: the "image of the dance forbids us to think of God as solitary."[12] However, this last quotation from LaCugna also emphasizes what is weak about this relational model of perichoresis if taken on its own. Whatever its attractions in expressing the dynamism of God, this way of understanding perichoresis clearly falls short of explaining or defending God's unity. The dance partners are just that: partners. They are two or more, not one. Moltmann's view of perichoresis is too limited.

At this point, my third way of viewing the Spirit offers explanatory aid. I turn aside now from considering the Spirit as a person. I return to impersonal ways of viewing the Spirit, but this time consider the impersonal Spirit as an entity rather than in purely functional terms. This supports the unity of God in indicating the *pervasion* of the being of God by the Spirit. While the Father is only and always the originator of the persons

9. See, e.g., Parry, *Worshipping Trinity*, 20; Yong, *Spirit-Word-Community*, 53, 56; Volf, *Exclusion and Embrace*, 129; cf., in fiction, Lewis, *Voyage to Venus*, 177 ("Some say there always is . . . dancing in Deep Heaven"), 181–88.

10. LaCugna, *God for Us*, 271–72.

11. For Barr's contribution, see Cotterell and Turner, *Biblical Interpretation and Linguistics*, 113–15.

12. LaCugna, *God for Us*, 272.

and actions of God, I seek to find this pervasion in the Spirit's impersonal being and activity, understanding that the Father pervades all that is God by means of the Spirit. I do not begin my discussion with reference to the Johannine Christ's declarations that he was in the Father and the Father in him (John 10:38).[13] My avoidance of this starting point is not so much that Jesus prayed for this dynamic to be shared by his followers (John 17:23), for even this creaturely perichoresis could be understood as engaging in the gracious overflow of the divine interpenetration. It is rather that I very much doubt whether any reference to ontological unity is intended here. It seems more likely that "in" is used in this context to express with great intensity what might be expressed less forcefully as "with." So, for example, if I were to say that my wife Alison is "in" me, I would not be claiming some perichoretic quality to our relationship on a par with that of the Trinity. I might rather mean that her cumulative influence on me after decades of marriage is so great that it pervades my being—it is "in" me—she is "in" me. I could make this point in mutual terms, without there necessarily being any sexual connotations: I am in my wife and she is in me. So in the case of Jesus and the Father, it seems more likely in the whole context of John's gospel that Jesus was claiming the utterly pervasive *influence* of the Father in all his being and doing rather than claiming an *ontological* pervasion.

Where then to start? I begin with my experience of the Spirit, trusting that I can assume that many of my readers share experiences in common with me. In contrast to my experience of the Father and the Son, my experience of the Spirit is such that I find it relatively difficult to distinguish between "the Spirit in me" and "me in me"—myself.[14] I claim no pantheistic ontological participation in the being of God. I simply mean that, in keeping with Paul's declarations in Romans 8:26–27, I sense that the Spirit crosses the "line" between divinity and humanity, coming to my side of the gulf and participating in my actions—in the case of Paul's reference, prayers—towards God and towards others. But I sense more: I sense that the Spirit participates not only in things as "superficial" as my actions, but participates in—has the upper hand in—my very being. If I say that the Spirit is "in" me, I mean more than when I say that my wife is "in" me. The Spirit reaches to the core of my being. The Spirit upholds the very fabric of

13. Unlike Volf, *Exclusion and Embrace*, 128.

14. Contrast Gunkel's interpretation of New Testament Christians' experiences, as reported by Rabens with reference to "a foreign being inside themselves" (Rabens, "Power from In Between," 139).

my existence. And I believe firmly that this is true for all life, let alone all humanity, while recognizing that Christians have a particular perception of it.

When I read the Gospel presentations of Jesus of Nazareth, I sense, by means of imaginative analogy, that Jesus participated in this same experience of the Spirit, though I read that in his case this was without limit (John 3:34), and so we must not be arrogant enough to imagine that we experience anything like all of the Spirit that Jesus did. My christology tells me that this participation in the life of the Spirit that was enjoyed by the human Jesus of Nazareth was at one and the same time experienced by the incarnate *Logos*—the eternal Son. By further extension, I can "cross the bridge" from the economic Trinity to the immanent Trinity at this point. For all eternity, I suggest, the Son experiences the Spirit in and as the very fabric of his own being, while also experiencing the Spirit as a gift from the Father. Thus the perichoresis of the Son by the Spirit is pervasive, not just relational. It is also reciprocal. The perichoresis of the Spirit by the Son is evident to our eyes only after Pentecost, but is thereby evident to our faith for all eternity. If a Christian such as the apostle Paul receives the Spirit *and thereby experiences the presence of the Son* then without doubt the person of the Son pervades the being of the Spirit.

Reciprocal pervasion between the Spirit and the Son, then, is relatively easy to suggest. It becomes harder to demonstrate when we move to consider pervasion by the Father, and pervasion of the Father by the Son. However, in the former case, there is another line to be pursued. It is the monarchy of the Father. As the fount of all that we call "God," the Father holds the Son and the Spirit in his being. He has not offered them the individuation that would have come about had he created them. They are eternal and uncreated. They are divine. This divinity is received from the Father but it remains the Father's divinity, for all divinity is from the Father. Thus in this sense at least, the Father's own being—his divinity—pervades the other two persons. I have explored this in chapter 4 in terms of the Father *giving* the Spirit to the Son—giving the Son the fabric of his own life and being. That leaves the pervasion of the Father by the Son. Beyond resort to "proof-texting" ("I am in the Father"; John 10:38), which I have already questioned, and resort to the argument of balance, I can offer no argument to support this aspect of pervasive perichoresis. I do not on that account suppose that it does not exist. I just sense that I cannot demonstrate it. Perhaps that is useful, for the post-incarnate Son is not just divine but human:

the Word became flesh and has not ceased to be thus. It might be going too far to say that we can demonstrate that the human *pervades* the divine.

I have discussed reciprocal divine pervasion at some length to show that the unity of God is thus defended: the persons do not just dance round each other; they permeate each other, to use LaCugna's term.[15] This idea of pervasion can also be expressed in terms of perichoresis, by drawing on another possible derivation of this word. Perichoresis does not only need to be understood in terms of a dance. It can also be understood, admittedly in a more static way, as penetration or containment. Each person penetrates the other; each person contains the other. This view of the word's etymology is probably better founded: it is more likely that the word "perichoresis" comes from the Greek for to "encompass," to "make room," or to "contain."[16] Each person contains the others in the sense of having the others within. I suggest that to maintain God's unity in the face of the sociality of the persons, one must hold onto this idea of perichoresis as well as the more dynamic, dance-like, one. LaCugna presents both these aspects. She refers to the "active sense" and the "passive sense" of perichoresis, indicating that the former is expressed also by the technical term "circumincession" and the latter by the confusingly similar term, "circuminsession."[17] Torrance too makes reference to both aspects of perichoresis: "the notion . . . has an active nuance as mutual movement as well as mutual indwelling."[18] In conclusion to this last part of the section, an impersonal but ontological view of the Spirit has helped to explicate a pervasive view of perichoresis that firmly articulates the unity of God. The one God pervades all of God's own being, speaking, and acting. God is, as Father, Son, and Spirit. The one God pervades God. There is one God.

A TRIAD OF TRINITARIAN MODELS

How might one conceive of the Trinity? What metaphorical models are available that enlighten our thinking? My pneumatological trinitarianism suggests three, following the three ways of viewing the Spirit that I have set out. In suggesting three models, I want to claim that there is no reason to be hesitant about resorting to more than model. It is quite acceptable to have

15. LaCugna, *God for Us*, 271.

16. Ibid., 312 n. 94; Torrance, *Trinitarian Perspectives*, 141.

17. LaCugna, *God for Us*, 272.

18. Torrance, *Trinitarian Perspectives*, 141.

two or more different models for the Trinity that can coexist. We recognize that all our views about God are limited by our finitude and the finitude of our environments. God is above and beyond, as well as within and beneath, our limited and finite thinking. Therefore, even the most helpful things we succeed in saying about God are only a partial reflection of the truth. Much or all of what we say about God is based on analogies with other phenomena from our finite environment—there is a metaphorical quality to it. Therefore models are both acceptable and necessary. Volf puts it well:

> Our notions of the triune God are not the triune God, even if God is accessible to us only in these notions. A certain doctrine of the Trinity is a model acquired from salvation history and formulated in analogy to our experience, a model with which we seek to approach the mystery of the triune God, not in order to comprehend God completely, but rather in order to worship God as the unfathomable and to imitate God in our own, creaturely way.[19]

No one model will capture the whole truth of God. Indeed, all of them put together will fail to do this, but as with many aspects of theology, a combination of models will help us to say something more useful about God than one model alone. The combination of such models is necessary, for as Volf observes, "each model is inadequate to the extent to which it fails to accommodate the truth of the other."[20] Each can enlighten the others, balance the others, and offer insights closed to the others. In this section, I will first summarize what my three models are and then consider how they might be seen to relate to each other.

The first model that I have been referring to is usually called a social model, though I think that the term "relational model" might be just as helpful. It focuses on the Father, the Son and the Spirit as persons in relationship with each other. Thus, particularly as it contrasts with the other models I will be suggesting, it could also be called a tri-personal model. It coheres remarkably with what I have been exploring concerning kenosis. Given that kenosis has been a central theme of my exploration, it naturally follows that I not only accept this model but also celebrate it. In fact, I suggest that it is the main model—the controlling metaphor. Its strength is in the relational dynamics of kenosis and exaltation that it explores with

19. Volf, *After our Likeness*, 198.

20. Volf, "Being as God Is," 5. For Volf's discussion of the models promulgated by Gregory of Nyssa (social) and Augustine (modal) and the ways that they both accommodated their models to the realities suggested by the other, see "Being as God is," 5–6.

respect to the Trinity. However, there are weaknesses. First, biblical foundations for viewing the Spirit as personal are sparse. So too are data from the early church: it would not be right to assume that teachers in the early church meant by "person" precisely what I have been meaning in this book. My answer to this first challenge has worked on the basis that once any justification emerges for seeing the Spirit in personal terms (which it does) then the Spirit's kenosis is seen in a considerable number of aspects of the economy. A second potential weakness is that there is debate about how this model can result in genuine trinitarianism rather than tritheism. My answers to this second challenge have drawn from both the concept of the Father as sole source and cause, and from the idea of perichoresis. However, I also want to stress in response to both challenges that what protects this model in my scheme, however vulnerable the model *on its own* might be to the charges, is precisely that it should not be regarded on its own. If it is held in creative paradoxical tension with the other models, this possibility is avoided.

The second model I have been setting out is an instrumental one. This model continues to regard the Father in personal terms but takes a different view of the Spirit or of both the Spirit and the Son. In the former case, the Son too is seen in personal terms. However, the Spirit's impersonhood comes into focus. The Spirit is regarded instrumentally as the means by which the Father and/or the Son act. In the latter case, the Son too is regarded impersonally. It seems to me that the former case gains common currency in typical modern Pentecostal worship and spirituality, where believers may equally pray, "Father, come by your Spirit" or, for example, "Jesus, heal by your Spirit." On the other hand, the latter picture, in which the sole person of the Father—God—acts by means of both the Son and the Spirit, coheres more with biblical imagery of the word and breath of God and with early church ideas of the Son and the Spirit as the right and left hands of God. This view of the Trinity can help to express the unity of God and the degree of inner coordination in divine being and actions. Smail expresses something of this when he writes: "If Son and Spirit are the two hands of God, as Irenaeus taught, they are, on all the New Testament evidence, closely clasped hands."[21] Equally, this view lends itself to a focus on the outward actions of God. Thus, with a slight change in the metaphor, Volf refers to the two arms of God, "by which humanity [is]

21. Smail, *Giving Gift*, 125.

. . . taken into God's embrace."[22] One might say that God's hands are open, not closed.

This model presents the hazard that the Spirit, or both the Son and the Spirit, may be regarded as starkly relegated beneath the person of the Father. An undue subordination may be inferred, not least because to the Father (and possibly the Son) is ascribed not only personhood but also ontology, while to the Spirit (and possibly the Son) no such ontology is ascribed but only functionality. I repeat, however, that the model is not to be seen in isolation but in creative paradoxical tension with the others. I also stress that I am not imagining that there are two different Spirits, one personal and the other functional. I am offering two models—two complex metaphors—that help us to imagine something of what the Spirit is and therefore something of what the Trinity is.

The third model is one I am calling a "substantial" model. It is likely to be the most controversial. It might be argued that it is unnecessary once the first two have been conceptualized or that it has no biblical foundation (see chapter 2). In this third model, the Father and the Son are once more seen in personal terms. The Spirit alone is seen as an impersonal divine entity entirely pervading both the persons and the relations of the Father and the Son. The difference between this third model and the second one is this. The instrumental model, set out in the previous paragraphs, does not regard the Spirit as an entity. The Spirit is a mode of operation, a means of expressing or achieving the words and actions of God. To put the matter in a brutally grammatical way, the Spirit is by that account an adverb, not a noun. For God to act "by the Spirit" is for God to act "spiritually." However, in this third model, the Spirit has entity. The biblical foundation is sparse, I admit. Perhaps the descending dove at Jesus' baptism comes to my rescue, though biblical metaphors of oil and water are not without merit. However, the conceptual foundation seems to me to be strong. If God is an entity—a noun, not merely an adverb or a verb—and as God is spirit, then "spirit" is likely to have ontology. I acknowledge that this syllogism may not make this conclusion logically or demonstrably necessary but it strikes me as likely. And a further likelihood is then that the Spirit has entity. However, the logical argument might be that divine being is personal: there can be no divine "member" that is not personal. I sought to address these concerns in chapter 2. I see good reason for maintaining a perspective on all three divine persons that allows for an impersonal approach as well as a personal

22. Volf, *Exclusion and Embrace*, 128.

one. I simply claim that the one where this is most obvious is the Spirit: the Spirit can be regarded as an impersonal entity. The value, then, of this third model is that it helps to make concrete the idea of divine pervasiveness. As long as the Spirit is only seen instrumentally as a mode of action, then divine pervasion, whether this be of another divine person or it be of creation, is likely only to be seen in terms of influence. "The Spirit in me," whether spoken by the Son or by a Christian, means no more than "God's (spiritual) *activity* within me." Once the Spirit is seen ontologically, "the Spirit is in me" can mean, "God's being is actually within." This third, substantial model strikes me as especially important in helping one to conceptualize the idea of *pervasive* perichoresis.

Insofar as three distinct models are all potentially helpful but only if not held in isolation, the question immediately arises about how they may fit together. Two answers can be given. First, they must simply sit in paradoxical tension with one another. This is such a common feature of ways in which we humans conceive God that I hope it needs no further introduction here.[23] It only needs to be repeated that trinitarianism itself is replete with paradox. The other answer is that these three models can work together in "perichoretic" unity. At this point, I am actually taking a leaf out of trinitarianism itself to explain the relationship between the models. I am suggesting that the very idea of perichoresis, developed to describe the relations of the three persons in the unity of God, functions as a good way of seeing the relationship between these three models of the Trinity. As in the case of the Trinity, this can be both a relational and a pervasive perichoresis. They are in *relation* to one another analogically, for they all refer to the Father, the Son, and the Spirit, and are in a sense metaphors of each other. They belong together, inform one another, "dance" together, and as such contribute each to the dynamic of the other: they work next to each other in dynamic symbiotic relationship, informing each other usefully. But these models must also *pervade* one another, so that none can be allowed to develop at the expense of the others. Each must be "shot through" with the others. One must not be allowed to raise its own voice to the exclusion of the others. As soon as one is mentioned, the others must immediately be brought to mind.

Having delineated these three models of the Trinity and their relationships with each other, I must indicate that my emphasis is on the social,

---

23. On the place of paradox in theology see, e.g., Baillie, *God Was in Christ*, chapter V.

relational model. It cannot function as the sole model but, overall, it does have more explanatory power than the instrumental model or substantial model. The social side to the Trinity is most obvious in the relationship between the Father and the Son, and this in turn is the *relationship* that is most obvious in the history of God's dealing with the world. Furthermore, as I have sought to indicate throughout the book, personal, relational kenosis lies at the heart of the Trinity. It is not surprising, therefore, that this model of trinitarian relations shines most brightly. The instrumental and substantial models, as important as I think they are, rest most firmly on the impersonal side to the Spirit's being and on how the Father and Son relate to this impersonal Spirit. As the Spirit is the least distinct of the trinitarian persons, it is not surprising that these instrumental and substantial sides of the Trinity are less explicable or describable. They are, however, indispensible.

TRINITY AND HUMANITY

It would be tempting at this point to add a final chapter of the book that sets out to relate my suggestions so far concerning the Trinity to various aspects of human life. It is tempting to consider a wide range of possible relations and discuss much of what has been written by a host of modern and ancient authors.

For example, worship and prayer springs to mind. I take to task the naivety that leads to such prayers as, "Father, thank you that you died on the cross for us" and "Father, thank you that you were born as a baby." I have heard these with more frequency than I would care to mention. However, beyond the need to "tighten" the vocabulary of Pentecostal prayer, there is a broader vein of practical theology to be mined: the persons of the Trinity are involved in exalting the others but primacy must be given to one aspect of this dynamic: the role of exalting the Father. First Corinthians 15:28 says as much, at least in respect of the Son's relationship to the Father. We have no reason to assume that the Spirit's relation to the Father would be any different. On that basis, as the church is called to walk in step with the Spirit and follow the path of the Son, the church's ultimate task is to glorify the Father.

Is worship of the Son, or indeed of the Spirit, then in some way wrong? Is prayer to either wrong? Robin Parry makes a call for worship and prayer to the Spirit in today's churches.[24] He notes that the Nicene Creed as developed in Constantinople in 381 contained the well-known words about the Spirit, "who with the Father and the Son together is worshiped and glorified." The absence of such worship and prayer in the New Testament does not worry Parry, who rightly sees the New Testament as setting up trajectories that in due course take Christian belief and practice beyond what was actually explicated in the New Testament. Of course, trinitarian doctrine and worship is an example of just this process. Parry's positive call is, however, carefully nuanced: the only worship of the Spirit that can properly be called Christian is that which recognizes wholeheartedly that the Spirit is the Spirit of God, the Spirit of Christ. This worship will always connect the Spirit to the Father and the Son. As Parry observes, the "Spirit's mission is tied up with Christ's mission, and worship focused on the Spirit *to the neglect of Christ* is dishonouring to the Spirit."[25] This matter of trinitarian worship deserves further careful discussion.

Another practical outworking that I would be tempted to explore would be the connection between the Trinity and Christian mission. This could be taken in several directions. Of relevance to this book's focus, for example, is Daugherty's conceptual link between kenosis in God and missional contextualization.[26] Implicit in this link is a suggestion that, as God is kenotic, so too should God's people be kenotic in their mission towards others. Of interest too would be the exaltation that follows kenosis; and this thought can be applied in a distinctively pneumatological way. In texts like James 4:10 ("be humble in front of the Lord and he will exalt you") we hear an echo of the Son's trinitarian relationship with the Father. Because we hear this echo, and emboldened by certain related New Testament promises (e.g., Rev 3:21; cf. 1 Cor 6:2–3) we dare to believe that the exaltation we will experience in the eschaton will in some way graciously reflect the ascension-exaltation of the Son to the Father's right hand, referred to in Acts 2:33. It is clear from these New Testament promises that they will not be fulfilled in and for us until that eschatological event. However, it is equally clear from numerous New Testament references that the Holy Spirit brings a foretaste of the eschaton to Christian experience during the church age.

24. Parry, *Worshipping Trinity*, 112–21.
25. Ibid., 119.
26. Daugherty, "*Missio Dei*," 165.

With all these factors in mind, one might be justified in daringly speculating that, just as the Holy Spirit proceeds in eternity from the Father through the exalted Son, and just as the same Spirit proceeds in time from the Father through the exalted Jesus, so too the Spirit proceeds to the world, during the church age, from the Father through the continuously-being-exalted church. We tread on sacred ground here. The church is not Christ. It is not the incarnation of the Word or the Son. But there are echoes of the Son's ministry in that of the church and there are echoes of the Son's exaltation in every way that the Father graciously fulfils his promise to lift up his people. It would be worthwhile to explore, from the perspective of the trinitarian discussion in this book, the church's calling to bring the Spirit to the world. When a Christian calls upon the Spirit to come in Jesus' name, or more daringly says words to the effect, "I anoint you with God's Spirit in Jesus' name," I suspect the Christian does not blaspheme.[27] This is perhaps an implication of John 20:21–22 and of the whole tenor of Acts that deserves further consideration.

Yet another matter about which this book invites further thought is that of the Trinity and leadership. Moltmann's trinitarianism fits his espousal of "flat," egalitarian forms of society. The one set out in this book, which gives more attention to the monarchy of the Father, coupled to loving kenosis, fits the servant leadership that the New Testament champions. Jesus did not exclude leadership but called for its underpinning in service and servanthood. The findings expressed so far in this book suggest to me that when Jesus called for his followers—those who aspired to leadership—to be "servant-leaders," he was not only calling them to follow his own example but was also calling them to follow the example that he saw set by his loving eternal Father, who led the Son and did so kenotically as a servant.

Finally, a topic that trinitarian discussion brings to the surface is that of gender. There are two related questions. One is of any possible genderedness in God. The other is whether the nature of the Trinity offers any lessons for human gender relations. On the first question, Thompson speaks for many in offering the "standard" answer: "There is, it is argued correctly, no gender in the deity."[28] Moltmann takes a more courageous stance: God "is a motherly Father. He cannot be understood to have a single sex, mascu-

---

27. I do not seek to judge the hearts of individuals. God alone knows if these words have ever been said blasphemously. I only wish to suggest that they are not necessarily blasphemous in and of themselves.

28. Thompson, *Modern Trinitarian Perspectives*, 115, cf. 116–17.

line, but must be understood to be bisexual or transsexual."[29] It may be that there is value in both Thompson's and Moltmann's assertions. Just as I have found warrant in viewing God as both personal and impersonal, so too there may be a case for seeing God as both ungendered and gendered. To accept only the former suggests a "neutered" God; to accept only the latter risks anthropomorphism. God may be ungendered and gendered because God is more than gendered. If so, the statement, "God is feminine," for example, may be one of a several true statements that can be offered concerning God and gender. Nevertheless, I have chosen to use the traditional masculine terms, "Father" and "Son" in this book, not least because of their rich scriptural heritage, and have therefore referred to these persons using masculine pronouns (he; him; his). However, I have not used masculine pronouns of God (referring consistently to "God's own self" rather than to "God himself" or "God herself" or God itself").[30]

Turning from the issue of gender in God to that of the impact of trinitarian discussion on gender relations among humans, Giles discusses at length a debate among evangelical Christians concerning the Son's eternal subordination to the Father and the impact this supposedly has on whether women should submit to men.[31] However, note the assumptions that are being made in this debate. Insofar as the Father and the Son have any gender ascribed to them implicitly by the use of those very terms, they are both masculine. So why does the Father stand for men in this debate and the Son for women?[32] Could it not just as easily be the other way round? Or might it not more directly offer an analogy that suggests children should obey their parents? The more significant assumption, however, is that one particular relation within the Trinity should be set up as determinative of one particular set of relations within humanity. It would be more helpful, I submit, for

---

29. Moltmann, *History and the Triune God*, 22. D'Costa is sharply critical of Moltmann's approach (*Sexing the Trinity*, 86–88).

30. Nor have I used pronouns with reference to the Spirit. I am uncomfortable with implicitly ascribing masculinity to the Spirit by the use of masculine pronouns. Neither do I see any value of redress by implicitly ascribing femininity with feminine pronouns. (Yong ascribes at least grammatical femininity by fairly consistently referring to the Spirit as "she" throughout *Spirit-Word-Community* [there are exceptions; Yong uses "it," 64]). Despite my focus on the impersonhood of the Spirit, I also shy away from referring to the Spirit as "it."

31. Giles, *Trinity and Subordinationism*, throughout.

32. I acknowledge the relevance to this debate of 1 Cor 11:3 but wish to suggest that a single "proof-text" is a slender base for a far-reaching conclusion.

the dynamic reciprocal relations of kenosis of the self and exaltation of the other to be expressed in all human relations.

Having listed several important topics that might potentially arise from the trinitarian discussion I have offered in previous chapters, I need to indicate why I have chosen *not* to include detailed discussion of these topics in this volume. One reason is simply that there is so much to cover that a whole further book would probably be required! However, there are two other important reasons. One is that I do not wish to make undue assumptions, as I suggested in the previous paragraph, concerning any postulated applicability of the Trinity with respect to humanity. Book subtitles such as *The Church as the Image of the Trinity* and *The Trinity Imaged in our Humanity* can be found.[33] Implicitly, they rely on the concept of humanity created in the divine image. However, no easy assumptions can be made about the degree to which trinitarian relations as such are imaged in us humans. As attractive as I find it to extrapolate, for instance, from the kenosis and exaltation I have been exploring in God to the call for servant-leadership among Christians, I must not assume an assured analogical basis for doing so.[34] I am not claiming that no analogical case can be made. The prayer of the Johannine Jesus in John 17:22–23 might be a starting point for building this case. I simply wish to point out that the nature and degree of the analogy must not be assumed.

The second important reason for my reluctance to "apply" my trinitarian discussions arises from the accusation of pragmatism levelled by Moltmann against the Christian church and referred to at the outset of chapter 1. My intention is absolutely not to give the impression that the only reason of us Christians to study the Trinity is so that we can then more helpfully answer the practical questions we face. That is surely to demean God, for God thereby becomes a means to our advancement. We are called at times simply to gaze at God—to stop everything else and worship—and if we love God then it is a pleasure to do so, even though we realize that we risk blinding dazzlement in the process. Thus I end this section and this book here, without exploring practical features of human living. You may well not agree with all of the suggestions I have made about the nature of the Trinity, but please join with me to pause here, even if there are further conversations that we must have in the future, and worship.

33. Subtitles of, respectively, Volf, *After Our Likeness* and Smail, *Like Father, Like Son*.

34. The analogical argument that I put forward in chapter 1 for reasoning from the economic to the immanent Trinity is stronger.

Bibliography

Ackley, A. H. "He Lives! He Lives! Christ Jesus Lives Today." In *Redemption Hymnal*, hymn number 631. London: Elim, 1951.

Alexander, Estrelda, and Amos Yong, editors. *Philip's Daughters: Women in Pentecostal-Charismatic Leadership*. Eugene, OR: Wipf and Stock, 2009.

Alexander, Paul, Jordan Daniel May, and Robert G. Reid, editors. *Trajectories in the Book of Acts*. Eugene, OR: Wipf and Stock, 2010.

Anderson, Allan. *An Introduction to Pentecostalism*. Cambridge: Cambridge University Press, 2004.

Atkinson, William. P. "Angels and the Spirit in Luke-Acts." *Journal of the European Pentecostal Theological Association* XXVI.1 (2006) 76–90.

———. *Baptism in the Spirit: Luke-Acts and the Dunn Debate*. Eugene, OR: Pickwick, 2011.

———. *The "Spiritual Death" of Jesus*. Leiden: Brill, 2009.

Balthasar, Hans Urs von. *Mysterium Paschale*. Translated by Aidan Nichols. 1970. Reprint. San Francisco: Ignatius, 2000.

Barth, Karl. *Church Dogmatics Volume I: The Doctrine of the Word of God*. Translated by G. W. Bromiley. Edinburgh: T. & T. Clark, 1975.

Bauckham, Richard. "Moses as 'God' in Philo of Alexandria: A Precedent for Christology?" In *The Spirit and Christ in the New Testament and Christian Theology*, edited by I. Howard Marshall et al., 246–65. Grand Rapids: Eerdmans, 2012.

———. *The Theology of Jürgen Moltmann*. Edinburgh: T. & T. Clark, 1995.

Beasley-Murray, George R. *John*. Word Biblical Commentary. Dallas: Word, 1987.

Bennema, Cornelis. "The Giving of the Spirit in John 19–20: Another Round." In *The Spirit and Christ in the New Testament and Christian Theology*, edited by I. Howard Marshall et al., 86–104. Grand Rapids: Eerdmans, 2012.

Boyd, Gregory A. *Oneness Pentecostals & the Trinity: A World-wide Movement Assessed by a Former Oneness Pentecostal*. Grand Rapids: Baker, 1992.

Bruce, F. F. *The Acts of the Apostles*. London: Tyndale, 1951.

Cartledge, Mark J. *Testimony in the Spirit: Rescripting Ordinary Pentecostal Theology*. Farnham, UK: Ashgate, 2010.

Conzelmann, Hans. *Acts of the Apostles*. Translated by James Limburg, A. Thomas Kraabel, and Donald H. Juel. 1963. Reprint. Philadelphia: Fortress, 1987.

Cotterell, Peter, and Max Turner. *Linguistics & Biblical Interpretation*. London: SPCK, 1989.

Crisp, Oliver D. "Problems with Perichoresis." *Tyndale Bulletin* 56.1 (2005) 119–40.

Daugherty, Kevin. "*Missio Dei*: The Trinity and Christian Mission." *Evangelical Review of Theology* 31.2 (2007) 151–68.

D'Costa, Gavin. *Sexing the Trinity: Gender, Culture and the Divine*. London: SCM, 2000.

Deere, Jack. *Surprised by the Voice of God*. Eastbourne, UK: Kingsway, 1996.

Dixon, Patrick. *Signs of Revival*. Eastbourne, UK: Kingsway, 1994.

Duce, Philip. *Reading the Mind of God: Interpretation in Science and Theology*. Leicester, UK: Apollos, 1998.

Dunn, James D. G. *Baptism in the Holy Spirit: A Re-examination of the New Testament Teaching on the Gift of the Spirit in Relation to Pentecostalism Today*. London: SCM, 1970.

―――. *The Partings of the Ways: Between Christianity and Judaism and their Significance for the Character of Christianity*. London: SCM, 1991.

―――. *Romans 1–8*. Word Biblical Commentary. Dallas: Word, 1988.

―――. *Unity and Diversity in the New Testament: An Inquiry into the Character of Earliest Christianity*. 2nd ed. London: SCM, 1990.

Dye, Colin. *Revival Phenomena*. Tonbridge, UK: Sovereign World, 1996.

Fee, Gordon D. *First Epistle to the Corinthians*. New International Commentary on the New Testament. Grand Rapids: Eerdmans, 1987.

―――. *God's Empowering Presence*. Peabody, MA: Hendrickson, 1994.

Garland, David E. *1 Corinthians*. Baker Exegetical Commentary on the New Testament. Grand Rapids: Baker Academic, 2003.

Giles, Kevin. *The Trinity and Subordinationism: The Doctrine of God and the Contemporary Gender Debate*. Downers Grove, IL: InterVarsity, 2002.

Green, Joel B., and Max Turner, editors. *Jesus of Nazareth: Lord and Christ*. 1994. Reprint. Eugene, OR: Wipf and Stock, 1999.

Gregersen, Niels Henrik, Willem B. Drees, and Ulf Görman, editors. *The Human Person in Science and Theology*. Edinburgh: T. & T. Clark, 2000.

Greig, Gary S., and Kevin N. Springer, editors. *The Kingdom and the Power*. Ventura, CA: Regal, 1993.

Grenz, Stanley J., and Roger E. Olson. *20th Century Theology: God and the World in a Transitional Age*. Downers Grove, IL: InterVarsity, 1992.

Gunton, Colin E. *The Actuality of Atonement: A Study of Metaphor, Rationality and the Christian Tradition*. London: T. & T. Clark, 1988.

―――. *The Promise of Trinitarian Theology*. 1991. Reprint. London: T. & T. Clark, 1997.

Hanson, R. P. C. "Introduction." In *Historical Theology*, edited by J. Danielou et al., 9–22. Harmondsworth, UK: Penguin, 1969.

Harris, John. "Four Legs Good, Personhood Better!" *Res Publica* IV.1 (1998) 51–58.

Hefner, Philip. "Imago Dei: The Possibility and Necessity of the Human Person." In *The Human Person in Science and Theology*, edited by Niels Henrik Gregersen et al., 73–94. Edinburgh: T. & T. Clark, 2000.

Hurtado, Larry W. *Lord Jesus Christ: Devotion to Jesus in Earliest Christianity*. Grand Rapids: Eerdmans, 2003.

―――. *One God, One Lord: Early Christian Devotion and Ancient Jewish Monotheism*. London: SCM, 1988.

Jeeves, Malcolm A., and R. J. Berry. *Science, Life and Christian Belief: A Survey and Assessment*. Leicester, UK: Apollos, 1998.

Johnson, Luke Timothy. *Religious Experience in Earliest Christianity: A Missing Dimension in New Testament Studies*. Minneapolis, MN: Fortress, 1998.

Jones, D. Gareth. *Valuing People: Human Value in a World of Medical Technology*. Carlisle, UK: Paternoster, 1999.

Jowers, Dennis W. "The Theology of the Cross as Theology of the Trinity: A Critique of Jürgen Moltmann's Staurocentric Trinitarianism." *Tyndale Bulletin* 52.2 (2001) 245–66.

Kelly, J. N. D. *Early Christian Doctrines.* 2nd ed. San Francisco: Harper and Row, 1978.

Kenney, Garrett C. *Translating H/holy S/spirit: 4 Models: Unitarian, Binitarian, Trinitarian, and Non-Sectarian.* Lanham, MD: University Press of America, 2007.

Knell, Matthew. *The Immanent Person of the Holy Spirit from Anselm to Lombard: Divine Communion in the Spirit.* Studies in Christian History and Thought. Milton Keynes, UK: Paternoster, 2009.

LaCugna, Catherine Mowry. *God for Us: The Trinity and Christian Life.* New York: HarperCollins, 1991.

Lane, Anthony N. S. "Cyril of Alexandria and the Incarnation." In *The Spirit and Christ in the New Testament and Christian Theology*, edited by I. Howard Marshall et al., 285–302. Grand Rapids: Eerdmans, 2012.

Lartey, Emmanuel Y. *Pastoral Theology in an Intercultural World.* Peterborough, UK: Epworth, 2006.

Lederle, Henry I. *Theology with Spirit: The Future of the Pentecostal and Charismatic Movements in the 21st Century.* Tulsa, OK: Word & Spirit, 2010.

Levison, John R. *Filled with the Spirit.* Grand Rapids: Eerdmans, 2009.

Lewis, Alan E. *Between Cross and Resurrection: A Theology of Holy Saturday.* Grand Rapids: Eerdmans, 2001.

Lewis, C. S. *Undeceptions: Essays on Theology and Ethics.* London: Bles, 1971.

———. *Voyage to Venus (Perelandra).* 1943. Reprint. London: Pan, 1953.

Lossky, Vladimir. *The Mystical Theology of the Eastern Church.* Translated by members of the Fellowship of St Alban and St Sergius. 1944. Reprint. Cambridge: James Clarke, 1957.

Macchia, Frank D. *Baptized in the Spirit.* Grand Rapids: Zondervan, 2006.

Marshall, I. Howard et al., editors. *The Spirit and Christ in the New Testament and Christian Theology.* Grand Rapids: Eerdmans, 2012.

McFague, Sally. *Metaphorical Theology: Models of God in Religious Language.* Philadelphia: Fortress, 1982.

McGrath, Alister E. *Historical Theology: An Introduction to the History of Christian Thought.* Oxford: Blackwell, 1998.

———. *Theology: the Basics.* Oxford: Blackwell, 2004.

———. *Understanding the Trinity.* Eastbourne, UK: Kingsway, 1987.

McKnight, Scot. *A New Vision for Israel: The Teachings of Jesus in National Context.* Grand Rapids: Eerdmans, 1999.

Menzies, Robert. *Empowered for Witness: The Holy Spirit in Luke-Acts.* Sheffield, UK: Sheffield Academic Press, 1994.

———. "The Sending of the Seventy and Luke's Purpose." In *Trajectories in the Book of Acts*, edited by Paul Alexander et al., 87–113. Eugene, OR: Wipf and Stock, 2010.

Mittelstadt, Martin William. *Reading Luke–Acts in the Pentecostal Tradition.* Cleveland: CPT Press, 2010.

Moltmann, Jürgen. *The Crucified God.* 2nd ed. Translated by R. A. Wilson and John Bowden. London: SCM, 1973.

———. *History and the Triune God: Contributions to a Trinitarian Theology.* Translated by John Bowden. London: SCM, 1991.

―――. *The Trinity and the Kingdom.* Translated by Margaret Kohl. 1980. Reprint. Minneapolis, MN: Fortress, 1993.

Moo, Douglas. *The Epistle to the Romans.* New International Commentary on the New Testament. Grand Rapids: Eerdmans, 1996.

Nolland, John. *Luke 1:1—9:20.* Word Biblical Commentary. Dallas: Word, 1989.

O'Neill, J. C. *The Bible's Authority.* Edinburgh: T. & T. Clark, 1991.

Otto, Rudolf. *The Idea of the Holy.* Translated by John W. Harvey. 2nd ed. 1917. Reprint. Oxford: Oxford University Press, 1950.

Parry, Robin A. *Worshipping Trinity: Coming Back to the Heart of Worship.* Carlisle, UK: Paternoster, 2005.

Pennington, Jonathan T., and Sean M. McDonough, editors. *Cosmology and New Testament Theology.* London: T. & T. Clark, 2008.

Perriman, Andrew, editor. *Faith, Health and Prosperity: A Report on "Word of Faith" and "Positive Confession" Theologies, by The Evangelical Alliance (UK) Commission on Unity and Truth among Evangelicals.* Carlisle, UK: Paternoster, 2003.

Peterson, Michael, et al., editors. *Reason and Religious Belief: An Introduction to the Philosophy of Religion.* 2nd ed. Oxford: Oxford University Press, 1997.

Pinnock, Clark H. "Foreword." In Roger Stronstad, *The Charismatic Theology of St. Luke*, vii–viii. Peabody, MA: Hendrickson, 1984.

―――. *Most Moved Mover: A Theology of God's Openness.* The Didsbury Lectures. Carlisle, UK: Paternoster, 2001.

Pinnock, Clark H., et al. *The Openness of God: A Biblical Challenge to the Traditional Understanding of God.* Downers Grove, IL: InterVarsity, 1994.

Polkinghorne, John. *One World: The Interaction of Science and Theology.* London: SPCK, 1986.

Powers, Janet Everts. "Pentecostalism 101: Your Daughters Shall Prophesy." In *Philip's Daughters: Women in Pentecostal-Charismatic Leadership*, edited by Estrelda Alexander and Amos Yong, 133–51. Eugene, OR: Wipf and Stock, 2009.

Rabens, Volker. *The Holy Spirit and Ethics in Paul.* Tübingen: Mohr Siebeck, 2010.

―――. "Power from In Between: The Relational Experience of the Holy Spirit and Spiritual Gifts in Paul's Churches." In *The Spirit and Christ in the New Testament and Christian Theology*, edited by I. Howard Marshall et al., 138–55. Grand Rapids: Eerdmans, 2012.

Rahner, Karl. *The Trinity.* Translated by Joseph Donceel. 1967. Reprint. London: Burns and Oates, 1970.

Reed, David A. *"In Jesus' Name": The History and Beliefs of Oneness Pentecostals.* Blandford Forum, UK: Deo, 2008.

Robinson, John A. T. *Honest to God.* London: SCM, 1963.

Rudolph, Kurt. *Gnosis: The Nature and History of Gnosticism.* Authorized translation edited by Robert McLachlan Wilson. 1977. Reprint. Edinburgh: T. & T. Clark, 1983.

Schmidt, Friedrich Wilhelm. "Christian Revelation and Dogmatic Theology." In *Twentieth Century Theology in the Making*, edited by Jaroslav Pelikan, 56–61. London: Fontana, 1970.

Smail, Tom. *The Forgotten Father: Recovering the Heart of the Christian Gospel.* 1980. Reprint. Carlisle, UK: Paternoster, 1996.

―――. *The Giving Gift: the Holy Spirit in Person.* London: Hodder & Stoughton, 1988.

———. *Like Father, Like Son: The Trinity Imaged in Our Humanity.* Grand Rapids: Eerdmans, 2005.

Soards, Marion L. *1 Corinthians.* Peabody, MA: Hendrickson, 1999.

Society for Pentecostal Studies. "Oneness-Trinitarian Pentecostal Final Report, 2002–2007." *Pneuma* 30 (2008) 203–224.

Stronstad, Roger. *The Charismatic Theology of St. Luke.* Peabody, MA: Hendrickson, 1984.

Teske, John A. "The Social Construction of the Human Spirit." In *The Human Person in Science and Theology,* edited by Niels Henrik Gregersen et al., 189–211. Edinburgh: T. & T. Clark, 2000.

Thompson, John. *Modern Trinitarian Perspectives.* Oxford: Oxford University Press, 1994.

Torrance, Alan J. *Persons in Communion: Trinitarian Description and Human Participation.* Edinburgh: T. & T. Clark, 1996.

Torrance, Thomas. F. *Theology in Reconstruction.* London: SCM, 1965.

———. *Trinitarian Perspectives: Towards Doctrinal Agreement.* Edinburgh: T. & T. Clark, 1994.

Turner, Max. *The Holy Spirit and Spiritual Gifts: Then and Now.* Carlisle, UK: Paternoster, 1996.

———. "Luke and the Spirit: Studies in the Significance of Receiving the Spirit in Luke-Acts." PhD diss., University of Cambridge, 1980.

———. *Power from on High: The Spirit in Israel's Restoration and Witness in Luke-Acts.* Sheffield, UK: Sheffield Academic Press, 1996.

———. "The Spirit of Christ and 'Divine' Christology." In *Jesus of Nazareth: Lord and Christ,* edited by Joel B. Green and Max Turner, 413–36. 1994. Reprint. Eugene, OR: Wipf and Stock, 1999.

Vermes, Geza. *The Complete Dead Sea Scrolls in English.* London: Penguin, 1962.

Volf, Miroslav. *After our Likeness: The Church as the Image of the Trinity.* Grand Rapids: Eerdmans, 1998.

———. "Being As God Is: Trinity and Generosity." In *God's Life in Trinity,* edited by Miroslav Volf and Michael Welker, 3–12. Minneapolis, MN: Fortress, 2006.

———. *Exclusion and Embrace: A Theological Exploration of Identity, Otherness, and Reconciliation.* Nashville, TN: Abingdon, 1996.

Volf, Miroslav, and Michael Welker, editors. *God's Life in Trinity.* Minneapolis, MN: Fortress, 2006.

Walton, Steve. "Whose Spirit? The Promise and the Promiser in Luke 12:12." In *The Spirit and Christ in the New Testament and Christian Theology,* edited by I. Howard Marshall et al., 35–51. Grand Rapids: Eerdmans, 2012.

———. "'The Heavens Opened': Cosmological and Theological Transformation in Luke and Acts." In *Cosmology and New Testament Theology,* edited by Jonathan T. Pennington and Sean M. McDonough, 60–73. London: T. & T. Clark, 2008.

Warrington, Keith. *Pentecostal Theology: A Theology of Encounter.* London: T. & T. Clark, 2008.

Welker, Michael. "Is the Autonomous Person of European Modernity a Sustainable Model of Human Personhood?" In *The Human Person in Science and Theology,* edited by Niels Henrik Gregersen et al., 95–114, Edinburgh: T. & T. Clark, 2000.

Williams, Don. "Following Christ's Example: A Biblical View of Discipleship." In *The Kingdom and the Power,* edited by Gary S. Greig and Kevin N. Springer, 175–96, Ventura, CA: Regal, 1993.

Bibliography

Witherington, Ben III. *The Acts of the Apostles: A Socio-Rhetorical Commentary*. Grand Rapids: Eerdmans, 1998.

Witherington, Ben III and Laura M. Ice. *The Shadow of the Almighty: Father, Son, and Spirit in Biblical Perspective*. Grand Rapids: Eerdmans, 2002.

Yong, Amos. "The Spirit and Creation: Possibilities and Challenges for a Dialogue between Pentecostal Theology and Science." *Journal of the European Pentecostal Theological Association* XXV (2005) 82–110.

———. *The Spirit Poured Out on All Flesh: Pentecostalism and the Possibility of Global Theology*. Grand Rapids: Baker Academic, 2005.

———. *Spirit-Word-Community: Theological Hermeneutics in Trinitarian Perspective*. Eugene, OR: Wipf and Stock, 2002.

Zizioulas, John D. *Lectures in Christian Dogmatics*. Edited by Douglas H. Knight. London: T. & T. Clark, 2008.

Subject Index

Abraham (patriarch), 18, 59, 101
absentee christology. *See* christology, absentee
adoptionism, 65, 87–88, 120
analogy, 14–16, 25–26, 28–29, 31, 35, 37, 39, 42, 52–53, 56, 63, 74, 76, 85, 96, 98, 102, 115, 122, 125–26, 132, 135, 147, 156, 158, 161, 165
angel, angels, 23, 32, 45–48, 79, 86, 92, 100, 119
apotheosis, 85
Aquinas, Thomas, 14, 104
Arianism, 84
ascension, 24–25, 48, 61, 67, 79–80, 82, 88, 131, 147
attributes, communication of. *See* communication of attributes
Augustine, 9, 54, 76, 104, 158

Baptist, John the. *See* John the Baptist
binitarianism, 3, 8–11, 23, 38, 87–88, 90, 105–6
breath of God. *See* God, breath of

Cappadocian doctrine, fathers, 125
cause, eternal, Father as, 34, 56, 125, 128, 136–43, 148–50, 156, 159, 164
Chalcedonian settlement, 84
christology, absentee, 82
christology, divine, 81, 84, 110, 156
christology, functional, 12, 115

christology, incarnational, 8, 12, 115, 120, 143
christology, *logos*, 61, 75, 82, 156
christology, parabolic, 12
circumincession, 157
circuminsession, 157
classical theism. *See* theism, classical
communication of attributes, 93
Constantinople, Council of, 52, 163
Council of Constantinople. *See* Constantinople, Council of
Council of Florence. *See* Florence, Council of
Cyril of Alexandria, 35, 130

dance, dancer, 36, 146, 150–51, 154, 157, 161
ditheism, 34, 86, 152
divine christology. *See* christology, divine
divine image. *See* image, divine
divine unity. *See* unity of God
dualism, 26
dynamism, dynamics, 33–34, 36, 38, 63, 76, 109, 131, 157

economic Trinity. *See* Trinity, economic
economy, 28, 76, 99, 108, 111–12, 123–24, 126–27, 130–31, 135, 142–44, 146–48, 159
emancipation of women, 138
eschatology, 34, 54, 91, 93, 103, 105, 108–10, 112, 136, 142–43, 146–48, 150, 163

Author Index

Author Index

Ancient Document Index

Lightning Source UK Ltd.
Milton Keynes UK
UKOW04f1422150813

215424UK00001B/35/P